The Film Business

Also by Ernest Betts

Heraclitus: or the Future of Films
Inside Pictures (editor)
The Private Life of Henry VIII
Jew Suss

The Film Business

A History of British Cinema
1896–1972

ERNEST BETTS

PITMAN PUBLISHING CORPORATION
NEW YORK / TORONTO / LONDON

Pitman Publishing Corporation
Library of Congress Catalog Card No. 73-93699

Erratum: page 279, last paragraph, should
read '1958' not '1968'.

Printed in Great Britain

To
Leonard and Nancy Schuster

Acknowledgements

I would like to thank Sir Michael Balcon for his kindness in reading the proofs of this book and for correcting a number of errors. I am also grateful for interviews and information to the late Lord Rank, to Lord Bernstein, Sir John Davis and Robert Clark; to John Terry of the National Film Finance Corporation; to Victor Saville; John and Roy Boulting; Frank Launder and Sidney Gilliat; to Mrs Gwyneth Dunwoody, director, and J. P. H. Walton, secretary of the Association of British Film Producers, and to Raymond Williams for permission to quote from a BBC broadcast.

There are many others whom I must thank for their interest and help: Edgar Anstey, Felix Barker, Thorold Dickinson, Cyril Hicks, Ivo Jarosy, David Jones, Oscar Lewenstein, Roger Manvell, Michael Medwin, Stanley Reed, Tony Richardson, Peter Rogers, Ernest Lindgren, J. C. Trewin, Ben Weinreb, to whom I owe the title, and Philip Unwin, for his unfailing courtesy and care.

I am indebted to Dr R. P. Thomas of the Science Museum for reading my account of the first inventors of film apparatus. Regarding the general background of the silent cinema, Anthony Slide has provided me with some valuable material. F. E. Hutchinson, a former head of Paramount in London, gave me some interesting details of the film business in the 1900s. For the use of privately owned stills and information about early film production I have to thank John M. East, and for details of G. B. Samuelson's career, Harold M. Dunham and the Samuelson family.

No one can embark on a study of the film industry without acknowledging a debt to Rachael Low's *History of the British Film*, Paul Rotha's *The Film Till Now*, and Charles Oakley's *Where We Came In*. To these I would add PEP's *The British Film Industry* (1952 and 1958), a key work for the clarification of the background.

I must also acknowledge with gratitude the specially written article on documentary by the late John Grierson which appears as an Appendix to this book. Grierson was kind enough to set down what would appear to be his final reflections on the movement he founded in response to a request I made for his views. I regret that he never saw the article in print but some corrections he made are incorporated in it and Mrs Grierson was kind enough to check the work for me.

I must also say how grateful I am to the various departments of the British Film Institute whose staff have responded so efficiently to my incessant raids on the Library, the National Film Archive, the Information Department and the Press Office. Finally, it is impossible to say how much I owe to my wife, preserver of order and sanity, for debts of gratitude without end.

Acknowledgements are due to the following for permission to use stills: MGM-EMI; Paramount Film Service; United Artists; 20th Century-Fox; the Rank Organisation; Associated British Picture Corporation and John M. East.

Preface

This book surveys the British film industry from 1896 to 1972. It considers not only the films themselves but their financial and political background, British films being pre-eminently a concern of the State.

But the most striking fact about the British film industry is that it is not British. Since 1914 and even earlier it has undergone a piratical process of Americanisation, until by the 1960s it is as much American as British, if not more so.

This is said in no chauvinistic spirit but as a thing well known, though seldom challenged. Apart from government White Papers and those authors whose work I acknowledge elsewhere in this book, there have been few attempts to examine this state of affairs, to put together in a single volume the facts about British films, to trace the course they have taken and assemble the opinions of critics about them. Nor has there been much detailed examination of the political and financial set-up or of the personalities who created the film business and made it what it is. This gap I have tried to fill.

For critical opinion on British cinema I have plundered the writings of critics past and present, here and in America, occasionally adding, as a second opinion, my own. Quotation proved a harder task than I anticipated. Brief extracts do not adequately represent a critic's judgement or point of view; longer extracts can give a wrong emphasis to work of perhaps minor importance.

My aim has been to indicate through contemporary opinion the artistic or commercial value of the work discussed, or to draw attention to some significant aspect of it and so help to place the film in cinema history. Whether I have succeeded or not is for the reader to judge. I hope I have not unfairly represented the work of any critic or colleague, to whom I gratefully acknowledge my indebtedness.

For the factual account of British films I have relied on the usual sources, on material of my own, and on a number of interviews. These are by no means complete: books, like politics, are the art of the possible. For the omissions I take full blame, together with those doubtful dates which seem inseparable from an industry as careless about itself as the film industry.

Whether a British film business could exist or have existed without the Americans, whether my view of it is correct, whether it matters to the art of the film, are questions producing a variety of conflicting opinions. The art is in the hands of those who are not businessmen and the business is in the hands of those who are not artists. It is arguable that it would be better for the business if there were no art and better for the art if there were no business. But this is to separate things that are indivisible and to be blind to the laws of the game.

The choice of films I have made to develop this theme may not recommend itself to everyone, but it is intended to cover the ground as fully as possible and provide a factual record which can be generally useful, especially perhaps for more complete study by others.

In the case of Alfred Hitchcock and Victor Saville I have considered only the films they made in England, though some of their best work, at least in Hitchcock's case, was done in America. Newsreels, cartoons and educational films, with one or two exceptions, I have excluded.

The film industry is well known as 'the crisis industry', for it has, for most of its history, failed to solve its problems and put its affairs in order. It has bungled its way through the century, turning to the Government or to America whenever in trouble, and frequently making things worse 'by paving the way for more extensive and more destructive crises, and by diminishing the means whereby crises are prevented'.

Through this comedy of errors the individual film-maker has had to find his way and seek a mode of expression. His efforts to do so and the success or failure that attended them form the recurring theme of this survey.

Contents

Illustrations

Part I

Beginnings

Chapter 1

The Threepenny Cinema

The history of the film may be seen as the struggle of the film-maker to ascertain the nature of the medium, to discover its laws and properties and to make the best use of them he can. His efforts have been both advanced and retarded by problems peculiar to the film and to no other medium, at least in the same degree—problems of machines, of chemistry, of finance, of censorship, of the national interest, of government intervention, of American domination, and so forth. After more than three-quarters of a century the British film-maker has gained a measure of independence, but rarely has he won total freedom. The explanation must be sought in the organisation of the film industry itself.

The cinema begins with the machine, and with the men from the circuses and music halls who saw it as a profitable addition to the clowns and acrobats of the traditional show. The cinematograph arrived during the 1890s and was one of the last great scientific inventions of the Victorian age. Though launched as a money-making device it enabled an art to be born, the most potent and significant of our time and the most immediately exciting.

The credit for this new invention belongs to many hands and minds. Britain played some part in it and a Bristol man, William Friese-Greene (1855–1921), must be mentioned for his contribution. The cinematograph patent he took out in June 1889 for a projector is 'the prior patent of the world' in this particular field and was upheld as such in the American courts against a counter claim by Thomas Edison, whose patent was not granted until 1893, and then only in the United States.[1]

Friese-Greene never got to the point of demonstrating

21

his invention. Edison, for his part, did not trouble to take out a patent in France or England, contending that it was not worth the 150 dollars it would cost him. But he succeeded in projecting films experimentally. Moreover, he owed a great deal to his English assistant, William Kennedy Dickson, and to a Frenchman, Eugene Lauste, who was the first to reproduce sound on film, though not the first to record it. Others such as Edison and Graham Bell succeeded in doing this on a photographic plate, but could not reproduce it.

Eugene Lauste, who in 1900 was working in a studio at Brixton, had the true passion of the scientific investigator. In America, where he was one of Edison's assistants, 'he lived with his work and slept on a cot in the corner of the room'. He is one of those little-known men of importance and has been called the father of the talking picture.

Of course there were many promising or crackpot inventions of a cinematic kind before either Edison or Friese-Greene. Terry Ramsaye, not surprisingly in a history of the American film, makes large claims for Edison as inventor of 'the motion picture film machine' and dismisses Friese-Greene with contempt. All such inventions, he declares, are 'descended by traceable steps' to Edison's own invention, the kinetoscope.

But the kinetoscope, we are told later, 'was not the motion picture as we know it now, but only its immediate ancestor'. It was in fact a peep show. Edison had some way to go before reaching Friese-Greene's position but he just did not trouble to go there because he failed to perceive what a tremendous thing it was, and was occupied with other problems. Whether Friese-Greene could ever have projected his films we do not know, we only know that he was in a position to do so before Edison, and Edison had to wait for George Eastman to invent the roll film before he could operate his own machine. Perhaps Friese-Greene was waiting for the same thing.

Scientists studying the motion picture had been busy with the problems of optics and the chemistry of photography since early in the nineteenth century and had produced some strange instruments with daunting names—the thaumatrope, a British invention of 1825, the praxinoscope from France in 1877, the kinematoscope from America in 1861, and the kinetoscope of 1891 to which I have referred. Some of these can be seen in the Science Section of the Victoria and Albert Museum. The prettiest of them is the zoetrope. It had the fascination of a toy, which indeed it was, for the movements of figures could be observed in seeming continuity through the slits of a revolving drum. To the uninstructed eye the zoetrope is the clearest demonstration of the kinetic principle. But all these machines, crude as they seem to the eye today, strove to marry motion to picture.

Perhaps the best known attempt to produce a motion picture is that of Eadweard J. Muybridge who, in 1877, using a battery of cameras, photographed the running horse. He was followed by that romantic figure, Louis Aimé Augustin le Prince[2] who did much of his work in England and tried to create movement by passing strips of sensitised paper in front of lenses. This apart, the most interesting thing about him is that in 1890, while in France, he boarded a suburban train for Paris and disappeared.

The distinction of putting on the first commercial film show is given by general consent to the Lumière brothers of France who presented one-minute films in Paris in 1895 and at the Regent Street Polytechnic in London on 20 February 1896. This was by the use of their *cinematographe*, a term they invented. In the same year (March 25th) an Englishman, R. W. Paul (1869–1943), who was a film manufacturer, showed his Animatographe at the Alhambra Theatre, Leicester Square. Edison in America came a month later (April 23rd) with his Vitascope show at Koster and Bial's Music Hall in New York.

We notice, from the coincidence of the dates, the keen awareness in one country of what was going on in another, and the need on strictly commercial grounds to be first in the race.

One of these pioneers, an Englishman who worked a good deal in Germany and was held in great respect there, was Birt Acres. He was the first to project moving pictures effectively in Britain. He produced a film of the opening of

23

the Kiel Canal and of Kaiser Wilhelm with his troops in 1895. Details of Birt Acres' life were published in a German pamphlet in 1962. The writer, H. Tummel, complains of the neglect of Acres, and refers to the filming of the Kiel Canal film as an achievement virtually unrecognised, and to Acres himself as 'almost forgotten'.[3] Yet from what we know of him he must have been a man of genuine scientific bent, constantly making discoveries in cinematography and pushing them forward. Between 1891 and 1898 he took out numerous patents varying in kind from stereoscopic photography to camera projection.

Birt Acres was born in 1854 of English parents who lived in Virginia and died in the American Civil War. He was educated in Paris, settled in England in the 1880s and after working as manager for a manufacturer of dry plates, he built a laboratory in High Barnet which later became the Northern Photographic Works. This was about 1895.

His first attempts at moving pictures were photographs of clouds taken at brief intervals which he then projected with a dissolving lantern in rapid succession giving an illusion of motion. These he showed with approval to the Royal Photographic Society.

In 1895 he patented the kineopticon or kinetic lantern 'for the taking and viewing of cine-film' and the first pictures he shot were of his own home in Barnet and 'of a haycart crossing Hadley Green'. His apparatus was sufficiently advanced by that year for him to film the Derby and the Boat Race and the films in Germany to which we have referred.

Acres was clearly a first-rate showman and he appears to have found favour with royalty wherever he went, exhibiting his work to the Prince of Wales in England and to a whole string of princes and nobles in Germany. The Prince of Wales gave the name *Cinematoscope* to Acres' apparatus, thus adding one more monstrosity to the terminology of the day.

'Without any doubt', says Tummel, 'the projector of Birt Acres was the first usable instrument in England.' Acres also devised a shutter allowing variable time-setting in

24

cinephotography which he called the Birtac and combined a camera with a projector. His inventiveness furthered the technique of the camera in his day and entitles him to high pioneer status, for he was always making and doing. Even the problem of sound did not daunt him, for he placed a man behind the screen to make the appropriate noises and the sound of a rough sea he simulated with a tray of peas.

Britain, though far from lacking in able technicians, did not derive much benefit from master patents or from the photographic machines her inventors put on the market. Her genius was in showmen, salesmen and entrepreneurs. They are the most active at the birth of the cinema, pushing and promoting, selling and exploiting, buying and building. They created an industry. The film itself hardly matters to them.

Why did it arrive at this moment? It arrived because the means existed. Every invention has its hour, and the hour for the cinema struck at the close of the nineteenth century. Its development beyond its circus origins can be traced to the social needs of the time. There was little amusement for the working class. The whole nation yawned with boredom during weekends and was ready to put a fortune into the hands of anyone who could relieve the tedium.

Marghanita Laski has pointed out that in Edwardian times working-class families spent six shillings a week on intoxicants . . . 'but with homes which of their nature could provide no pleasure or relaxation' she writes 'there was little else for the poor to do'.[4]

It was then that the picture palace arose, the threepenny cinema, bringing luxury to those who had none and new worlds at bargain prices. The threepenny cinema, a penny less or more, was the foundation of the film industry. Cheapness and the desire of the human spirit for refreshment speeded its success.

On a higher level various theories have been advanced to account for the rise of the film as an art. One example may be given from a BBC broadcast by Raymond Williams.[5] 'What most impresses me', he said, 'is the seeming co-incidence of two facts: that the motion picture was invented and began to be popularised in the eighteen-nineties; and that in the same period the most experimental and *avant-garde* European drama—that of Strindberg—had reached the creative point at which something like the motion picture is necessary. In the apparent context of their time, no two developments could seem more widely separated. Strindberg was experimenting on paper and in minority theatres. The peepshow and the nickelodeon must have seemed a world away.

But I think this may be a case not just of the lucky discovery of a technical form, which, as it developed, major artists were able to use, but of some deep cultural situation out of which, as apparently separate facts, new moves were made, at very different levels, and indeed quite quickly though not deliberately came together.'

Dr Williams shows how the dramatic forms invented by Strindberg and Ibsen 'where men struggle to get out of the trap between past and future' and events 'unroll' in time and space, were peculiarly suited to film expression.

'If there had been film then, in any normally available way, there can be little real doubt that Strindberg would have written for it. For he was writing a process of projection, of constantly altering angle, proportion and emphasis, of interacting and dissolving places and times, which with the new techniques was to become directly realisable and in the end even commonplace.'

At the turn of the century entertainment was addressed mainly to the middle and leisured classes. The Common Man had not yet arrived. J. M. Barrie was writing *The Admirable Crichton*, Kipling was deep in patriotic gore, H. G. Wells was publishing *The First Men in the Moon*. Middle-class families crocheted and played whist. Fortunate were those who owned a piano and could listen to an esteemed aunt singing *Pale Hands I Loved* or reading selections from Ruskin or George Eliot.

But as we have said, perhaps the most remarkable thing about those days was the silence, a condition which has since been amply rectified by the introduction of organised noise and uproar. In the early 1900s there was a deplorable

26

absence of sound except that of buses, trams and the whistling of schoolboys. There was no BBC, Speed had not been invented, the Wright brothers had not yet got off the ground, Ford was to come. Such an atmosphere, lacking the din of propaganda and canned entertainment, makes one wonder how mankind lived through the twenty-four hours.

What better moment than this for the pictures to arrive? The nation asked to be amused, to be moved out of itself into action and life. On the physical side this was to be realised with the invention of the motor-car, a revolution greater even than that of the cinema. The car satisfied the universal lust for movement culminating in space travel and in flights to the moon. The film satisfied the lust of the eye.

On the cultural level other things were happening. By a coincidence the cinema, the cheapest and most challenging of pleasures, came in with the most extravagant and traditional—the ballet. In 1909, the Russian ballet 'first exploded upon Paris', followed a year later by the fantastic opening of *Scheherazade* at the Opera, which Marcel Proust and Reynaldo Hahn attended, a triumph described as 'instant and tremendous'.[6] Not long after, the Diaghilev Ballet came to London for a season at the Alhambra Theatre. Ballet and film were motion in differing dimensions and were soon to be found together in the same music hall programme.

But we must return for a moment to the time when Robert Paul showed his Animatograph in 1896. He, like Lumière, produced a revolution in entertainment, the animated picture. In 1898 he made a one-minute film of *The Last Days of Pompeii*. Long before Paramount or Metro, the bioscope flickered at the Empire Theatre, Leicester Square, where Adeline Genée or Phyllis Bedells topped the bill, while Pavlova was making her dying fall in *The Swan* at Covent Garden. These brief history-making films were mere fill-ups between the acts or were used to create a diversion for the audience as it left the theatre. They consisted of newsreels or topical events; of trains arriving and storms at sea, or they presented flower shows, fetes, egg-and-spoon races and other actualities. They created an illusion of life and were true marvels of the age.

27

So it was with slapstick in the 1900s. The first slapstick pictures caught life in mid-air, it scarcely mattered how it was done, the art was unpremeditated. Only much later did these improvisations develop into a conscious art. In the comedies of early Hollywood spontaneity often outdid calculation, and the gag or business which the comedian seemingly introduced by accident was so successful that it became a part of the act. Max Beerbohm said of Dan Leno: 'He selected and rejected according to how his jokes, and his expression of them, "went"; and his best things came to him always in the course of an actual performance, to be incorporated in all the subsequent performances.'[7] This could as well be said of Charlie Chaplin or any of those rare spirits from Mack Sennett to Buster Keaton who were his contemporaries and whose influence on our own film comedies was so great.

The earliest acted films were not so much imitations of life as fragments cut out of it. However defined, they caused an immense expansion of interest between 1906, let us say, and 1914. By then a more sophisticated film was growing up in better surroundings than those of tents and fun fairs.

The threepenny cinema had brought into being a fabulous world of imagination conjured up out of children's pocket money. Higher prices brought greater luxury. J. B. Priestley recalls that 'for sixpence you were not only offered the film programme but a cup of tea and a biscuit'.

All this did not happen at once, but the movement was rapid. In 1904, A. C. Bromhead, who later became chairman of the Gaumont-British Picture Corporation, surprised the City of London by putting on a permanent show, *The Daily Bioscope*, in Bishopsgate. It was not by any means a marble hall but a converted shop able to take a hundred people. Bromhead had already opened an outdoor studio at Loughborough. These brave captains pioneering the film industry were always mixed up in both production and exhibition, they jumped impartially on the swings and roundabouts, they plunged and they gambled.

Bromhead had been connected with Leon Gaumont in France, a manufacturer of cameras who also had his own

28

company in Britain. We find others of energy and imagination getting into the act. Among them were Charles and Emile Pathé whose trade mark of the crowing cock circled the globe. They were originally agents for Thomas Edison whose Kinetoscope they put on in Edinburgh, and they already had film studios in Vincennes and in London. Charles Pathé thought that as producers we lacked boldness and vision. He and his brother continued actively in England and were an important part of the scene.

Georges Méliès (1861–1938), a less successful but more original character who might have been a disciple of H. G. Wells or Jules Verne, is of greater interest to us. He has been described as 'the second great figure in the French cinema', Louis Lumière being the first.[8] He perceived the film as an art and he had imagination and a strong picture sense. Méliès was by profession a conjuror and magician and owned a theatre in Paris, the Robert Houdin, and a studio of his own at Montreuil, made largely of glass. But he was obviously far more than an entertainer. One of his first pictures was a dance by a row of chairs. He had a considerable influence on American cinema, and according to Terry Ramsaye, believed in what he called 'artificially arranged' scenes, or 'events to be created for the camera'. He was one of the first to realise the possibilities of the cartoon in pictures.

His *Trip to the Moon* (1902), judged by the designs for it, suggests something of Fritz Lang's *Metropolis*. The man who also produced *The Voyage Across the Impossible* (1904), *The Conquest of the Pole* (1912) and scores of other beautifully constructed fantasies clearly knew the meaning of film and had marked gifts of poetic invention. He is linked to the career of Charles Urban, an important figure in British films who photographed Edward VII's Coronation from a reconstruction of the scene which Méliès had made in Paris.

Urban was both impresario and film-maker and was co-inventor of the colour process on which nearly all subsequent systems were based. This was Kinemacolour which he produced in 1906 with G. Albert Smith, an inventor who had a studio at Brighton. An American, Urban had settled in

29

England as head of the Warwick Trading Company in Warwick Court, Holborn, and although he laboured long and hard to establish his own colour process he was finally edged out of it by the very Americans who had made a tentative bid of $250,000 for the process.

In 1908 he had shown his colour process to the Royal Society of Arts and again at the Palace Theatre in London. It was a year after this that his New York friends dropped him. Terry Ramsaye gives a lively account of this incident.[9]

He relates how in 1912 Urban, who was desperately ill, showed his colour picture of the Delhi Durbar to King George and Queen Mary at the Scala Theatre, London, but was unable to be present himself. It was a brilliant success. But it was followed by a court action which William Friese-Greene brought against him for infringement of his patent. The case went to the House of Lords and Urban lost it. Nor did Friese-Greene gain anything by it, for the legal verdict 'threw the Kinemacolour process open to the world'.

That was the end of Kinemacolour for Charles Urban but not of Urban himself, who had enlarged his image as a showman by opening Urbanora House in Wardour Street, (where it still is) and was perpetually on the move as a film distributor and head of his own trading company. On the film itself he had little influence but he encouraged the production of films in others.

Cecil Hepworth joined him at the Warwick Trading Company where his technical knowledge led to great improvements in film developing processes. Charles Urban organised, expanded, and advertised the film industry and he gave it prestige, and this was a considerable achievement in those days.

Yet he belonged to the pioneers who leave no legends. They lay the bricks and mortar, are immersed in money-making and end by being fundamentally uninteresting people. They possess the single merit, if it is one, of having been in at the beginning.

George Hale, also an American, belongs to this period and is indeed more picturesque, for in 1906 he opened one of the first commercial cinemas in Oxford Street, known as Hale's

Tours, and he demonstrated how easy it was for an American citizen to gain a hold on the British film industry and open it up to invasion.

As a piece of cinema, Hale's idea was well ahead of its time. His tours consisted of an imitation railway coach which rocked and swayed and made train-like noises, while its occupants, who paid sixpence, watched a travel film on the screen as if they were actually going on a train journey.

George Hale of Kansas City, by trade a fireman, indeed the chief fireman of that city, was one of the first to make a large fortune from movies. He was typical of those vigorous Americans who are always to be found starting from nowhere and getting somewhere. His portrait, for which he wears his fireman's cap and silver badge, is like that of some bourgeois citizen from the pages of Balzac, with full moustache, a lively expression, and a nose which juts forward and is always on the move.

Other names, remembered or forgotten, need to be spoken of, for this was a period of risk and adventure when any man could climb to fortune, and thin partitions divided the real thing from the fake, the successes from the failures. It is surprising how many who do so well suddenly give it all up and disappear. Among the successes we may count Herbert Ponting who went with Scott to the Antarctic in 1910, and Cherry Kearton, a newsreel maker with his own studio in London who excelled in travel films. He had an artist's eye and an explorer's passion. He accompanied Theodore Roosevelt on a hunting trip to Africa and filmed in many parts of the world. His shows at the New Gallery Kinema in Regent Street before the 1914 war were fashionable events rivalling the craze for tango teas.

To Kearton and Ponting we must add some names of greater importance—W. G. Barker of the Barker Motion Picture Photography Ltd., George Pearson of the Welsh-Pearson Company, and Ralph Jupp who founded a cinema circuit—these were shaping British films before they became an industry. Cinemas and studios sprang up in many parts of Britain. There was no direction, the industry was a mass of shifting interests. It was still emerging from the penny gaff

31

stage into the universal grading of threepence, sixpence and ninepence. The crowds were forming and the excitement was visible.

In Russia, France and Italy the same ferment was brewing, something new, something great was in the air. Jay Leyda quotes Tolstoy's remark in praise of the film: 'You will see that this little clicking contraption with the revolving handle will make a revolution in our life—in the life of writers. It is a direct attack on the old method of literary art.' A new form of writing will be necessary which commands 'the sea, the coast, the city, the palaces—there is always tragedy in palaces'.[10]

This was written in 1908 when few people brought much imagination to the medium or had any real understanding of it. Indeed, we notice a fearful poverty of thought directing the machine. It is still being used as a stunt, its highest flights are travelogues and newsreels, pictures of durbars, funerals and calamities, and this continues for several years. In fact little of importance was produced during the first ten years following the cinematograph's invention, and nothing of artistic significance. Yet the turn of the camera by hand, like the cranking up of Ford's engine, brought a social revolution to every country in the world.

In America in 1903 Edwin S. Porter had made *The Great Train Robbery* in which gun fights, chases and armed hold-ups were portrayed in roaring theatrical style and set a pattern for the first Western films. The picture ran for only eight minutes but it caused a prodigious stir among audiences and tempted studios to work on a grander scale. In France the Comédie Française took to the screen in *Film d'Art* but with no great success. The French stars could not adapt themselves to the new techniques. Bernhardt, Rejane and other divinities quickly faded out.

In our own studios *The Life of Charles Peace*, produced by Hepworth's contemporary, Walter Haggar, in 1905, was as important in its way as Porter's film. Its realism, as of people suddenly exposed in their homes or in the street, was for those days a sensation.

In 1904 Sir Oswald Stoll opened the London Coliseum,

and a few years later we find the Bioscope is an important item in the Coliseum programme. It was a sign of the film's increasing prestige that the most respected and plushiest of variety theatres in London, dedicated to Sarah Bernhardt, Ellen Terry and Diaghilev, was now to show pictures every week. The Pathé Gazette was already in existence in 1909 and studios at Shepherd's Bush which were to be of great consequence to the British industry were opened in 1914.

Stoll later took to film production himself and in 1919 opened impressive studios at Cricklewood. He brought Sessue Hayawaka from Japan to make pictures and employed many British directors—A. E. Coleby, Maurice Elvey, Sinclair Hill and J. Stuart Blackton (an American), who made some expensive flops. He was not a success as a film impresario, but he did much to advance the industry. It is astonishing how rich the cinema becomes, and how soon.

A technique was being formulated, an art was being explored. Nevertheless, it was still a diversion for slow afternoons and for slower weekends. 'Sundays here are ages long,' said Apollinaire, and they were, the diversions during that decade being Votes for Women, Lloyd George's oratory, German bands and Thomas Beecham conducting at the Queen's Hall. Diabolo, a game, consisting of a top spun on a cord, relieved the tedium for children.

England not only prospered in the arts, she was booming commercially. There was plenty of money to launch a film industry. City men began to see that films, as Bernard Baruch the banker put it, were 'a pot of gold', and they poured money into them. Indeed one of the most pleasing reflections for those engaged in the film business is that money is never very far off; art or not, it must be accepted with a good grace.

Growth and enterprise is everywhere seen and the narrative film becomes a vast trade soon to encircle the globe. Features grew in length from a few hundred feet to 6,500, as in the production of *East Lynne*, which W. G. Barker made in 1913. He had already produced a film about Henry VIII in 1911 and his sense of showmanship is evident in engaging the full stage company for it from London, with Sir Herbert Tree,

B

33

Violet Vanbrugh and Arthur Bouchier heading the cast. Clearly, stars were invented earlier than we supposed. It was natural that the screen, having no ready-made personalities of its own, should create them from the material at hand. In America this process had already begun by 1910.

George Robey, Bransby Williams and Fred Evans, renowned in the music hall, brought a passing lustre to the film, and so too did Henry Ainley, Sir Johnston Forbes-Robertson and Sir Seymour Hicks. These nobly strutting players were the progenitors in England of the star system, though England did not in fact possess a system. They were joined by such eminences as Arthur Collins, the Drury Lane producer, and Herbert Darnley, the variety comedian, and this must have been when Dan Leno was at Drury Lane in pantomime. Unhappily we do not hear of any Dan Leno films.

But players are beginning to arrive who are of the film only and who owe their fame entirely to it—Florence Turner, an American who filmed in England, Alma Taylor, Chrissie White, Henry Edwards, Violet Hopson, John Stuart, Guy Newall, Stewart Rome—all of them leading players in the 1920s and decades later. Their profiles were advertised on picture postcards and cigarette cards. By 1914 the commercial film was expanding at a prodigious rate and reaching a full awareness of its powers.

Yet British producers were painfully slow to learn what films were about and showed a deplorable provincialism of outlook compared with Europe and Hollywood. Boldness was not their aim but caution. We are not surprised that Arthur Knight, the American historian of the cinema, declares that 'we (the British) muddled through the silent era without distinction or success',[11] or that Paul Rotha finds few films earlier than Maurice Elvey's *High Treason* (1929), Grierson's *Drifters* (1929), and some of Asquith's films, worthy of mention.[12]

Nevertheless, advances were being made and these were in the direction of the full-length fiction film. On this the whole world of cinema entertainment was to prosper. In England our own studios, taking their cue from the playwrights and novelists of the time, brought a more adult conception of film to the screen and a stepping up of production plans.

Most potent of all for the British film among these new influences was the American participation.[13] By 1914 America was already flooding the market with pictures. Exhibitors protested and campaigned against it, they would be ruined, our pictures were better, something must be done, and so forth. But nothing was done. There was no effective leadership and British cinema owners readily booked the productions they condemned as ruinous to themselves.

This acquiescent attitude perfectly suited the emerging cinema groups, and indeed many individual showmen; for their policy, as far as they had one, was already pro-American and heartily in favour of handing over their screens to the American industry. This is how it came about that from the year 1918 or so we forfeited our independence as an industry. The war had reduced our own studio output to a shadow, we needed the films, we needed the business, and we were ready to pawn our future to that need. As Chateaubriand said, an Englishman will go to any lengths to sell a yard of calico.

Chapter 2

First Features: Hepworth and Others

It is difficult to evaluate the first feature-length films. A feature in the 1900s could be anything from a few hundred to a few thousand feet in length. Seen through the spectrum of our own day they can look crude and inept. Some of them undoubtedly were. But their interest lies in their visible growth and development. They were evolving a method of expression when the film as an art scarcely existed. They succeed, moreover, in telling us a great deal about the manners and morals of the time and far more vividly and memorably than by other means. If we are to judge them it can only be by those standards rather than by our own. These early films were not merely reflections, examples, criticisms of life, they were a new experience, they had hypnotic powers.

However crude *Black Beauty* (1907) or *The Road to Ruin* (1913) may have been, they revealed for ordinary people an unsuspected truth, namely that the moving picture could make an appeal to the senses of infinitely greater force than the written word.

Those who had been reading Dickens or Mrs Henry Wood responded with even greater delight to films of *Scrooge* or *East Lynne*, however indifferent in quality they might be. Films did not talk then, they were confined to captions. 'Come at once . . . Too late! . . . Dead!', etc. Action told everything and had a beauty, a completeness of its own. Film was the poetry of the Common Man and spoke directly to the heart and mind. Writing was tame and never more so than when used to describe the stuff of the cinema.

36

Of those making reputations before and during the 1914 war the most renowned are Cecil Hepworth, R. W. Paul, W. G. Barker, George Pearson, Maurice Elvey and Florence Turner, an American who made a number of comedies, now almost forgotten, with Larry Trimble.[1]

R. W. Paul, who was skilled in the construction of trick films and indeed became a leading producer, withdraws from the scene in 1910. He had made *The Soldier's Courtship* in 1898 and said of a reissue of it that it was 'extremely comic, and a fine film'. Film-makers had to speak for themselves about their work, for nobody else did in those days.

W. G. Barker, who had considerable flair as a showman, followed his *Henry VIII* in 1911 with *East Lynne* in 1913 and *Jane Shore* and *Brigadier Gerard* in 1915. *Jane Shore*, 5,500 feet long, seems to have been quite a smash hit, though 'it is hard to imagine any audience being stirred' by it, says Rachael Low. The important thing, however, was to produce a classic and one learns of the Gaumont Company making *Romeo and Juliet* as early as 1908 with Godfrey Tearle in the lead.

The subjects chosen in the 1900s already show the beginnings of a film tradition—*Dick Turpin, The Life of Shakespeare, Tragedy in the Alps,* archetypal themes. These were produced by Barker for the British and Colonial Kinematograph Company, which also filmed *The Battle of Waterloo* in 1913. It was intended to stun the eye with crowds and spectacle in the Italian manner but it was not a success. The company then decided on a new challenge to public taste and made a series of dashing productions with Percy Moran as star under the title *Lieut. Daring,* anticipating the novelettish heroes of later days.[2]

In 1908 the names of Cricks and Martin appear. They made the first feature film in Britain, 945 feet long, and at one time turned out a picture a week. They flourished exceedingly, largely with the production of comedies, but by 1914 they were overtaken by their competitors, of whom one, the London Film Company, is most to be noted.[3] Others came and went. Everyone was jumping on the bandwagon and it is not always easy to distinguish the passengers from the driver.

One of the more important travellers was the celebrated Dr Ralph Jupp, already mentioned, who promoted one of the largest cinema circuits in Britain, and laid the foundations of the exhibiting industry. The doctor is already active in 1909 and has introduced Sir Max Aitken (later Lord Beaverbrook) and the sporting and affluent Sir William Bass to the film trade. Jupp's passion for collecting cinemas is to affect profoundly the shape of things to come.

In Dr Jupp we discern the unsleeping entrepreneur, the master mind and prototype of all the barons of cinema history. For the moment he is to be observed only as a producer and as the guiding force of the London Film Company. He engaged American players and producers and assisted the process of linking the British film industry to the dollar. The London Film Company had considerable flair and a high degree of professionalism and employed actors of the calibre of Henry Ainley, Sir Cyril Maude, Charles Rock, Gerald Ames and Mary Brough, all eminent on the London stage at that time. Its pro-American policy however was much criticised.[4]

In 1914 the company cast Sir Herbert Tree in *Trilby*, and was making films of two to three thousand feet in length. They had studios at Twickenham. Harold M. Shaw, an American producer, was responsible for most of the films and he too came under fire as an American when it was thought that a British producer might have been chosen. Yet American producers, it must be admitted, had greater expertise than the British. *A Bachelor's Love Story* and *David Garrick* which Shaw made are typical of a thousand similar subjects reflecting the choice of the studios.

Both the London Film Company at Twickenham and the Hepworth Company helped to give the film industry a solid foundation and a needed prestige. So too, did the Williamson company which had studios at Brighton and produced, among a number of features, *Williamson's Animated Gazette*. It enjoyed a brief fame and departed. So it was with many companies which came and filmed and went.

One of these can claim the distinction of having pioneered Boreham Wood in Hertfordshire as an ideal centre for film production. This was the Neptune company formed by a group of men from the theatre who had worked for the London Film Company. They were Percy Nash (1869–1958), John M. East (1860–1924), actor-manager, and Gerald Lawrence (1873–1924), who was Henry Irving's juvenile.

Like others whose ambitions were thwarted by boardroom policies, Percy Nash and his friends felt they must establish themselves independently, and under the guidance of A. M. Lawrence, Gerald Lawrence's brother, who raised the large sum, for those days, of £40,000, they formed the Neptune company and bought seven acres of land at Boreham Wood, Elstree. Here they built one of the most advanced studios in Europe.

Well-known names from the Edwardian theatre formed the Neptune stock company—John M. East himself, Gerald Lawrence, Fay Davis, May Whitty, Ben Webster. Gaby Deslys, the French cabaret star for whom J. M. Barrie wrote his one revue, *Rosy Rapture* (1915), was a guest star for Neptune with the youthful Alfred Willmore (better known to us as Michael MacLiammoir). Neptune held the film rights of all Barrie's plays, and not only filmed *Rosy Rapture* (with Gaby Deslys), but also *The Little Minister* and *What Every Woman Knows*.

In 1915, after boardroom disagreements, Percy Nash resigned from Neptune, and two years later the company abandoned production. Actors and technicians were being conscripted for the war, money was slow in coming in from the distributors, and 'a crippling flood of American pictures coming into Britain free of import duty' was a heavy blow to the company.

In 1918 Neptune was taken over by Ideal Films and in 1921 was wound up. Percy Nash retired when sound pictures came in.

Besides Neptune, there were thirty or forty studios in operation from Manchester to Brighton and in many other parts of the country. If little of their work remains to us except in archives and catalogues or in old newspaper files the reason is obvious. It was industry only, it lacked the preservative of art. There is nothing of what came to be known as editing, the grammar of the film is still being explored, the text books are still to be written.

Cecil Hepworth (1874–1953), who largely dominates the scene in the early days, was born in London and made an immense number of films, but the majority of them were only a few hundred feet long and were produced in a week or so, sometimes less. He had the devotion and thoroughness of the craftsman joined to the qualities of an engineer. He loved machines and lamps and he made improvements to them. Will Barker was perhaps as skilled, certainly as industrious, but it is Hepworth's work which catches the imagination and remains a live force in the records.

'Fate had a very clear idea from the beginning of what she intended to do with me,' he declares in his autobiography.[5] His father was a photographer and popular lecturer and early introduced him to the camera trade. With the enthusiasm of the neophyte, young Hepworth, then 21, made himself known to Robert Paul on an occasion which was to be historic— Lumière's first Cinematographe show in London. Shortly after this performance he bought a projector for the sum of a pound.

He is soon discovered working for Charles Urban at the Warwick Trading Company. In 1898 he filmed the Boat Race and a year later was producing fifty-foot films of his own, of which the first was *Express Trains in a Railway Cutting*.[6] He describes one picture he made in his garden, *The Egg Laying Man*, in which his own head filled the whole of the screen. This incident leads him to deny D. W. Griffith the credit for inventing the close-up; it was first used, he declares, in *The Kiss*, a film which he claims was immensely popular at fairs and circuses. We have not been able to identify it. What is important is that Hepworth stands for the producers of that time who were creating the elements of a new art and the methods he employed are of interest for that reason. Most films were made outdoors in natural light. A good light being imperative, even interiors were built in the open air, painted flats and floorboards being assembled in a garden or field to represent a kitchen or a drawing-room. The sets were amateurish but they were conditioned by the meagre resources of the director and his limited expenditure, which had to be counted in shillings rather than pounds. Hepworth's *Rescued by Rover* (1905), one of his successes, was made for a few pounds and is noted as one of the first films to obtain its effects by editing.

At the turn of the century film producers could not expect to rival the theatre on those qualities of casting and staging which made it pre-eminent among civilised entertainments. They could not afford sophistication or extravagance. Hepworth's wife played in his pictures to save money and so did he. She was the White Rabbit in *Alice in Wonderland*.

It was not until he made *Hamlet* (1913) with Sir Johnston Forbes-Robertson that he could afford well-constructed interior scenes or castles of canvas and plaster which he built into cliffs. He had owned a studio at Walton-on-Thames since 1899.

Hamlet however was not his own production, it was made for the Gaumont Company and is of little interest except for the appearance in it of Forbes-Robertson and his wife. Many a grandee of the theatre, moved by the promise of a renewed fame, roared his lines at the camera in films which vanished as soon as seen. By 1912 the lines of development of the film were being more firmly drawn and in the production of mass entertainment they have not basically changed since. Blood, thunder and romance were taken over as fixed elements in the human comedy, as they are to a great extent still.

Stars were not chosen for any knowledge they possessed of the new art—they had none—but because they were already stage or society names. If they had no name or fame they had alluring faces and figures and that was good enough. Sets were constructed for their photographic value, as they are today, but were used over and over again. The castle in Hepworth's *Hamlet*, for example, was also used for *The Princes in the Tower*. Novels and plays were bought because they were successful. Publicity was a blend of bluff and impudence. Only film scandal had still to be invented.

Hepworth had conventional ideas but he also had a real film sense. He had used tracking shots and close-ups at

41

Walton studios, he had studied the American technique which in so many ways freed the camera, and he claimed, at least in this country, to have originated the dissolve.[7] He was skilled at composing a shot and in avoiding too literary a script and he wasn't at all sure that the theatre provided the right material for a film, or that the stage star was suited to the camera.

He liked to create his own stars, not take them ready-made, and this he achieved with Gladys Sylvani, Alma Taylor, Chrissie White, Stewart Rome, Violet Hopson and Hay Plumb. He was one of the few to acknowledge that American pictures at that time were superior to our own and he had learned in encounters with John Bunny and Florence Turner, who used his studios, what progress was being made in American production and what direction it was taking.

Yet, although a craftsman and a man of warm sympathies, an examination of his career shows an extremely limited outlook compared with the Americans or his contemporaries in Europe—for example, the Germans.

He produced many films from impeccable sources, *David Copperfield* (1912), *The Old Curiosity Shop* (1914), *The Vicar of Wakefield* (1914), and *Far from the Madding Crowd* (1916). He strove to reflect the dramatic taste of his time in such plays as Pinero's *Iris*, which he filmed with Henry Ainley and Alma Taylor. Eden Philpotts and Temple Thurston figure among his authors and he describes a visit to America in which he sees much of Charlie Chaplin.

Clearly he was something of an international figure about this time and ranks with the film industry's most influential men. His reigning star, Alma Taylor, is declared to be the most popular in Britain.

But summarising his productions, what is his achievement? He considers his most important picture to be *Comin' Through The Rye* (made twice, in 1916 and 1923) and his most successful, *Alf's Button*. Iris Barry, writing of the film at this time, has described *Comin' Through The Rye* as 'a most awful film'.[8] Judged by the variety and number of his pictures his contribution to British films is phenomenal; but on artistic grounds there is not much to be said for him, a judgement that applied to most of his contemporaries. Yet he leads as a producer for several years and he did much to establish the commercial cinema.

When at length Hepworth failed through financial difficulties he felt that all his work for the industry had been in vain. His stars deserted him and nobody would entrust him with a production. Indeed, he shares with certain birds the fate, when wounded or afflicted, of being pecked to death by their own kind. His place in British films is best judged by the stimulus he gave to films as a whole, and not by any one picture.

To modern eyes he seems provincial, in Renoir *père's* sense of 'an inability to discern', a criticism which could be levelled at most British films of that period. A comparison with the American cinema of the same period is very much to the point. D. W. Griffith had made *The Birth of a Nation* (1915) and in the following year *Intolerance*, films of deep commitment and visual excitement. They widened the bounds of technique, indeed the whole art of cinema. Charlie Chaplin had made *Tillie's Punctured Romance* and *The Champion*.

Italy had produced the spectacular *Cabiria* with a script by d'Annunzio (1913). France, so strongly to influence our own directors, was always keenly aware of the artistic possibilities of the cinema and could point to the work of Abel Gance, Jean Epstein and René Clair. German filmmakers, in their Expressionist phase, had joined with the foremost painters, writers and designers to create a film art of their own. Their work is seen in *The Cabinet of Dr Caligari* (1919) and *The Golem* (1920), in *Destiny* (1921) and *Warning Shadows* (1922), brilliant examples of silent film unsurpassed at the time.

Russia was in the middle of a revolution and had not entered films but we know what Lenin said about them. Sweden could put forward serious claims to the film as an art in the work of Mauritz Stiller and Victor Seastrom and in the phenomenon of Greta Garbo's magnificent film, *The Atonement of Gosta Berling* (1923). By comparison the British cinema has a dreadfully philistine air.

In all these European countries a different spirit, a deeper understanding prevails. The film is first of all a means of expression, its success at the box office is a secondary matter.

Of course, as with ourselves, these countries made bad films too. They were by no means indifferent to monetary success. But it did not take them twenty years or so to discover that the cinema was an art. In the early 1920s our directors and studio executives can hardly be mentioned in the same breath with their continental rivals or for global success with the Americans. They suffered a narrowness of outlook which was often to cripple the work of Elstree and Shepherd's Bush and this is one among several reasons which led in later years to crisis and failure.

Chapter 3

Early Influences

George Pearson and Maurice Elvey bring us within range of our own time, but before we consider them we must note the conditions prevailing in those early days.

Several influences, varying in importance from the American interest to the introduction of film censorship and Sunday opening were already deciding the character of the industry and its future workings.

Censorship had its origin in the Cinematograph Act of 1909 which was purely a safety measure to guard against the risks of inflammable film stock and fire in cinemas. It empowered local authorities to grant licences only to those cinemas that fulfilled the fire regulations.

But exhibitors saw that under cover of these regulations wider powers might be used to decide how the film business should be conducted and the character of its entertainment. A case in which the Act was invoked by the London County Council to deal with Sunday opening made this evident. It was the abuse of the Act and the supposedly corrupting influence of the cinema as an engine of opinion and taste that led to the creation of a censorship board.

As the cinema becomes a vast apparatus of communication these influences tend to multiply and to become more powerful and binding. Especially did conditions in the American film industry determine the course of affairs in England.

In 1910 the leading American production companies, ten in all, combined to form a monopoly of the industry through the Motion Picture Patents Company. The case makes a stormy chapter in the politics of the American film. No independent producer, distributor, or exhibitor could operate outside the ring unless he accepted its terms, and this meant bowing to a dictatorship.

The prospect of a single group dominating the American industry could not be tolerated. It was crushed by the action, among others, of William Fox (progenitor of 20th Century-Fox) who was joined by Carl Laemmle of Universal Pictures and Adolph Zukor, of Famous Players, independent showmen who could not be bluffed, still less intimidated by threats or legal bluster. It was not long before they destroyed the ring, and with the breakup of the Motion Picture Patents Company (or more accurately, the General Film Company under which it functioned) American film men were free to make and sell pictures in any part of the world, and the part of the world they favoured most outside the United States was Great Britain.

From that day they established themselves here as salesmen and manufacturers. We constantly hear in the time of Cecil Hepworth, Will Barker and their successors of the ruinous competition from this source. The complaint is aggravated with the years, indeed is an unending theme of protest.

The period during which the Americans captured the British film industry is usually assigned to the years 1914 to 1927 and it is easily explained. Their films were better than ours.[1] Audiences were more receptive to John Bunny, Charles Ray, Maurice Costello and Pauline Frederick than to Alma Taylor, Henry Edwards, Chrissie White and Stewart Rome. The challenge was that of the star system joined to a highly efficient screen technique and to the brilliance of American showmanship. We lacked the expertise, the imagination and the money to compete on equal terms. A Betty Balfour or an Ivor Novello might arise and prove immensely popular, but British stars, it became evident, were made in Hollywood and Hollywood stars made British films.

Great personalities like Ronald Colman or Clive Brook, born in England, were luxuries a British film company could not afford, for they were paid twice or three times the money in Hollywood. Built up by brilliant advertising campaigns all over the world, they soon held the world's attention. We lacked the flair and the confidence. Nor did we feed the appetite for surprise and sensation which America supplied in such abundance.

It was Hollywood that brought British filmgoers the thrills and scandals of the front page, the squalid affair of Fatty Arbuckle and Virginia Rappe, the disappearance of beautiful women from the yachts of film stars, the sexual orgies which we may safely say did not take place at Shepherd's Bush. On the screen Gloria Swanson and Lillian Rich made such things fashionable, they introduced to films Roman vices and Swinburnian passions and empurpled the passages of Elinor Glyn's novels.

It was this unhealthy Hollywood background as well as the films themselves which eventually brought censorship to the American movie business. This was not until 1922 when the Hays office was established to clean up the movie industry and restore its reputation. Will Hays, its chief executive, had been postmaster-general in President Harding's administration and he laid down a code which made a great many specific and often absurd prohibitions. They created problems for British as well as American producers.

In Britain the anomolies of film censorship have held it up to constant ridicule. It has a long history of petty controversy justifying Macaulay's saying that 'nothing is so ridiculous as the British public in one of its periodical fits of morality'.

Censorship is already a familiar story by 1910 when a film of the Johnson-Jeffreys fight was condemned by the Watch Committee in Walsall because it tended to 'demoralise and brutalise the minds of young persons'.[2] The London County Council passed a resolution that it was undesirable to show the film and it notified all the music halls and other places under its jurisdiction to this effect.

The Council however had no power to forbid local authorities to show such a film; if the offence were repeated or flagrant it could withhold its licence, which came to the same thing. Local watch committees could do likewise. 'The local authority acts as the final arbiter and censor of films in its own area.'[3]

At Blackburn in 1911 the Justices made it a condition of issuing licences that films should be submitted to the Chief

Constable before they were shown. Thus the whole confusing ritual of censorship began in Britain, to be even worse confounded when in later years Hollywood brought in its own form of censorship.

In those days the issue of freedom of expression was not so acute as it was destined to become, but because of the inconsistencies and differences of practice in different parts of the country, and the genuine anxieties overhanging society at the time, some official form of censorship was considered imperative. The trade took action and on 22 February 1912 a deputation of film manufacturers and renters submitted a scheme of censorship to the Home Secretary, Reginald McKenna.

He approved the idea in principle but did not want the Government to be further involved. They should seek the co-operation of the local authorities, especially the London County Council. In short, it was left to the film trade to set up its own organisation. It had the right to appoint its own president, who was to be some public figure, but the choice must be approved by the Home Secretary.

It was thus that the British Board of Film Censors came into existence, with G. A. Redford, a former examiner of plays at the Lord Chamberlain's office, as its first president.

The London County Council had no desire to act as official censor or to exceed its existing powers. It granted licences to cinemas on the broad principle that the films shown 'should not be subversive of public morality'. To this broad prohibition the British Board of Film Censors added rulings of its own which classified films as 'A' for adults and 'U' for children. As a matter of fact the Board had no written code and there were only two absolutes in its ruling: no nudity and no portrayal of Christ.

By 1913 the Board was properly constituted and from March of that year every film had to carry its certificate. The president was assisted by four examiners who had no connection with the industry or interest in it. As *The Factual Film* points out, 'it claims to be independent in its decisions' but as it is financed and maintained by the film trade its degree of independence may be judged.

48

Promptly in the year of the Board's formation a Darlington cinema owner was prosecuted for showing *Sappho*, and at Dewsbury *Dante's Inferno* was banned. Clearly there was to be no censorship without plenty of censoring.

In 1915 *Five Nights*, the film of Victoria Cross's novel, was given an 'A' certificate but ran into trouble in St Helen's and other towns on the ground that it was 'objectionable and indecent'. The sequel in the courts was inconclusive. It turned on what was reasonable, and this seemed to vary with different judges.

In 1916 G. A. Redford died and was succeeded by T. P. O'Connor, member of Parliament and journalist. The *Five Nights* case led to a campaign in the trade for an official censorship board backed by the Government such as no council could over-rule. After lively discussions with the various trade organisations the Government decided to bring in an official censorship in 1917 and this was formally approved by McKenna's successor at the Home Office, Sir Herbert Samuel.

But at the end of 1916 a new Government came in and with it a new Home Secretary, Sir George Cave. He was altogether opposed to an official censorship, as the film trade was, too, when it learned in more detail what it meant. And so the matter was allowed to drop and the BBFC retained its powers, subject always to the rights of local authorities to make decisions of their own in defiance of the Board's ruling.

Though it could not satisfy everyone, voluntary censorship proved a good compromise. It was complicated when the American film industry introduced their own censorship in 1922 in the form of the Hays organisation. The Hays office, as it was called, had its own production code which, as Hunnings points out was not dissimilar from ours though it was written and ours was not.* British producers, we are told, preferred to deal direct with the Hays Office rather than the BBFC, and there was an office in New York to deal with British scripts.

In 1920 the film of Brieux's *Damaged Goods*, made by

* For a full discussion of the British and American film censorship see *Film Censors and the Law* by Neville March Hunnings, Ch. 4.

49

Samuelson, was banned under the Venereal Diseases Act of 1916 for being 'of a sexual and sensational nature'. So too, in the following year was *Auction of Souls* which pleaded the cause of Armenian refugees expelled from Turkey. The objection here was that the film made political propaganda. 'In spite of the independent status of the Board of Film Censors', says *The Factual Film*, 'there can be little doubt that this body is susceptible to Government influence.' Herbert Wilcox's *Dawn*, which dealt with the Edith Cavell case, was banned on political grounds so as not to offend Germany. In America some years later a film could be censored because of the use of such a word as 'damn' or 'bloody'. On both sides of the Atlantic the activities of film censors make sad reading.

Two other matters of policy had a marked effect on cinema owners and on the public—entertainments tax and Sunday opening. The entertainments tax was introduced as the Amusements Tax in 1916 to raise revenue during the war. In succeeding decades it produced hundreds of millions of pounds and in a single year £37,200,000. The tax applied also to theatres, music halls and other entertainments (not sport), but the cinema was obviously marked down as the richest source of revenue, there being some 4 to 5 thousand film theatres at that time in the country.

Cinema prices varied from a penny to a shilling and the tax began with the imposition of a ha'penny on seats up to 2d and as much as a shilling on 12s 6d seats, these of course being in the live theatre.[4]

It was bad news for the exhibitor. In the first years of the 1914 war the weekly profit of a small cinema owner might be only a few pounds, and the tax, trifling though it seems, could mean the difference between profit and loss. Attempts were made in Parliament to establish the sixpenny seat as the lowest to which the tax should apply but the Chancellor was unsympathetic and would not be moved.

Sunday opening of cinemas had been almost as deep a grievance among exhibitors as the tax. They knew that the

Cinematograph Act of 1909 which had been designed simply to ensure safety in cinemas could extend its authority to other matters—to the days, for instance, on which cinemas were allowed to open. This is exactly what it did. Licences were only granted for six days and this gave power to county councils to stop Sunday performances. They stopped them and the usual uproar followed.

In 1910 a court case arose when an exhibitor defied the Sunday ruling. He won his case, it being held that the London County Council had no power to act except in matters of safety.[5] The Council appealed and the decision was reversed. The wrath of exhibitors knew no bounds. A campaign was waged to fight the decision.

But in 1911 the LCC relented and Sunday opening was permitted provided the profits went to charity. A confused situation continued among other councils. The position turned on legal hair-splitting about the use of inflammable film, this being the whole *fons et origo* of the first Cinematograph Act. Eventually, in 1915 the courts ruled against Sunday opening altogether.[6] Those who on religious or other grounds had no taste for entertainment on Sunday were satisfied. The others, that is to say the great mass of working people, fell again into the Great Boredom. It was to be with them for years.

Chapter 4

Pearson, Samuelson, Elvey and their Contemporaries

George Pearson (1875–1973), formerly a schoolmaster, entered the film industry in 1913 at an unpropitious moment when 'British films', he declared, 'had reached a final twilight of surrender to their foreign competitors'.[1] He understood popular taste and had a gift for original stories, and he did not begin his film career until he was 36, when, with no experience as a producer, he joined Pathé Films in their Great Portland Street office. Pathé were in a commanding position in the industry then, and indeed in the world. Pearson was not with them for long but his experience showed how ambitious the movies were becoming, for one of his jobs was to edit a version of *Les Miserables*, lasting three hours.

In 1914 he left Pathé to join G. B. (Bertie) Samuelson (1886–1947), a bright young man in his twenties who was soon to make his mark in the production field.[2]

Samuelson's career in its beginnings and development is characteristic of the time. Born of a show business family— his brother was Julian Wylie, the West End theatrical producer—he began as a film renter in Southport with the Royal Film Agency.

In 1913 his ambition led him into production and he rented Will Barker's studios at Ealing to produce *Sixty Years a Queen*, a picture filmed 'in one long scene', taking about 20 minutes to photograph. Barker and Samuelson were both men of strong patriotic feeling and the film was their joint effort, Barker directing and Samuelson taking an active interest in the details of production.

52

He was then 26, but he did not long continue this association. In 1914 he and George Pearson built the Worton Hall
Studios at Isleworth for a thousand pounds and made their
first film there, Conan Doyle's *A Study in Scarlet*. The pace
appears to have been too hot for Pearson however and they
parted. At Worton Hall Samuelson made a number of major
pictures, *John Halifax, Gentleman* (1915), *My Lady's Dress*
(1918) and *Hindle Wakes* (1918), which Maurice Elvey
directed.

'Samuelson's hey-day', says Harold Dunham, who has
made a study of the period, 'was probably just after the First
World War. He had a number of directors working for him
at Worton Hall including Rex Wilson, Alexander Butler (an
American), Albert Ward and Fred Paul.' In 1919 he took a
company to America and rented studio space at Universal
studios, where he made six pictures, a fact surprising enough
for those days.

In short, he was a considerable figure if not the wholly
dedicated film man, for in 1921 during a railway strike he
conceived the idea of launching a fleet of coaches to provide
transport for stranded travellers. In 1922 however he is back
in films and joins up with S. W. Smith to promote Napoleon
Films, making *A Royal Divorce* (1924), *Pagliacci* (1923) with
Adelqui Millar and Lilian Hall-Davis, and *She* (1925),
produced in Berlin with the American stars, Betty Blythe and
Carlyle Blackwell.

But by 1926 Samuelson's influence was beginning to
decline, 'things were just ticking over' says his manager,
Arthur Alcott, though in that year he made an ambitious
come-back with *If Youth But Knew*, engaging a starry company. Yet in the following year he was turning out quota
quickies and by the 1930s his output was sadly reduced, his
last picture being *The Crucifix* (1934), a 50-minute quota
production.

Harold Dunham speculates on this strange ending to a
notable career. 'Why did it end in failure?' he asks, and puts
it down to a number of causes. 'All British producers in the
silent era labour under difficulties,' he observes, 'and in fact
the most obvious one may have been the most important—

sheer lack of finance. . . . He must have taken great losses over the coach business, which I would doubt if he ever recouped. . . . Once he had been reduced to the level of directing quota films there was really no future for him and in the early thirties he realised this.'

It is remarkable that men who were so ambitious and could attract the highest talent among authors and players leave so little trace behind them. They did not always know the value of their own work but sank it all in commerce.

George Pearson had been associated with Samuelson in the making of a patriotic film, *The Great European War* (1914), in which Lord Kitchener, Lloyd George and the Kaiser were portrayed. It was made in ten days, Pearson tells us in *Flashback*, his autobiography, and was 'an instant success.' His account of it shows his keen awareness of the film's powers and his imaginative use of them. Pearson decided on 'a technique of brevity and speed . . . a sense of rushing history . . . moments of patriotic symbolism . . . a flag unfolding, a lion rampant, German hands tearing a parchment treaty to pieces'.[3]

Pearson left Samuelson in 1915 and went over to the Gaumont Studios at Lime Grove, Shepherd's Bush, as their senior film director. Here he met Thomas Welsh, head of the studios, and two years later they formed the Welsh-Pearson Company with a capital of £6,000. Various persons of eminence were associated with him—Ward Price, the war correspondent, Herbert Ponting, the naturalist and photographer, H. de Vere Stacpoole, the novelist, and Reginald Bromhead of the Gaumont Company.

Pearson had to find a subject which would correspond in popularity to the latest French success, *Fantomas*, a fabulous character who defied the law for noble ends. He invented *Ultus, the Man from the Dead* (1915), which tells how a crook steals his partner's diamonds in the Australian desert and leaves him for dead. But the partner returns in the form of Ultus the Avenger, and retribution follows.

Pearson wrote and produced this story and was forced rather against his will to make three more, *Ultus and the*

Grey Lady, *Ultus and the Secret of the Night* and *Ultus and the Three Button Mystery*, the last being written in a week and produced in a month. They were full-length features of between four and six thousand feet, given ornamental subtitles, an idea borrowed from America. Aurele Sydney, an Australian whom Leon Gaumont discovered, played the lead. He was a dashing character and people spoke highly of him, but he died of a fever a few years later.

Pearson points out that his players looked after their own make-up, there was no continuity girl to keep time and place in order and check every detail. Work, which began at nine in the morning, often continued until late at night. 'No one ever grumbled', Pearson says.

In 1917 British films were still at a low ebb, many of the best men from the studios had gone to war, and Pearson, who had recently made Temple Thurston's novel, *Sally Bishop* in the middle of the *Ultus* series, had nothing much to do. He worked on a number of Edgar Wallace's stories but they did not materialise and we next find him producing *The Better 'Ole*, a burlesque based on C. B. Cochran's stage show at the Oxford Music Hall in London. This again was derived from Bruce Bairnsfather's celebrated war cartoons published in *The Bystander*. They described the life and times of Old Bill, the Cockney soldier at the front.

Filming was made difficult by war-time restrictions and by air raids which hit studios and homes alike. The war was bleak. Men of 45 were being called up. Films were needed to stiffen morale and take people's minds off the fighting.

The Better 'Ole, in which Charles Rock played Old Bill and Lilian Hall-Davis his daughter, repeated the success of Pearson's earlier productions and enabled him to build his own studios at Craven Park, Harlesden. The possession of a studio was the mark of success. He had made this film for £5,600 and it had brought him in £40,000. Thereupon he produced a naïve little story about a failed actor, *Nothing Else Matters*. Utterly commonplace, it received an excellent press and brought Betty Balfour, the first considerable British star, into pictures.

She had been introduced to Pearson at the age of 18 by

55

Leon Gaumont and had the brash, wild-cat personality so beloved of movie audiences. With her came Mabel Poulton, a typist working at the Alhambra Theatre who was recommended for a film part by Charles Penley, the theatre's manager.

Pearson put Betty Balfour into a film called *Squibs* (1921),[4] about a Piccadilly flower girl in love with a policeman, and this production inspired an unparalleled enthusiasm in innumerable hearts. The producer finished the picture and thought no more of it, but William Jury, the distributor, later of Jury-Metro-Goldwyn Pictures, saw in it a chance to hit the jackpot and insisted on a series. We notice how the film renter early exercises his influence on the creative talent and becomes the dictator thereof.

Squibs was followed by *Love, Life and Laughter* (1923) the story of a London chorus girl, and by *Reveillé* (1924) about a mother and her three sons in the war, again with the much-adored Betty Balfour and such accomplished players as Sydney Fairbrother, Henrietta Watson, Stewart Rome and Frank Stanmore. Pearson considered *Reveillé* to be his masterpiece and quotes a characteristic comment by James Agate: 'This film may not be as great as *The Trojan Women*, but it is two thousand years nearer the human heart.'

The Welsh-Pearson Company, though booming, appears to have met financial trouble shortly after this and it parted from the Gaumont Company,[5] to be rescued, surprisingly, by an Old Etonian, Myles Corry, whose father was chairman of the Cunard Line. He too disappears after negotiating a Harry Lauder film in America and is a loss to the picturesque history of the time. Competition is now increasing, the field is widening and getting tougher for all. Other good pictures are receiving attention—*The Lodger, Nell Gwynn, Mademoiselle from Armentières*. But George Pearson at this moment was again without a subject.

He had produced a de Vere Stacpoole novel, *Satan's Sister*, which caused little excitement. Now, conscious of veering winds, he turned to a different type of film, *The Little People*, a story of Italian puppets with a moral. Thorold Dickinson, then at Oxford and soon to become a

distinguished film director himself, has recorded his experiences with Pearson, with whom he collaborated in the making of *The Little People* (1925). He describes him as 'the outstanding personality in British silent cinema'.[6]

The story, inspired by an advertising stunt he and Pearson had encountered in Paris, 'dealt with a peasant family', writes Dickinson, 'who had travelled the Mediterranean coast with an itinerant puppet show. We visited an old puppet theatre in Milan and studied behind the scenes. . . .

'In a week or two George lined up the cast and the unit and the costumes, writing all the time. My great coup was to assemble the puppeteers and to persuade André Derain to lend us his priceless collection of eighteenth century puppets. The art directors were to be Albert Cavalcanti and Erik Aes.'

They worked long hours, unencumbered by trade unions, and 'the whole film, including exteriors on the French Riviera, was made for around £8,000. Alas, it was a resounding flop because it was unprecedented as a British film; there was no art house movement in those days.'

Pearson made only one more film of importance, *Journey's End* (1929), which he made for Gainsborough and James Whale directed. It proved to be highly profitable but soon films were at their lowest ebb and Welsh-Pearson were forced into liquidation. He worked on a number of quota productions, always with the same keenness and professionalism, his faith and enthusiasm remain. But in 1937 there was another film crisis and he could get no further backing. He withdrew from feature film making and joined the G.P.O. Film Unit under Cavalcanti, and later the Colonial Film Unit, as instructor in films to overseas film students, and there he remained for fifteen years 'in a field in which I was a novice'.

Like Samuelson's, it was an extraordinary end to the career of a man who had such a record of success, who was one of the great figures of the silent film, and was a founder of the London Film Society. He himself described his withdrawal in *Flashback* as 'a mortifying curtain on ambitious hopes'.[7] He had entertained vast numbers of people and to all outward appearances was solidly established in the industry. But the movies were moving on and the new men coming in. No longer are films an inferior entertainment, no longer an unpremeditated art. True, there is not much art in films of any kind, but an aesthetic is being studied, and is a matter of passionate concern to film-makers, to students of cinema and to the readers of *Close Up*, the avant garde magazine produced by Bryher, which was the focus of critical opinion in the 1920s.

In the meantime the burden of production is carried on, among others, by Maurice Elvey, (1887–1967) whose career of forty-four years takes us from the silent era into sound.

Elvey made scores of films of every kind, most of them unashamedly commercial. A Yorkshireman, born in Darlington, his real name was William Seward Folkard. He seems to have had little formal education, but went early into the theatre as actor and director.

He founded the Adelphi Play Society in 1911 and put on plays by Shaw, Strindberg, Ibsen and Chekhov. He was engaged by Granville Barker to produce plays in New York, and this, for one of small experience, was an unexpected distinction. He loved the theatre and had an instinct for it.

In 1913 he joined the Motograph Film Company for whom his first assignment was the classic *Maria Marten, or Murder in the Red Barn*. In 1914 he went to the British and Colonial Kinematograph Company. He seems always to have been working for different concerns—for Hepworth, Butcher's, Ideal Films, and in 1919 for Sir Oswald Stoll, for whom, if we are to believe it, he made scores of films.

Then comes his Hollywood experience which he did not much care for and of which little is known, but we have it on the authority of Victor Saville that he went there. The lover of the theatre was directing films for Fox. The year 1926 finds him working for Gaumont-British and the 1930s at the Gainsborough Studios in the back streets of Islington. In largeness of output few can have rivalled him. Leslie Halliwell lists thirty-four of his more important films between 1912 and 1956 but there must be a great many more.

For the most part they are stagey transcriptions of successful novels or popular plays—*When Knights Were Bold* (1916), *Bleak House* (1920), *The Wandering Jew* (1923), *The Flag Lieutenant* (1926). Occasionally he struck a richer vein as in *Don Quixote* with George Robey. According to the records he must sometimes have produced four full-length features in a single year.

A contemporary of his with a briefer career must also be mentioned. He is Sinclair Hill whose life was cut short by an RAF flying accident when he was 49. For many years he managed the Stoll Studios at Cricklewood and among his silent successes as a director was *The Guns of Loos* (1928), in which Madeleine Carroll played the lead.

His films bore such titles as *Dark Red Roses* (1929) and *Greek Street* (1930), which dealt with life in Soho, an area not yet discovered by the screen. He directed Somerset Maugham's *The Man from Toronto* for Gaumont-British and his career illustrates the dilemma of film directors moving from silent pictures into sound. Of a film he made in 1930, *Such is the Law*, *The Times* critic observed: 'The talking element acts as an elucidatory framework to a film acted silently . . . in striving to give freedom to the spoken and silent form it evades the responsibilities of both.'[8] In short, the treatment did not work and the story, about a divorce case manipulated by a woman as a warning to her daughter, suffered from being in two minds.

Graham Cutts (1885–1958), a more sophisticated film-maker, seemed likely to become a major talent in British films with *Woman to Woman* which he directed in 1922. Cutts had a polish, a know-how, an intimacy with wordly affairs which impressed the ordinary filmgoer. An American, Betty Compson, starred in the film with Clive Brook at the fantastic fee, then, of £1,000 a week and this drama of women in conflict gave a prestige to British pictures which they badly needed.

The Rat, *The Wonderful Lie* and *The Blackguard* which Cutts made in the 1920s showed a director who had learned much from the continental school and could match Hollywood in technical virtuosity. *Woman to Woman* concerns a young married officer's love affair with a dancer during the war which has tragic consequences. He loses his memory and on his return to England does not know that she has borne him a child. The film did well, especially in the United States, and this was largely because it had an American star in it. The starring of Americans was soon to become standard practice.

In British production the only films that mattered at this time were war films. They did not need so much originality or inventiveness, but a good deal of technical know-how and something of the sergeant-major, and this was a thing our directors understood, as Hollywood understood gangsters and big business.

Bruce Woolfe, of British Instructional Films, who originated the famous *Secrets of Nature* series in 1922, is associated with some of the best British war films of the 1920s. *Zeebrugge* (1924) and *The Battles of the Coronel and Falkland Islands* (1927) directed by Walter Summers, were memorable for their documentary qualities and for their fervent patriotism at a time when patriotism could be felt and flags could be waved.

These films, with others like *Mons* and *The Somme*, were immensely popular. *Zeebrugge* brought great prestige to the cinema for it was the first film to be seen with an audience by a reigning monarch. George V attended the opening at the Marble Arch Pavilion (now a shop). After that the highest in the land could go to the pictures without losing face.

Norman Walker (b. 1892), must also be given a place as a pioneer of those days, for he turned out some admirable things for the cinema of the 1920s and years later was partly instrumental in persuading Lord Rank to enter the industry. He was to play a considerable part in a field of interest generally ignored by the film industry, that is to say, religion. Viewing the total scene this was a bad time for our studios, as George Pearson had observed.

J. Stuart Blackton, an American producer from the Vitagraph Company, made *The Glorious Adventure* (1922) for Stoll and with characteristic enterprise cast Lady Diana Manners for the lead, the society beauty whom Rheinhardt

60

had starred in *The Miracle*. But she made little impression as a movie star and the film lost money. Stoll's ambitious production of *The Prodigal Son* (1923) magnificently put on at Covent Garden was an equal disaster, and in the following year the Hepworth Company failed. In 1926 only twenty-six British features were made and most of what was screened came from abroad, that is, from America.

These were some of the worst years in film history. Hollywood was pushing British films off the map—films all too frequently characterised by mediocrity and timidity, those Ugly Sisters who too often turn up at the British film party. It is no surprise that Paul Rotha, surveying the industry at this moment, observes: 'The British film is established upon a hollow foundation . . . it rests upon a structure of false prestige . . . it has been built up by favoured criticism and tolerance of attitude . . . it is spoon-fed by deceptive praise and quota regulations,' and he quotes the much-quoted remark of Leon Moussinac: '*L'angleterre n'a jamais produit un vrai film anglais.*'

Rotha was writing in 1929 when our greatest achievements of the period, again to quote him, were such films as *Splinters*, *Tip Toes*, *The Co-Optimists*, *A Sister to Assist 'Er* and *The American Prisoner*. He is nevertheless at pains to single out Grierson's *Drifters* as a production apart, pre-eminent in the British cinema, and has some appreciative things to say of Miles Mander's *The Firstborn* and on Anthony Asquith's films.

The hollowness of the foundation to which Rotha refers is seen in the crises, defeats and bankruptcies that followed. Art is slow to come and makes no noticeable advance in Britain. In Germany it is the year of *The Blue Angel*, in France of *Sous les Toits de Paris*, in America of *The Love Parade* and *All Quiet on the Western Front*.

British directors had not yet acquired enough prestige to influence production and little original work appeared.

Chapter 5

Sound Erupts in the 1920s

The cinemas were easier to build than the films. The much harder task fell to the film-maker seeking stable conditions for his work and some understanding at the top of what he was trying to do. In the 1920s Hepworth and his contemporaries had established the film of fiction as the universal pattern of entertainment, as in a more sweeping and imaginative way Griffith, Rex Ingram and de Mille had done and were doing in America. The medium was insatiable, it swallowed everything good or bad. But an immense field of narrative remained to be explored which could satisfy a more sophisticated taste and rise to more adult levels of appreciation.

The Quota Act of 1927 meant that anyone who could make a British film of average competence could be certain it would be shown. That was indeed a gain, though it was offset by the abuse of quickies. By the late 1920s the British film had acquired form and character, it was on good visual terms with itself. It was a premeditated art able to bear comparison with those other arts to which it was related. The language and grammar of the film were established and its terms were in common use. These advances were of little value without a stable background of production and release and this was defeated by the revolution in sound.

Sound was a severe shock to the whole industry and struck at its very foundations, and this when the laws of the silent film, according to its most devoted practitioners, were still being formulated. All techniques were brought to nothing and the art had to begin again.

The centre of this cataclysmic change was America. During the second half of the 1920s films were on the decline in every part of the United States. The story is almost too old to tell of how the Warner brothers, on the verge of bankruptcy in 1927, were saved by the voice of Al Jolson in their first-full length semi-sound production and brought a renewed prosperity to themselves and the American motion picture.[1]

About this time, too, various experiments with sound were being made in Britain such as British Acoustic which Gaumont-British favoured and the De Forest Phonofilm. In Germany Tobis Klangfilm was developed and was being used at Welwyn studios.

The talkie age really begins for Britain with the flood of all-talking, all-singing, all-dancing productions launched on the world by Hollywood and shown in London in the late 1920s. The sound tracks of these early productions were provided by gramophone records. They frequently broke down but it was accepted as part of the entertainment. Early examples of such films are *The Broadway Melody* (1929) directed by Harry Beaumont in which Bessie Love and Anita Page starred. It 'has no spark of originality', said *The Times*, but 'as a further experiment in synchronization, in wrought with some striking colour sequences, it has interest'.[2]

Gloria Swanson in *The Trespasser* (1929) comes off slightly better in sentimental melodrama, and John Boles a good deal worse in *The Desert Song* (1929), a pageant 'paralysed by stage conventions'. Hollywood set the pace as usual but Britain soon joined in with the work of Graham Cutts, Alfred Hitchcock, Anthony Asquith and Victor Saville.

Immense technical and physical problems confronted film directors, many of them solved by ingenuity or guesswork or the wit of acoustic experts. It was no time for aesthetics. Solution of the artistic problems, first understood and unravelled by the Russians, had to wait in Britain while a succession of static comedies and thrillers photographed direct from their stage originals were rushed onto the screen.

Elstree looked to Frederick Lonsdale, Noel Coward, Sean O'Casey and John van Druten for words, or indeed for any sound, noise, voice or mummery that could make money. Audiences were still theatre-minded and accepted with enthusiasm whatever they were given. Indeed, the cinema has never completely abandoned the technique of the theatre despite all that has been said about it as a purely visual art. Yet it still depended for its very existence and for the character it was to assume on a vast investment of capital. All problems of film production yield to the electronic will and the City men. Soon the lesser systems are swept aside and the citadels of power are occupied by Western Electric and RCA.

It was in this atmosphere of creative and financial chaos that the major studios found themselves when Al Jolson spoke and sang. British film-makers proceeded with caution and while making great technical advances were still far behind Europe in discovering the film's poetic and intellectual virtues, and in the creation of a style. The French critic, Jean Georges Auriol, deplores the fact that Great Britain 'neglected the film so long as a means of expression and self-projection'. In Germany Fritz Lang had made *The Nibelungs* (1924) and *Metropolis* (1926), films which gave full scope to the camera and the actors and to the imagination of designers and architects. F. W. Murnau astonished the critics with *The Last Laugh* (1924) and E. A. Dupont with *Vaudeville* (1925). The centre of artistic growth was on the continent.

In France René Clair had made *Entr'acte* (1924) and *The Italian Straw Hat* (1927) and was moving towards his own form of elegant social satire. Jean Epstein, Carl Dreyer, Man Ray, Jean Renoir hold a position for which there is simply no artistic equivalent in England.

America poured a stream of pictures into Europe of boundless vitality and richness. Griffith towered above everyone. And these American films joined an assured technique to an imcomparable flair for entertainment. They reflected America in a thousand ways, from the clowning of Mack Sennett and Hal Roach to the more studied flights of Buster Keaton and Harold Lloyd. And again, on a different level, Hollywood showed its supremacy in such war films as *The Big Parade* and *What Price Glory*, both 1926.

In point of showmanship Britain lagged far behind Cecil B. de Mille who proclaimed the glorification of bodies and bathrooms and of queens bathing in milk of which *The Golden Bed* (1925) is a fair example. Even then the record is

64

far from complete and should include Chaplin's *The Gold Rush* (1925), Josef von Sternberg's *Salvation Hunters* (1925) and James Cruze's epic of all the epics, *The Covered Wagon* (1923). These indicate the weight of competition British films had to fight, indeed there were few bolts they could fling at a Goliath so well armed.

Intellectually this is a barren period. There is no sign of interest in politics or affairs, in the lock-outs, hunger marches, deep social divisions of the time, in the rise of feminism or the phenomenon of the motor-car.

The silent films do not fall into any well-defined category except perhaps that of theatre or music-hall. Films seem to be picked with the inconsequence of a raffle. In the late twenties we find *Shooting Stars, Quinney's, The Farmer's Wife, A Little Bit of Fluff, Tesha* and *Underground*. Film directors have little to say, they are content to amuse, and in this Elstree excels and is prolific.

Michael Balcon is already making his name as a producer and heads his own production company, Gainsborough Pictures. Before long he is controlling the Gaumont-British studios at Shepherd's Bush as well. In these two studios the early Alfred Hitchcocks, Victor Savilles and Walter Fordes are made. Balcon began to build up a team of writers and directors, among them Angus MacPhail, Ivor Montagu, Sidney Gilliat and Frank Launder.[3] He scanned the American skies for stars and brought them down to Shepherd's Bush—Alice Joyce, Jane Novak, Victor McLaglen; and at home Clive Brook, Ivor Novello, John Stuart. It is an important phase of film history.[4]

The background of production is still tenuous and uncertain and provides a precarious foothold for the creators of film fiction. Those, like Alfred Hitchcock and Anthony Asquith, who brought a new imagination and thinking to the British film, did not find it either easy or secure, it was full of doubts and compromises. The cinema was always short of directors, its strength was in writers, composers, designers, the men and women on the studio floor. Here were two film directors totally different in style on whose gifts much good cinema was to be built.

Chapter 6

Of Cinemas, Societies and Institutes

During the 1920s and 30s the commercial film enjoyed an unchallenged monopoly of interest. While it was successful and making a profit the industry felt there could be no reason to encourage any other kind of film. Filmgoers had no choice, they took whatever British or American programme was offered.

But there were signs of a deepening awareness of the part the cinema should play in the life of the community. Equally there was apprehension at what might happen if the cinema were left entirely to its own devices. A report, *The Film in National Life*, published in 1932 by the Commission on Educational and Cultural Films led directly to the creation of the British Film Institute, whose aim was primarily one of education and instruction. It expanded into wider fields and carried out many of the recommendations of the Radcliffe Report (1948) appointed to consider the Institute's scope and constitution.

The creation of the Institute corresponds to parallel movements among students and the more informed sections of the film industry who felt that cinema programmes were stereotyped and unadventurous. Something should be done to make available the more challenging work of the European studios. This was felt early in the 1920s when the German cinema was at its highest point of development and in France the names of Abel Gance, Renoir and Clair, among others, were creating attention.

It was in this context that the London Film society was formed in 1925 and the Institute a few years later. The Film

Society's leading spirit was Ivor Montagu who was himself engaged in film production and had all the needed contacts and persuasiveness for such an enterprise. George Pearson and Hugh Miller, the actor, joined Montagu in forming a society that would enable professional film-makers and the ordinary filmgoer 'to see the progress made in the film medium by the *avant garde* in Europe, that is to say Russia, Germany, France and middle Europe'.

Montagu requisitioned for the Society's monthly performances the New Gallery Kinema in Regent Street, then the most prestigious of all London cinemas, and here, and at the Tivoli in the Strand, shows were given on Sunday afternoons each month. Artists, intellectuals, producers, technicians and what was left of society gave their strong support, and among the founder members were Bernard Shaw, H. G. Wells, Roger Fry, Jack Isaacs, Augustus John, and J. B. S. Haldane. Iris Barry, then film critic of the *Spectator*, joined Montagu on the council with Sidney Bernstein (now Lord Bernstein), Adrian Brunel, and the former film critic, Walter Mycroft.

The London Film Society was undoubtedly a turning point in the cultural life of the film in Britain. Its Sunday afternoons were occasions of strenuous debate and a reminder that the art of the film was engaging some of the acutest minds of the age. The colour abstractions of Len Lye, the experiments of Louis Delluc and René Clair, the cartoons of Anthony Gross and Hector Hoppin were evidence of a new spirit and a new intelligence in films.

The first programme, on 25 October 1925, consisted of Ruttman's *Absolute Films*, Essanay's *How Broncho Billy Left Bear Country*, Paul Leni's *Waxworks* with Emil Jannings, Werner Kraus, and Conrad Veidt, and Chaplin's *Champion Charlie*.

Such films were held to be 'commercially unsuitable for this country'. Among those shown later were Stroheim's *Greed*, Lubitsch's *Marriage Circle*, Renoir's *Nana*, Grierson's *Drifters*, Paul Rotha's *Shipyards*, Maurice Elvey's *Maria Marten* and *The Glad Eye* (part only).

One of the best things the Society did was to break down trade prejudice and opposition to work of originality or

distinction, especially from abroad, and to encourage others
to follow suit. By so doing it inspired a film society movement
which was in time to cover the whole country.

The London Film Society continued its seasons for fourteen years until 1939, by which time, having achieved its aim
and brought numerous other societies into existence, particularly in London, it was felt expedient to leave the movement
to develop independently.

In various pockets of the commercial cinema experiments
of a similar kind had been tried out and drew enthusiastic
audiences. One of these was at the Shaftesbury Avenue
Pavilion (now the Columbia Theatre) which in 1927 began
seasons of continental programmes on the same lines as the
Film Society. This theatre belonged to the Davis family, well
known exhibitors in the industry, and for two years was
managed by one of its younger members, Stuart Davis, with
great success. Then one of those reshuffles of ownership took
place and the Avenue Pavilion became a newsreel theatre.

The example spread to the Polytechnic in Regent Street
and by the 1930s public taste was sufficiently advanced for
the Curzon, the Everyman, and one or two other specialist
cinemas to open. When, in 1929, the Avenue Pavilion became
a newsreel theatre the cause was taken up by Elsie Cohen at
the Academy Cinema in Oxford Street. Miss Cohen may be
truly described as a pioneer of the specialist film. She had
an intimate knowledge of European cinema and she planted
a strong continental tradition at the Academy which has
since flourished under George Hoellering and has become the
principal centre of advanced cinema in London outside the
National Film Theatre.

Miss Cohen has described how, in 1928, friends of hers
bought the Palais de Luxe, one of the oldest cinemas in
London 'and incidentally one of the most disreputable', and
ran seasons of continental films there, beginning with the
Russian film *Earth*, the Ufa films of Emil Jannings and
Conrad Veidt and others. 'This was in fact the first art
cinema in the world', said Miss Cohen.

After twelve months her lease expired and it was then she
learned that the Academy Cinema in Oxford Street was to

be pulled down to make room for a shopping arcade and she succeeded in persuading the owner to renounce his plan and allow her to put on continental films there. Silent films from all over the world were shown—Pare Lorentz's *The River*, Fritz Lang's *Kameradschaft* (which ran for two years) *Mädchen in Uniform, Le Dernier Milliardiare* and *La Grande Illusion*. Two films, *Professor Mamlock* and *Spanish Earth*, ran into censorship trouble on political grounds. 'I was always fighting with the Foreign Office and the censor', Miss Cohen recalls.

During the war Oxford Street was heavily bombed and the Academy Cinema more or less destroyed. When the war was over Miss Cohen found that the cinema had passed into other hands.[1]

Meanwhile a wider cultural movement was being sponsored with government support. The British Film Institute was set up in 1933 under the protection of the Privy Council. (It is now the responsibility of the Department of Education and Science.) Its first director was Oliver Bell, (1936–49).*

The Institute's objectives were clearly defined. It was to 'act as a clearing house for information on all matters affecting films at home and abroad, particularly as regards education and general culture; to influence public opinion to appreciate the value of films as entertainment and instruction; to link up the film trade and the cultural and educational interests of the country; to encourage research . . .' and 'to establish a national repository of films of permanent value'.[2]

The repository, or archive, was a first requirement among many proposed by the Radcliffe Report; second was the creation of a film library, together with books on the film and information for research; third was the provision of a lecture service; and fourth, the publication of authoritative work of high standard.[3]

The repository, or National Film Library, under its curator, Ernest Lindgren, became the National Film Archive, the first to be created. It began its work in 1935 and has pro-

---

* Bell was succeeded by Denis Forman (1949–55), J. F. C. Quinn (1955–64), Stanley Reed (1964–72) and Professor Keith Lucas (1972). Denis Forman became Chairman of the Governors in 1971.

gressed in the face of great financial handicaps to its present position as one of the most comprehensive collections in the world. Its aim in Lindgren's words is 'to build up and maintain by continual acquisition and preservation, a national collection of moving pictures, recorded on film or tape . . . which have lasting value as works of art or as historical records'.

But the cost, as with all things undertaken by the Institute, has always been a limiting factor and this has been aggravated with the years as economic conditions got worse. On the other hand, the film trade, far from clinging to its old prejudices, came in time to welcome the Institute as a means of preserving the best that is known in filmcraft, and has long given it unstinted co-operation. 'It is through the good-will and generosity of the industry', said a BFI report, 'that current films are acquired for the archive.'

Meanwhile, the laborious task of cataloguing the films has steadily proceeded and the first part of this catalogue dealing with silent news films from 1895 to 1933 was completed in 1951. It was a pioneering effort which other countries followed. As part of the Archive's services a Stills Library was formed, and by 1958 had acquired 130,000 stills.

The raw material for study is the Archive. The Archive is the cinema preserved, as the British Museum is the printed word preserved, but without the latter's immense resources in money, manpower and bequests. 'We are like the British Museum without the Reading Room', said Lindgren. The Archive, whose storage vaults are at Aston Clinton and Berkhamstead, contains newsreel and other material dating from 1895, including a royal garden party filmed in 1897. It also has in its keeping most of the Government-sponsored film of permanent value, and this includes some of our finest documentaries.

The Archive had some lean years during the war, confronted always with a shortage of funds and ever-increasing needs. It was difficult to get officialdom to appreciate that film was more than a commercial entertainment; it was 'a new form of communication, a new language, a new art, a new historical record'.[4]

70

The Institute's Education Department has its own distribution library and provides an education in film appreciation for students and young people. It books films to film societies and organises lectures in collaboration with local authorities, universities and colleges.

The whole area of film study for students and historians largely depends on the Institute's Library and Information departments developed from the days when it had its headquarters in Shaftesbury Avenue. There it built up a unique collection of books and technical journals dating from the pre-history of the cinema. Not only students, but the trade itself, deplorably ill-informed as it always has been, make constant raids on this department.

The BFI also publishes or collaborates in publishing books of its own. The launching of its quarterly *Sight and Sound* preceded the birth of the Institute by a year and may be said in some measure to be responsible for the Institute's existence, for as an educational journal with the sub-title *A Review of Modern Aids to Learning* it campaigned strongly for the BFI's foundation. It published reviews of films and it opened its pages to writers and critics of distinction, among them C. A. Lejeune, Paul Rotha and Alistair Cooke, and in the 1930s Graham Greene and John Grierson. As an independent critical journal strong in its foreign coverage it has acquired a reputation all over the world.

The Institute was in time to develop far beyond its statutory requirement of education, Archive and publication, and with its development went a good deal of internal strife and external criticism. These events belong to the later years.

Part II

Development

Chapter 7

Wardour Street: The Structure of the Industry

If in the development of British films progress was slow, particularly for the creative talent, it was due not so much to the opposition of Wardour Street as to the peculiar structure of the industry and the external pressures applied to it.

The two forces which more than any other have influenced British films are Parliament and the American film industry. We may think of the British film industry as a right-angled triangle whose three sides are formed by production, distribution and exhibition.

The square of the hypotenuse of the triangle is occupied on the one hand by Parliament and on the other by America. When these two combine they are more than equal to the sum of the squares on the other two sides—that is, to the producer and exhibitor. The distributor need not worry; he is the base of the triangle; he supports the whole structure. But in this arrangement there is not much geometry left for the independent producer or director. He must wage a continual war against the other two powers.

We have watched the silent cinema moving forward into feature production and gaining reputation. With its rise to power it left behind many of its old usages and abuses, its trading in basements and bargaining at street corners, methods that are picturesque enough in respect but have no future in the electronic age.

Prosperity changed this. The Wardour Street tradesmen settled down in a few years and became masters of an international business which they had themselves created. It began in a small way. From 1896 until the turn of the century films were sold at so much a foot—4d or 6d—in the open market. Or they were hired for a fixed period and then returned to the renter to be destroyed. The arrangement brought many disputes and price wars and when the feature film became big business shortly before 1914 it was to the advantage of the distributor or renter to make an outright sale.

The highest bidder bought the exclusive rights. Hence you will read in old trade paper advertisements the names of Ruffell's Exclusives, Walterdaw's Exclusives, and so on, the name defining the method.

Marketing and other problems, notably the monopolistic practices of the film manufacturers (or producers) which exhibitors strongly resented, forced the industry to put its house in order. It was getting impatient of disputes. The question always being asked was: Who is running this business? As in America during the Patents war, it was a question of control, and it took time to settle. By 1905 the electric theatres and picture palaces were rising everywhere and we can date the rationalisation of the industry on its present basis from this time.

F. E. Hutchinson, a trade personality of long experience, describes conditions as they were then. This was just before 1908 when he was working in Bradford and was a junior clerk with a British Company, the New Century Film Service. In later years he became head of Paramount Pictures in London.

'The only way to secure pictures in those days', he said, 'was to purchase outright, and as the public response to films was amazing, and a rapid extension of cinemas took place, the idea of a renting establishment quickly followed. Business grew by leaps and bounds. As the number of copies of a film on the open market failed to meet the demand, the idea was introduced of exclusive rights.'[1]

It does not appear, however, that renters were particularly anxious to sell British pictures. The first trade show of New Century, held at St George's Hall, Bradford, was not of a British film but of a Danish three-reeler by Nordisk, *In the Hands of the Imposters.*

New Century later merged with Jury's Imperial Pictures and this led to a further merger with Metro-Goldwyn under the name of Jury-Metro-Goldwyn. Thus the American invasion proceeded with increasing sounds of approval from the invaded.

Wardour Street became the centre of the film trade which gradually reorganised itself. The process of rationalisation applied less to the production branch of the industry whose principles of ordered chaos took longer to subdue. But in general Wardour Street took command and all wisdom and instruction flowed henceforth from there.

Why did the film men go to Wardour Street? They went because they had always been in business there or in some neighbouring part of Soho where they were engaged in photography or in the production of cameras and equipment; or they may have been furriers or tailors or in the rag trade.

In 1896 when the first stirrings of a commercial cinema are in the air there were no film names in Wardour Street, its shop fronts bear the signs of antique dealers, violin makers, print sellers, ivory merchants and café owners. It was a favoured market for such things and drew the town. Here, half a century earlier, Charles Lamb was accustomed to stroll on a summer afternoon in search of a book bargain, and so did Macaulay. Leigh Hunt has given an account of Lamb's visits there. John Flaxman earned his living at No. 27 where he worked for the Wedgwoods. William Blake was born round the corner in Broadwick Street and Hazlitt's grave lies in St Anne's churchyard which everyone must pass who walks up Wardour Street from the southern end.

The street is of a respectable age. In the history of London it is first mentioned in 1685 when it was only half the length it is now. The lower half of it was Princes Street and only became Wardour Street in 1843.

All this we must pass over to consider the state of affairs 230 years later. By 1915 the manufacturers and shop-keepers, the photographers and optical instrument makers, with allies drawn from elsewhere, form the three sides of the triangle—producers, renters and exhibitors.

Earliest to organise themselves are the cinema owners who

formed the Cinematograph Exhibitors' Association in 1912. They had as their president the eminent literary Irishman, T. P. O'Connor. The renters followed in 1915 with the Kinematograph Renters' Society, the most powerful in the trade, and they retained the 'K' of kinematograph into the second half of the century.

There had long been a related group, the Kinematograph Manufacturers Association formed in 1906—it still exists— who were not only renters of films but also producers, and were a focal point of controversy in trade affairs. But conditions changed and the Kinematograph Renters' Society which until then had been a somewhat vague body linked tenuously to the manufacturers, became an independent organisation under its present name.

The film producers, being by nature more independent, did not organise themselves until much later. Of the three associations which conduct the day-to-day affairs of the industry the exhibitors are the weakest part; in numbers and power they have been sadly diminished.

In 1917 they numbered four to five thousand and sustained the figure until 1950, when there were 4,583. But by 1965 there are only 2,047. The circuits, Rank and ABC, account jointly for 596, seven smaller circuits account for 296, and the remainder, some 1,555, consist of small groups or single cinemas. Of this remainder some 250–300 are represented by a splinter group, the Association of Independent Cinemas.[2]

Exhibitors have nearly always been at the mercy of the unforeseeable and the unmanageable. There is today very little real independence among them. In the 1930s, for example, new films arrived from Hollywood punctually every week, usually in double-feature programmes; there were plenty of films to choose from. But the British contribution tapered off, crisis followed crisis, and the market was in a constantly unsettled state. Exhibitors needed stability. They feared change. Perhaps this was why they opposed talkies, opposed Cinemascope and the wide screen, opposed the sale of films to television, and opposed Pay-TV.

In this commerce of the film it is always the renters or distributors who dominate the scene. If we follow the making of a British picture from start to finish, the renters, like the Church, are present at the beginning and the end. They provide the money or the guarantee of distribution that enables the independent producer to get his picture off the ground. The producer is in their hands from that moment until completion of the film. He hands it over to the renter. The renter recoups himself first for all the money he has lent and for all the expenses of distribution, advertising and so on, and the producer, if he is not by then in his grave, is permitted to take his percentage or whatever he can get out of it.

Though they are not bankers the renters act in a like capacity and in association with the banks, which means that they usually have the last word in all decisions of importance affecting production. The exhibitors take what films they can get and this is in strict proportion to the number of cinemas they control and to the bargaining power which fifty, a hundred, or more cinemas give them.

But the producers may also be renters. They may also be exhibitors. Producers who are exhibitors will naturally give preference to their own pictures, as we find with the Rank organisation or Associated British.

As for the independent showman with one or more theatres, he is at the far end of the queue and must bide his time until the crumbs fall from the rich man's table. He has in fact no independence but must console himself by digesting the various reports on tendencies to monopoly in the film industry.

Yet the renters and combines, the controllers of circuits and studios, at one time holding supreme power, have had that power considerably eroded by the laws of the land. At every turn they are confronted by the do's and don'ts of the Board of Trade (now the Department of Trade and Industry). What is good for the Board of Trade is good for British films. A good film is one which improves our balance of payments.

Parliament first laid its heavy paw on the cinema in 1909 to introduce safety regulations. It passed the first Cinematograph Films bill in 1910. Many other matters were causing concern, among them the wages and qualifications of projectionists.

In 1912 the Government again showed its interest in the film business, and the Home Office, as we have seen, gave its blessing to a British Board of Film Censors. These uninspiring events serve only to emphasise the course films were compelled to follow. The link between Whitehall and Wardour Street becomes ever stronger and opens the way for Parliament to interfere with increasing thoroughness and enthusiasm in the affairs of the film industry.

The structure of the industry is also interlocked with other interests, first, of course, with the trade unions. These, and the various associations, support when they don't divide the structure, for disagreements are constant. 'This industry', said Harold Wilson, in a much quoted *mot*, 'never agrees on anything as between producers and exhibitors.'[4] Mr Wilson said this in 1948 when he was president of the Board of Trade. He took a marked interest in film affairs, as events were to prove.

The growth of the unions in the film industry can be dated from 1907 when the projectionists (or operators as they were then called) formed a National Association of Cinematograph Operators, and this, again, was formerly the Bioscope Operators' Association. Unions or branches of unions spring up, join others, or disappear about this time, as various campaigns are fought over minimum wages, Sunday opening, training of operators and so on.

The Studios are not yet represented, but clerical workers or those on the staffs of cinemas joined the National Association of Theatrical and Kine Employees (NATKE), formed in 1910. It was then fighting for improved working hours and proper registration of operators and its membership included skating rink employees when, during the pre-1914 years, roller skating was a booming pastime.

Scarcely less important, as the cinema absorbed increasing numbers of people, were British Actors Equity (1930) and the Musicians' Union (1921) and the organisation for small-part workers and extras, the Film Artistes Association (1932). It was not until 1933 that the Association of Cine Technicians (now, with television, the ACTT) was formed. Oldest of them all is the Electrical Trades Union (1889). These various

80

bodies, of course, were outside the structure of the industry, but they could bend it, they could disrupt it, and sometimes they did so. But even by 1917 film workers were not properly organised, though the cinema was booming and 20 million people were going to the pictures every week.

They did not go to see British films, they went to see American ones. Bad British comedies and dramas, two or three reels in length, sometimes longer but woefully deficient in entertainment value had brought our pictures into disrepute. The Americans gladly made up the deficiency, their films had greater style, pace and expertise. Fatty Arbuckle, Mabel Normand, Bill Hart were coming up, Mack Sennett was working with Charlie Chaplin. American comedians were funnier, Americans stars more glamorous than ours, the American dream was infinitely more attractive than the British example at home.

As we have seen, conditions were ripe for a cornering of the market by US interests. War had severely curbed British film production and the continental studios which had been supplying us closed down with our own. The process of infiltration may be said to have begun before this, in 1910, when only 15 per cent of British films were of British origin.[5] By 1914 it had risen to 25 per cent, a figure bad enough.

But although the American predominance was so marked, British showmen continued to believe that it was a passing phase and that their audiences preferred British productions to all others. The truth was that Hollywood films were in every way superior to our own and that a campaign of conquest of the British film industry was being actively pursued. Fox already had a share in Gaumont-British in 1928. The American interest, destined to be so decisive, also had its advantages for British cinema owners: it supplied them with films. Exhibitors regarded it as a rescue operation rather than a danger. In 1927 a trade committee proposed that the Board of Trade should be given authority to prevent British films from being bought up by foreign interests, but nothing came of it. Post-war Britain was beset by more urgent problems than film production and this may account for the reluctance of Parliament to intervene.

There had been much talk of action. Lord Newton in the House of Lords, Mr Baldwin in the Commons, had called for a close look at the position of the industry in 1925 and the film press was worried about American trade practices, that is to say, block booking and blind booking of films.

It was not until eight years after the 1914 war, however, that our legislators went into action, spurred into it by another crisis. 'By 1927,' says the PEP report of 1952, 'the British film industry was well on the way to extinction. It could be saved only by voluntary trade action which meant, in effect, by American acquiescence, or by legislation.' 'Acquiescence' presumably meant that the industry could not act unless the Americans agreed.

And the truth was that in 1926 British films appearing on British screens were down to a mere 5 per cent, the majority were blind booked to our cinemas by American renters, that is to say they were sold in advance to exhibitors who had never seen them. The captains of the industry were powerless to act and the Government were driven in 1927 to introduce the Cinematograph or Films Act officially described as 'An act to restrict blind booking and advance booking of cinematograph films, and to secure the renting and exhibition of British films, and film purposes connected therewith.'

More plainly, its object was to reduce the number of American pictures shown on our screens and increase the number of British, a percentage of British films being enforced on a graduated scale.

The quota imposed took two forms, a renter's quota and an exhibitor's quota. The renter always had to produce more films than the exhibitor needed in order to give him a choice, so in this case it was fixed at $7\frac{1}{2}$ per cent as against 5 per cent for the exhibitor, rising to 20 per cent by 1935. The Act made blind booking and advance booking illegal. If the Government acted late, at least it acted effectively.

But the bill had the more serious consequence of changing the relations between the British and American industries. The law stiffened resistance to the American take-over—it did in fact provide the only resistance—and by the same token it stimulated British film production. But it did not

82

go far enough. There was nothing to prevent the Americans from turning out cheap films for quota purposes, which they did, and so the scandal of quota 'quickies' arose. We notice how the bill created ties with Whitehall which were closer, and looked like becoming permanent. It set up a Cinematograph Films Committee (now the Films Council) to advise the Board of Trade on the working of the bill and on the industry's own problems. The members of this committee were drawn from eight persons representing the trade and from seven who were outside it.

This was all very timely and necessary if Parliament was to be the catalyst and protector of the film industry; also the bill recognised for the first time that films were a national interest. They could not be allowed to wither or fail. Films had an educational value and were part of our culture, they sold British goods abroad and maintained our prestige. It would never do to allow this powerful medium to be dominated by another country. Indeed, a primary object of the Quota Act, as it was to be called, as important as guaranteeing screen time to British films, was *to establish an industry under British control . . . in the United Kingdom for the production of these films*[6] (my italics).

What actually happened was exactly the reverse. The industry, suffering repeated crises, unemployment, and enormous losses, could not manage its own affairs. It looked increasingly to Whitehall for aid. Interest and expediency brought it more and more under American dominion and prepared the way for a British surrender and loss of independence. C. M. Woolf and John Maxwell may have fought to avoid this but they were destined to be outwitted by superior forces and strategy.

Of the 1927 Act A. J. P. Taylor has said: 'It had little serious effect. Few British films made their mark. The actors were borrowed from the theatre and soon departed for Hollywood if they achieved any reputation. Only two British directors reached the front rank: Alexander Korda, an expatriate Hungarian, and Alfred Hitchcock, a successful maker of silent thrillers who went on to an equal success in talkies. Otherwise the Americans had it all their own way.'

83

Chapter 8

The Building of the Cinemas
Bromhead, Ostrer, Bernstein, Deutsch

The electric palaces and biograph theatres that flared up in the streets in Edwardian days soon ceased to be the wonders of the age. More ambitious schemes were being laid to bring more entertainment in greater luxury to larger numbers of people. It must be remembered that the music hall was still in its heyday, it was socially superior to the cinema, and a seat cost only threepence or sixpence, including an item from the bioscope. To pay so much for the pictures alone was unthinkable.

Then an event occurred which changed the scene. The Balham Empire opened in 1907 with a programme exclusively of films, the first theatre to do so. One may date the rise of the cinema from the threepenny stage to a dignity of its own to this period. Rachael Low puts it around 1908 and the three following years. In 1913 between five and six hundred companies were engaged in showing films and by 1914 a number of circuits had appeared of which the largest was Albany Ward's with twenty-nine theatres. We are still contemplating the pioneer days in which single cinemas were owned and run by showmen, some of whom did all the work themselves, from projecting the film to front-of-the house display.

But bigger things were on the way. By 1910 London, according to *The Bioscope*, had at least 300 cinemas and in 1915 Manchester had 111 and Liverpool 33.[1] Accurate figures are hard to obtain but the whole population was going to the pictures and builders and speculators were giving it every encouragement.

84

The boom in construction began in the 1920s with the coming of the fabulous marbled and mirrored halls, built to last. It reached its peak in suburbia and the provinces in the 1930s. Between the twenties and the thirties all the big West End Cinemas were built, three of them as shop windows for American companies.*

We have noticed already the activities of the ever active Dr Jupp, both as exhibitor and producer. He is important because in the bricks and mortar he so assiduously laid we can see the whole structure of the cinema rising in Britain.

He established two groups of theatres, Provincial Cinematograph Theatres (PCT) in 1909 and Associated Provincial Picture Houses in 1914, the latter being big enough to swallow the former. By 1920 these two Companies owned sixty-eight cinemas. This was the concern in which Jupp interested Sir Max Aitken (later Lord Beaverbrook), who was a large shareholder, and of which Sir William Bass became Chairman. Lord Ashfield succeeded him.

The lordly interest was an unmistakable sign of success, though Wardour Street was not paved with gold. Several companies which had begun well could not compete with the luxury and magnificence which the new men were providing. A number of them went bankrupt. Much of the history of British films is concerned with bankruptcy.

Light is thrown on the strange methods of business of those days by an energetic Wardour Street character who knew all sides of it. He was Sam Harris, a man of Dickensian exuberance and vigour, who flourished in the early days and was active well into the 1960s. He moved in the background and he can be considered one of the founders of the industry.

Harris founded an estate agency in 1910 dealing largely in theatres and cinemas and in property for the well-to-do in Mayfair and the West End. He owned a paper called *The Mayfair Property Gazette*, forerunner of the present *Cinema TV Today*, and he describes the rough and ready manner in which the film business was conducted in Wardour Street before it became rich and respectable.[2]

* These were the Plaza, the Empire and Warner Theatres. The London Pavilion was also converted into a cinema by United Artists.

85

'In 1909, to give you an example', he said, 'two West End theatre men, Horace Sedger and Edward Laurillard, called on me when theatre business in Shaftesbury Avenue was bad. They had plans for a cinema and I found premises for them in Marble Arch where the Cumberland Hotel now is. But the clients for whom I was acting (the Portland Estate) objected. 'We're not going to have these fly-by-nights ruining our property,' they said. 'Tell them to get out.'' '

It seems that they managed to make the building respectable by giving it a glass roof, a false ceiling and a sloping floor, and there it was—a cinema. 'These fellows never had any money,' said Harris, 'but they fitted up the place with carpets, luxury seats and everything to match. Then they organised a big gala opening for all the snobs in town. Unfortunately they didn't have the consent of Lord Portland to open, and Sedger only got it at the very last minute while the audience were waiting for the show to start. He arrived breathlessly in a hansom cab flourishing a permit.'

Harris speaks of a similar experience with Montague Pyke, an exhibitor well known in his day, for whom he found two draper's shops in Edgeware Road which were exactly suited to conversion into a picture palace.

'He didn't have a penny either but ordered everything as the other fellows did. He was soon in difficulties and I don't know what would have happened if Lady Battersea, Lord Rothschild's sister, hadn't subscribed £1,000 in shares and put the business on a proper footing.'

Pyke promoted Pyke's Circuit, and was apparently a good showman. His cinemas were prominent in the London of 1910 and Harris says he invented the phrase: 'The World Before Your Eyes'. But he gambled heavily, and of the thirteen companies he formed several went into liquidation.[3] Sam Harris, who later advised the film industry on what technical systems to use for the sound film, died in 1966. He was a fervent collector of antiques and among his other treasures at his Bournemouth home, such as paper-weights, he owned a superb collection of Japanese sword hilts.

The incidents he describes were not uncommon and were an invitation to more substantial interests to take over from the smaller men. Provincial Cinematograph Theatres and Associated British Cinemas, then evolving, were the foundation on which the two big combines were formed—the Gaumont-British Picture Corporation and the Associated British Picture Corporation. These giant concerns absorbed every cinema interest.

The origin of the Gaumont Company can be traced to the days of 1898 when films were shown on fairgrounds. The Bromhead name in Gaumont-British runs through film history from its beginnings, for Colonel Bromhead was the London agent to Leon Gaumont in France before the turn of the century and was already well established as renter and producer. Founded in 1898, it was not until 1922 that Bromhead and others bought the rights of the Gaumont Company from its French owners and Gaumont became British.

Bromhead's partners in this arrangement were the Ostrer brothers, Isidore, Mark and Maurice Ostrer, who were merchant bankers. In 1926 they bought Biocolour Picture Theatres, one of the larger circuits, consisting of seventeen theatres, and a year later the Gaumont-British Picture Corporation was formed.

This, again, absorbed other companies and other men— C. M. Woolf, head of the W. & F. Film Service, and Simon Rowson, the statistician of the film industry, who controlled Ideal Films. They joined the board of Gaumont-British and so did Alfred Davis whose family built the Marble Arch Pavilion (now demolished), and the vast Davis Theatre at Croydon. The Davis cinemas were added to the Biocolour group, making twenty-one in all.

A year later in 1923 we find that Gaumont-British own 187 cinemas, either built themselves or bought from independent owners. Colonel Bromhead is chairman and R. C. Bromhead is managing director, with Alfred Davis and others as directors. Woolf and Rowson were both on the board.

Amid all these complex shufflings of boards and people were two brothers, Philip and Sydney Hyams, owners of cinemas in the Denman circuit, and they too join the Board of the Gaumont-British Picture Corporation. Later the

87

Hyams brothers were to build huge cinemas in the East End of London.[4]

All these were an outlet for Gaumont-British films and show how the process of vertical integration was gradually taking shape. The building of cinemas necessitated studios to supply them. In 1920, as part of the Gaumont set-up, Gainsborough Pictures comes into existence, a company which made many good English films. C. M. Woolf is again on the scene as chairman, Michael Balcon is managing director and Maurice Ostrer a director. The Gaumont Studios (now occupied by BBC Television), were at Shepherd's Bush, the Gainsborough Studios were at Islington and were reconstructed from a former power station. Jesse Lasky records how Alfred Hitchcock worked for him there as a prop man for fifteen dollars a week. He liked the studios despite the risks of getting foggy weather there. In that grey Islington suburb many bright things were achieved and Gainsborough became a name in pictures.

In 1929 Gaumont vastly increased its strength by amalgamating with Provincial Cinematograph Theatres bringing its total of cinemas up to 287. Lord Ashfield resigned as chairman and was followed by Colonel Bromhead. Not long after that there was a further reshuffle, Bromhead left the corporation and was succeeded by Isidore Ostrer, with Mark Ostrer as vice-chairman and C. M. Woolf and Will Evans as joint managing directors. Roughly, the business is kept in the family but in all these vicissitudes Isidore Ostrer remains very much in the background. Aloof, veiled in mystery, he finds the money while Woolf and Balcon find the pictures, though in fact Woolf was not a producer but a salesman and promoter.

In 1935 he left Gaumont and began his association with Lord Rank, then Mr J. Arthur Rank, a step of great consequence to the film industry.

But other forces and men were striking out and completing the pattern. Associated British Pictures was formed in 1928 with John Maxwell as chairman, a Scottish lawyer and exhibitor. He was shrewd and ambitious and quickly gained eminence in the industry. While Dr Jupp collected cinemas,

Maxwell collected film companies—Wardour Films, Waverley Films, First National-Pathé, Scottish Cinemas and Variety Theatres, British Instructional Films, and that for which he was most renowned, the Elstree company of British International Pictures. In 1933 most of these came under the banner of the Associated British Picture Corporation, by which time Maxwell's circuit had increased to 147. It was still far behind Gaumont-British whose theatres he coveted with a collector's passion, indeed a Scottish collector's passion.

For the time being the pattern was set: the film industry, with some notable exceptions such as Sidney Bernstein and, a few years later, Oscar Deutsch, was in the hands of these two vertical combines. The Films Act of 1927 had favoured these designs. It had been a stimulus both to production and exhibition and had a transforming effect. Sound was an even more powerful catalyst. For these reasons—the passing of the Films Act, the formation of the combines and the revolution in sound—the years 1927 to 1930 have been called the most momentous in the history of the industry. Yet the transformation did not work out exactly as intended. The legislation which had furthered the plans of combines and producers and had put British films on the screen by law had later to go into reverse and restrain them. They were wasting money and going bankrupt. In later years Lord Strabolgi was forced to admit in the House of Lords that 'it (the Films Act) had not been the success that was hoped for at the time'.

Besides the two chains of cinemas set up by the combines there were a number of circuits of various shapes and sizes in various parts of the kingdom owned by individual showmen or companies. In 1927 there were twenty-two of them, of which the most notable for its growth and independence is Bernstein Theatres (since 1930 Granada) which rose from ten cinemas in 1927 to sixty in 1957. They were, and remain, a highly individual concern. Controlled by Sidney (now Lord) Bernstein, it formulated its own policy and did not follow the fixed patterns of the trade or conventional ideas of showmanship.

89

Bernstein's aim as an exhibitor, and later as head of Granada Television, was 'to entertain intelligently', which, in the broader context, meant to present the best of its kind in whatever field it might be. Moreover, to entertain intelligently applied as much to the way a film was presented as to the choice of programme and the management of the cinema. An off-beat film which received a favourable response could run its course without following a pre-ordained release pattern or reaching a required breaking figure. 'Providing worth-while entertainment', Bernstein declared, 'is not always as profitable as presenting second-rate entertainment.'

These unorthodox policies tended to set Granada apart in its aims and achievements and were not regarded with great enthusiasm by the rest of the film trade. Unlike his competitors, Bernstein is a left-winger in the centre of a predominantly right-wing Wardour Street and his interest in politics, in the arts, and in the film as a public service did not endear him to his Conservative opposite numbers.

In the building up of his cinemas he drew on the talents of such artists as Komisarjevsky and Frank Dobson. He was the first to open his cinemas to plays, opera and ballet. In the 1920s, when no one took the trouble to research into the needs of the industry, he sponsored an inquiry into the tastes and habits of 250,000 filmgoers and published the results. As chairman of a small group of cinemas he was of course freer to experiment; Granada policy was in fact a continuous experiment, prepared to discard old traditions and create new ones at any time.

There was one other notable exception to normal practice in cinema construction and that was the circuit built up by Oscar Deutsch known as Odeon Theatres and launched in 1933. A man of boundless energy, fertile in ideas and prompt in carrying them out, his unorthodox methods would have been sufficient to exclude him from the industry if he had not already, in a small way, been in it.

By trade a Birmingham metal merchant, he was associated with Balcon and Saville in Victory Motion Pictures, and had six cinemas of his own which grew to twenty-six by 1933. This naturally made him a member of the club. His grand ambition was to build a chain of 300 cinemas throughout Britain as a third circuit, a scheme unlikely to recommend itself to Gaumont-British or ABC. However, he needed no such recommendation. By 1937 he had already built 180 of them and was a visible threat to the two combines.

To put up a cinema at that time cost anything from £40,000 to £100,000. Oscar Deutsch's policy had always been to build a new theatre rather than to adapt an old one. Each one was to have a style and decor distinctively Odeon in character which would become as familiar to the public in the course of time as Selfridge or Hoover. Oscar Deutsch's wife, a professional in the business, contrived the decor.

It was a bold scheme and it had the virtue of simplicity. His method was to find local money in each town or city where he intended to build, the cinema was identified with its leading citizens and shopkeepers, and civic pride was linked to private enterprise. Each cinema was the focal point of a new shopping centre and a new one was opened usually every week and sometimes two on a single day. Deutsch had nevertheless to pay for his astuteness. New cinemas could not find audiences unless they were offered new and attractive films every week. Deutsch soon found himself frozen out by the two combines which owned 434 cinemas between them, Gaumont-British 287, Associated British 147.

It was an American company, United Artists, which saved the situation for him. As distributors they already had an interest in one circuit of fifty theatres, County Cinemas, and they were quite prepared to extend it. Odeon's predicament suited them. They bought a 50 per cent interest in the circuit and put three of their directors on the board. There is good authority for the story that United Artists paid £50 for shares of a nominal value of £25,000.[5] United Artists not only released their Hollywood films to Odeon, Alexander Korda's among them, but also their films for quota purposes. Thus Odeon could depend on a primary source of supply. United Artists meanwhile strengthened their hold on British films.

We see once again that it is through the renting of films that the Americans increased their power, and in 1935 they were releasing 60 per cent of all films shown in Britain. 'The

91

major American companies held absolute predominance',
say the trade economists, Klingender and Legg,[6] but on the
other hand United Artists were employing more British than
American producers for their films in Britain.

How favourable all these arrangements were to Odeon is
clear from its continuing growth and prosperity, for in 1937
the company absorbed County Cinemas and became a third
circuit 250 cinemas strong, only fifty less than Deutsch had
predicted. But for his death from cancer in 1942 there seems
no doubt he would have achieved his aim. Gaumont and
Associated British by now owned no less than 559 cinemas
between them representing an audience of 653,000.[7] They
were visibly shaken by the strength and rapidity of the Odeon
development and there was not much they could do. The
three groups remained in vigilant equilibrium until the
arrival of Mr J. Arthur Rank in 1932.

Chapter 9

The 1930s: Rank and the Great Carve-up of the Industry[1]

Both Arthur Rank and John Maxwell had believed that 'British production could only achieve lasting success in an industry free from American domination' and that this freedom could only be won by building up 'a powerful vertically integrated organisation combining the production, distribution and exhibition of British films'.[2]

Such was the conventional wisdom of the 1930s. It turned out otherwise. Indeed, it is surprising the number of people— Lady Yule, John Maxwell, Lord Rank—who believed in the principle of lasting success for British films but had been unable to make the kind of film on which lasting success depended. When Lord Rank went to the United States in 1945 with the object of getting his films shown over there he met Nicholas Schenck, at that time head of Loew's Inc. 'You're a flour miller,' said Schenck, 'you haven't got a chance.'[3] Events showed that he was right.

The facts about his entry into the film business in the 1930s are well known. A devout Methodist of enormous wealth, director of the great milling organisation built up by his father, he desired to make films in support of his faith. He was not interested in religious films that were mere entertainments, such as *The King of Kings*. He wanted simple, well-made productions that would preach the Gospel more effectively and movingly than it was taught in the chapel. This was his passionate concern and it led him to his first meeting with C. M. Woolf in Cork Street shortly after Woolf had left Gaumont-British and set up his own company, General Film Distributors. This was in 1935. The two men took an instant liking to each other, Woolf had all the secrets of the trade up his sleeve, including those of Gaumont-British, a circumstance bitterly resented by the Ostrer group. Indeed, the whole industry was sceptical about Mr Rank and had nothing good to say about him. They just wanted him to keep out. Instead, he put money into Woolf's new renting organisation.

Rank had a secondary motive for entering the film business. He had made a pleasantly English film, *The Turn of the Tide* at British National Studios, Elstree, owned by Lady Yule. Lady Yule was the widow of the jute millionaire and a firm believer in films of English character of which she had made several. But like Mr Rank, she did not approve of the way the film business was conducted. When one of her films was being produced on her own estate at Elstree she discovered that the union (ACT) forbade her grandson to move things in her garden, it must be done by a union man. This and various larger exasperations finally drove her out of films, and these exasperations she shared with Mr Rank, who on the contrary was driven deeper into film production than ever.

His complaint was that he could not get a fair release on the Gaumont circuit for *The Turn of the Tide*.

This treatment stiffened his resolve to gain control over his own productions and the manner of their distribution; he distrusted the whole film business and burned to put it right. With extraordinary promptitude he began to acquire a good half of the British film industry. At one time it looked as though a permanent partnership might develop between him and Lady Yule, a formidable alliance, but they were temperamentally far apart and shared only a patriotic belief in their kind of cinema.

Alan Wood says of Lady Yule that she once accused Rank of believing in 'Christianity with five percent', so it is hardly surprising that no partnership developed. One is prone to believe this story because Wood tries to be scrupulously fair in his assessment of Rank and of other personalities in Wardour Street.

Whatever inspired Rank to plunge into the industry, he was soon to meet some immensely complicated problems.

94

Excellent films were being made, many in Rank's studios, but they did not stimulate investment from the City until, from another studio, came Korda's *The Private Life of Henry VIII*. It started a wave of speculative film-making which back-fired on the industry and frightened the City out of its wits. There was no stability. It was stability that Rank wanted, and fair dealing.

Early in his plans and as a step towards cutting out the inefficiency he saw everywhere, he built Pinewood Studios in Buckinghamshire, and in this he had a partner in Charles Boot, a building magnate and, like Rank, chairman or director of innumerable companies. These studios, opened in 1935, consisted of a converted mansion standing in its own grounds and were designed by John Sloan, the studio manager. Pinewood was linked to British and Dominions Films of which C. M. Woolf, Herbert Wilcox and Richard Norton were directors.

The ramifications of the Rank empire have been the subject of several studies, in particular that of Klingender and Legg, already noted. The most important of a complex series of moves is his creation of a corporation known as the General Cinema Finance Corporation which took over Woolf's distributing agency, GFD, though he remained head of it.

General Cinema Finance has strong City affiliations, with Lord Portal as chairman. Paul Lindenburg, the international banker, Leslie Farrow, chartered accountant, and Lord Luke are directors, and of course Rank himself. They share seventy-five directorships between them 'in large-scale financial or industrial undertakings'. No film concern up to that time had been given such formidable City support.

It was significant, too, though not unexpected, that Rank should acquire an interest in the British end of Universal Pictures which in 1935 was merged with General Film Distributors. Thus he had a stake in the American parent company and the right to release Universal's Hollywood pictures. It was a similar arrangement to that made between United Artists and Oscar Deutsch, and Rank needed the films to fill all those cinemas.

Nor was this the end of his empire-building. For some time in the mid-1930s there had been rumours about the position of Gaumont-British, with its big production commitments, its sixty companies sunk in all kinds of entertainments, from variety shows to television, and its six-figure overdraft. Twentieth Century-Fox had long owned a slice of the Gaumont cake. It was said they wanted it all.

But the keenest bidder for Gaumont was John Maxwell of Associated British. Maxwell had made no secret of his ambition to gain control of the Corporation and in 1936 he announced to the press that he had done so. Henceforth he would be head of both Gaumont and Associated British.

The truth was otherwise. Maxwell could not buy himself into the Gaumont-British Corporation without sanction of 20th Century-Fox, and this sanction was not forthcoming.

Isidore Ostrer knew that if Gaumont-British went to John Maxwell, he (Maxwell), with a total of five or six hundred cinemas at his command, would be placed in a position of overwhelming power in the industry, a situation which he felt would do no good to British films and no good to the Fox Company in America to whom Maxwell would be able to dictate terms. And indeed, while Maxwell was negotiating in London with the Ostrer group, Isidore Ostrer, the *éminence grise* of the corporation, was negotiating in New York with Fox. He talked to its president, Joe Schenk. And between them, in Mr Goldwyn's picturesque phrase, they included Maxwell out. He sued the Ostrers over the sale of the shares and lost the case. But as a gesture of defiance he bought 136 more cinemas and demonstrated that his circuit was substantially greater than that of Gaumont-British. Thus the Napoleons of Wardour Street exhibit not only films but themselves.

Henceforth the Rank Organisation is the major influence in the industry and in its creation and rapid expansion Rank has acknowledged that he owed much to John Davis (now Sir John), later to succeed him.

Davis was born in 1906 and educated at the City of London School. An accountant by profession, he entered the film industry in 1938 when he was invited to disentangle the financial affairs of Odeon Theatres, then in a critical state. Odeon, back by Sir Edgar Mountain, had gone public in 1937, and when they lacked sufficient funds to run the business Sir Edgar asked Rank to join the company.

'So I got to know Rank', said Davis. 'When Deutsch died in 1941 I was appointed joint managing director, and then managing director in 1948.'[4]

He therefore controlled the day-to-day running of the organisation. He was soon confronted with a much larger financial crisis in film production which affected the whole industry. It involved the taking of some harsh measures.

Alan Wood, who does his best to make the black deeds of the industry look off-white, says of his episode: 'It is hard to imagine that anyone else would have matched the achievement of John Davis in straightening out and cutting down in the days when the Rank Organisation faced disaster.' He cut back production at Islington, Shepherd's Bush and Denham studios and this threw many people out of work. The documentary series, *This Modern Age*, which had gained a high reputation but was losing £40,000 a year, and Mary Field's children's films, which has acquired an almost classic status, were dropped. So too was the Independent Frame experiment after £600,000 had been spent on it.

Arthur Rank could not, according to Alan Wood, have made these drastic changes unaided. Unlike his father Joseph Rank, he lacked the necessary ruthlessness, and he must have been aware of it. He was, moreover, surrounded by Yes men. He turned to John Davis, for Davis above all things was a No man, and 'it is probably true', says Wood, 'that it was he who rescued the Rank Organisation from financial catastrophe: partly by his capacity for quick thinking and action, but partly also by the toughness, determination and frequency with which he said No. The only trouble was that he in turn began to risk the fate of all dictators: a tendency (with some notable exceptions) for him to end up surrounded by . . . Yes men of his own choosing'. 'He cannot', says Wood, 'be called a popular figure in the industry.'

In reviewing these operations it is noticeable once again

D

how remote from the task of film-making is the business of carving up the cinema for the benefit of the owners. In this manoeuvre the producers and exhibitors, considered as two sides of the triangle, though most affected by events have the least say in them. They must abide by the decisions of the two groups, and there are linked to over-riding American interests.

Rank, Maxwell and others who guided these decisions in the 1930s were producer-distributor-exhibitors formulating policies to serve the interests of their respective combines. The language of the shareholder falls naturally into place and that of the independent producer or director is more or less irrelevant or limited to the submission of projects.

The captains of industry however were by now confronted with increasingly stiff controls. The triangular structure is burdened with the weight of Parliament and again with that of the American industry.

Some authorities, of course, take a directly opposite view: that without the Americans, without the various pieces of protective legislation, there would be no film industry at all. However this may be, the two great presences, Westminster and Wall Street, were painfully evident in 1935, 1936 and 1937, when British film production, laden with gold and steeped in quotas, and in addition, cluttered up with a good deal of second-hand genius from the Continent, enjoyed its crowded hour of glorious life and entered into bankruptcy.

Chapter 10

Boom and Crisis in the 1930s

The decline in film production in the late 1930s came with devastating suddenness and was a blow to many hopes. The years 1933–1937 had brought a boom in production, new studios were opened and old ones were made active. By 1938 seventy sound stages were in use and films were being made on a high tide of quality and confidence. In that year 228 feature films were announced, but figures of this kind give little indication of the real state of affairs. How many were worth making or made a profit? 'One of the most striking features of this expansion from a financial point of view', say Klingender and Legg, 'is the fact that . . . it is based almost entirely on *expectation* (Klingender's italics) without any concrete results to justify that optimism, for the older companies that confine their activities to production . . . have for a number of years not been showing any substantial profits.'[1] It was not therefore a failure of the individual.

Maurice Elvey, for example, some of whose later work may be considered here, cannot be faulted on these grounds. *High Treason* (1931), a typical Elvey subject, described a war of the future between East and West, with flights of fancy into television and the use of a bizarre modern decor. In the same year he directed *The School for Scandal*, for he never lost his affection for the theatrical subject. He was a good popular showman and if there was nothing to say he said it in the handsomest way. Films did not have much sense of mission in his day, they were content to tell a story and please as many people as possible, and this was Elvey's philosophy so far as he had one.

Graham Cutts continued his career with a handful of films of no great consequence—*Aren't Men Beasts!* (1937) was one of them—and it is melancholy to see so much expertise applied to such material, for he had a talent, technically as finished as that of Hitchcock and a style of his own.

A glance at the films of the 1930s would give us, among a number of equal box-office merit, *Rome Express, Goodbye Mr Chips, The Private Life of Henry VIII, Victoria the Great* and *Pygmalion*. With these a number of documentaries should be mentioned, *Song of Ceylon* (1934), *Weather Forecast, Night Mail*, now part of the canon, for John Grierson was then guiding the movement which was to have so profound an influence on British film-making, and in fact, all over the world.

All these productions, feature and documentary, brought a buoyant sense of achievement to British studies and a conviction that they had a great future. Gaumont-British and Gainsborough are centres of a furious activity spotlighted by such names as George Arliss, Conrad Veidt, James Mason, Stewart Granger, Margaret Lockwood, Phyllis Calvert and Madeleine Carroll. Conrad Veidt, star of *The Cabinet of Dr Caligari* and of *Waxworks*, appeared in such thrillers as *I Was a Spy* and *Rome Express*. Madeleine Carroll, after a few successes, went to America. Jessie Matthews, having begun well in *Tne Good Companions*, seemed likely to become a big movie personality. And there were two bright British comedy stars, Jack Hulbert and Cicely Courtneidge, who appeared in energetic specimens of British humour and were widely popular.

During these booming days Balcon also put under contract a number of American stars, some of them in the first flight—Sylvia Sidney, Edmund Lowe, Richard Dix, Constance Bennett—in the belief that they would sell his pictures to America. Yet despite the money and resources poured out, (or perhaps because of them) Gaumont-British were again in trouble in 1936. There was a reorganisation, and at the end of the year Balcon left the corporation. The Ostrers, supposedly unshakable, were going out and Mr Rank was coming in.

100

Balcon's resignation was one among a number of moves he was to make as times change, the mighty fall, the humble rise, and the backbone of the industry suffers repeated dislocation. It becomes clear that however well established a producer is he can never be certain what the next day will bring forth, and this uncertainty penetrates right down the line, sinking all the creative elements with it. The buoyant future dissolves in the financial crisis of 1937.

Why did British production fail? For several reasons, first among them, high cost. But other factors complicate the issue and there is no simple answer. Certainly the cost factor is a decisive element, especially when unrelated to box-office values.

Rome Express (1932) directed by Walter Forde, was made for about £60,000 and did remarkably well. In the thirties £60,000 was big money. Korda's *Henry VIII* (1932), reached roughly the same figure and its success is a legend. But we also encounter films that have leapt to the £100,000 mark and do not always recover their cost. *Catherine the Great* (1933) would appear to be in this class. *The Scarlet Pimpernel* (1934), with Leslie Howard, reached well over £100,000 but scored handsomely at the box office. On the other hand, Max Schach's *Pagliacci* (1937) which Karl Grune directed, cost more than £100,000 and was a complete failure notwithstanding the performance of Richard Tauber, at that time high in popularity. *Love from a Stranger* (1937), directed by an American, Rowland Lee, with an American star, Ann Harding, was the only film Max Schach produced which was a real winner.

High cost can be equated with the delusions of grandeur British producers suffered in order to keep up with the Darryl Zanucks and Louis B. Mayers. They would put American stars under contract at salaries far above their true worth, usually when they were no longer wanted in Hollywood. Such a policy naturally brought inflation. With American stars went the big sets, the big publicity campaigns, the big transport and hotel costs for the star and her family and her maid and her hairdresser and her secretary and anything else she wanted. All part of show business, and in

101

those days a necessary part perhaps, except that Britain could not afford it and these things simply added to the tale of woe and bankruptcy.

A second reason for failure was that far too large a share of the profit was taken by the distributors, sometimes up to 35 or 40 per cent. Thirdly, notwithstanding inflated costs, producers failed to get the release in America they anticipated. Fourthly, the good films were accompanied by too many bad ones. The losses on these devoured the profits on the others. Fifthly, studio space was monopolised by the vertically integrated combines whose executives dictated policy. The voice of the independent with ideas of his own was seldom heard.

Sixthly, there was no permanent source of finance to guarantee both producers and studio workers continuity of employment, and without this it was impossible to keep costs down. All that had been built up in interest and loyalty during one production was thrown away because there was nothing to follow it, the crew were laid off, the studio was dark. These were commonplaces of the 1930s. In short, the production side of the industry had no policy of its own and no vision of things to come. It could not settle down and plan for the future.

Alexander Korda's *Private Life of Henry VIII* in 1932, as we have remarked, is usually credited with having launched the boom in the mid-thirties.* Its success in Britain and America made it easy for other producers to raise money for production, and many get-rich-quick promoters, some from the continent, joined forces with City under-writers in wild-cat production schemes.

Thus Korda, with a single picture, may be said to have achieved what the 1927 Films Act was designed to do but failed to do. By force of example he increased production in British studios on a considerable scale. That he incurred heavy losses later is true, but to nothing like the extent recorded of the Rank Organisation a few years later.[2]

In 1936 £4 million was borrowed for film production; in

---

* Jean Georges Auriol considers *Tudor Rose* (1936), directed by Robert Stevenson, the real starting-point for British films.

1937 the figure rose to £7 million. In that year Isidore Ostrer declared that unless he could obtain bigger returns on his films from America he must close down the Gaumont studies. In 1937, too, Gainsborough Pictures made a loss of £98,000 and a receiver was appointed for Twickenham Studios, where the independent producer Julius Hagen presided.

Max Schach, the lively impresario from Germany—he had been a journalist in Berlin—brought Karl Grune and Paul Czinner over to make a number of films, and put Elizabeth Bergner, Richard Tauber and Jimmie Durante under contact. At one time he challenged Alexander Korda but he did not survive long enough in films to make any lasting impression. Moreover, he was involved in litigation which threw a sharp light on the ways of film financiers, banks, and insurance companies. His organisation, Capitol Films, was the centre of a court case in 1939 in which the Westminster Bank sued a number of insurance firms for £1¼ million, two-thirds of which was lost.

In April only thirteen films were being produced in studio space with a capacity for fifty. With four or five thousand cinemas needing double feature programmes something like 600 films had to be found annually. It was hardly surprising that one of those critical House of Lords debates took place which the film industry knew so well.

'I don't believe it is possible by legislation', Lord Strabolgi had said of the 1927 Films Act, 'to compel people to go to a place of entertainment they do not find entertaining', thus putting in a nutshell the case against government intervention.

Whatever the causes of the production crisis—incompetence, extravagance, high distribution costs—the industry was only able to survive by showing American films. The triangular structure meanwhile was crumbling. In 1936 the Board of Trade set up a committee, The Moyne Committee, to see what could be done to promote 'the production, renting and exhibition of British films'. And what was done was in effect an appeal to Parliament, and so the passing of another Films Act in 1938. The Government had consulted the leaders of the industry, but as on previous occasions they

103

could not agree, so Parliament went ahead with its own proposals. Every disagreement of this kind lessened confidence in the power of the film industry to mind its own business, and every submission of its affairs to Parliament was an erosion of the industry's independence.

A consequence of the new act was to intensify American production in England and take it still further out of our own hands. The 1927 Act paradoxically had given this movement its first impulse when the U.S. companies formed production units of their own to make quota quickies. The new act emboldened them to bring over more stars, directors and technicians, not necessarily a bad thing within reason, but it was destined to become a habit, then by expansion in other directions, a takeover.

To check the abuse of quickies—and British quickies, it must be pointed out, were as bad as American ones—the Government had decided that only films of high quality would qualify for quota but without saying precisely what quality was. Now it was to be established on a basis of cost.

In 1938 Metro-Goldwyn-Mayer acquired their own studios at Boreham Wood. They bought the building which Paul Soskin had erected as Amalgamated Studios but never occupied. (Soskin made *Quiet Wedding* (1941) and one or two other pictures but did not stay long in the industry.)

Metro-Goldwyn-Mayer's first action on acquiring the studios, as we have seen, was to place Michael Balcon in charge of production. Victor Saville also joined them.

Warner's, RKO and 20th Century-Fox made similar plans, always a step ahead of ourselves. Thus the familiar pattern of American domination of the British film industry which it was the object of legislation to prevent was assisted by that very legislation. 'The British Government was not prepared to withstand American pressure at a time when it had other and apparently more vital interests to protect.'[3]

From 1938 then the Government became a policy-shaping instrument of the film trade and the main support of its structure. We hear the first murmurs of a films bank which was later, as the National Film Finance Corporation, to become the silk purse of the production industry.

The Moyne report had recommended some kind of organised finance or encouragement of finance to keep film production alive, but this proposal was dropped. So, too, was a recommendation for a Films Commission to operate the Films Act.

What the 1938 Act proposed was a continuation of the quota from the 1927 bill but with reduced percentage rates. It imposed a minimum cost test of £7,500 per film and it brought short films, hitherto excluded, within the scope of the bill. To encourage bigger and better features it offered producers an enticing quota scheme based on length of film and labour charges, so that the more money you spent on a film the greater its quota privileges.

Some odd definitions can be found in the bill. For instance, we learn that the author of a film 'shall be deemed to be a person directly engaged in the making of a film' but the person who is only 'financially interested' is not deemed to be making it. Yet in 1938 authors were usually the last people to take part in production and financiers the first.

It is only much later, largely as a result of the campaigning of the Screen Writers Guild, that authors are recognised as useful persons and permitted a deeper involvement in the creative process.

Where the bill was most valuable was in fixing conditions of employment, wages and contracts, and in deciding how disputes should be settled. The Act lays down strict rules for the registration of films, which are published in the *Board of Trade Journal*.

It again makes an attempt to define a British film. The maker of the film must be 'either a British subject or a British company', the studio must be 'within His Majesty's dominions' and the labour costs must be as prescribed in the bill.

In practice, about four-fifths of these costs must be spent on British labour or services. Two persons, one of whom must be an actor or actress, are excluded from this calculation. Thus a foreign star or director can be engaged without breaking the law and can of course angle the film to suit his own purposes.

Under the bill a Cinematograph Films Council takes the place of the old Advisory Council, but the independent members are increased by four to eleven and the Council is increased to twenty-two, of whom four represent film production. But only two of these four represent the producers, the others are employees. The bill barely recognises the fact that the key problem of putting the industry on its feet is one of production.

For reasons best known to the Board of Trade, an American was appointed to the Council and could be supposed to favour strongly the American interest, despite the fact that American competition was precisely what the Act was designed to oppose. 'The Council cannot therefore be regarded as the appropriate body', says *The Factual Film* report, 'to assist the British film industry.'[4]

As we have said, government intervention in the industry's affairs is now seen to be permanent. Whether the advantages of the 1938 Act would have increased the number of feature films it is impossible to say, for war was to bring all plans to an end. The City had already set up its own committee of investigation into the affairs of the film industry and this put a stop to any further investment. What money remained exacted a very high rate of interest, so that costs, already high, went higher still. 'There was for some years', said Sidney Bernstein, 'no relationship between costs of production and the potential earning power of the film made.'[5]

The full consequence of the crisis the new Act sought to resolve is not seen until the post-war years. We need note only this. In 1938 the American film industry has a far stronger hold over the British industry than it had in 1927. It is as deeply welded into the structure of British films as Whitehall.

Chapter 11

The Studios: Conditions of Filming

You see, the film studio of today is really the palace of the sixteenth century. There one sees what Shakespeare saw: the absolute power of the tyrant, the courtiers, the flatterers, the jesters, the cunningly ambitious intriguers. There are fantastically beautiful women, there are incompetent favourites. There are great men who are suddenly disgraced. There is the most insane extravagance, and unexpected parsimony over a few pence. There is enormous splendour which is a sham; and also horrible squalor hidden behind the scenery. There are vast schemes abandoned because of some caprice. There are secrets which everybody knows and no one speaks of. There are even two or three honest advisers. These are the court fools, who speak the deepest wisdom in puns lest they should be taken seriously. They grimace, and tear their hair privately and weep.
Prater Violet by Christopher Isherwood

The development of the studios ran parallel with the growth of the cinemas. They fill in the story of expansion from the 1900s to the 1930s, by which time a dozen or more production centres from Elstree to Beaconsfield supplied films to hundreds of Odeons and Gaumonts and three or four thousand independent cinemas.

The word 'studios' in those early days is a euphemism, for they were more often skating rinks, garages, sheds, Victorian greenhouses, even the roofs of buildings, anything that had space, light, and freedom from noise, and this was rare.[1] Life was rougher but more meaningful for the film-maker. Julius Hagen at Twickenham used to boast that he worked all night and nobody complained. There was a willingness, a devotion to the job which is singularly lacking later; the unions had not yet been formed, nor taught their members all the rules in the book.

Rachael Low gives a list of forty-two studios, major and minor, operating independently bstween 1906 and 1914, some of them—Twickenham, Merton Park and Hammersmith—still very active.[2] These old-time studios are usually identified with some well-known name—Hepworth, Samuelson, Kearton, Robert Paul, Hagen; but when the larger units at Elstree or Shepperton were formed and were let to all and sundry their identity was lost and the studio simply became a roof under which someone worked.

Soon the bright new factories, with instruments of wonderful precision, replaced the garages and conservatories and the mansions of Victorian brick that had served the pioneers in the first decade of the century. When the sound and dialogue film arrived the old studios became monuments to a silent age cut off in its prime. It was a sad end, like the closing of an old theatre or music hall; yet there was no alternative. Studios were at the mercy of acoustic experts and the engineers of Western Electric or RCA, while the whole technique of film-making was thrown into confusion.

Sound compelled a radical reconstruction of every important studio at immense cost and a revolution in filmcraft whose consequences could not be seen. Only the well-established companies could meet the expense, and they were few.*

Since the sound revolution the greater part of British cinema has been produced by a handful of studios—Shepherd's Bush, Islington, Elstree, Denham, Pinewood, Shepperton, Ealing, Beaconsfield and the Riverside studios at Hammersmith. The majority suffer the disadvantage of being ten or twenty miles from London and the time and money spent in getting to and from them adds a substantial item to the budget. The uncertainty of the English climate intensifies the wear and tear of putting a film together. These handicaps in the end give a certain character to British films.

Studios not only produce them, they condition the makers of them. The director must gear his subject to the dimensions of a large factory turning out goods for the world. Those

---

* See *Upton Sinclair Presents William Fox*, p. xvi. He quotes a figure of $20,000 per cinema (then about £5,000) for sound apparatus installation.

108

who built the studios were not usually film producers but entrepreneurs who thought in terms of manufactured goods to be sold at a profit. The size and costliness of a studio do much to explain the films produced in it. They place a heavy burden on the film maker who aims at the representation of his ideas by the simplest possible means. This he could achieve when the physical details of production were fewer, when he was not burdened with unions which undermined him or with huge vertical trusts which fell on top of him.

Shepherd's Bush studios, where George Pearson's *Ultus* series was made, were set up by Gaumont in 1913 and were developed by the Ostrers in the 1920s. They were linked to the smaller Islington studios as part of the Gaumont-British set-up and were, so to speak, the senior partner in production. Famous Players Lasky had made use of them in 1920 and Balcon took over in 1932. Under the Woolf-Balcon regime these two studios enshrine more history than we have room for, history of a more personal kind before the great amalgamations and industrial swoppings had rolled over the scene and flattened everything into big business.

Elstree studios, which have played a large part in the making of British cinema, owe their choice of site, as we have said, to Percy Nash. He recommended the location to an American, J. D. Williams, whose intention it was to launch British National Pictures on a large scale. Williams ran out of money and the studios were taken over by John Maxwell. On this Hertfordshire site of twenty-seven acres he founded British International Pictures in 1926 which later became part of the Associated British Picture Corporation.

The key figures of this period such as Maxwell, the Ostrers or C. M. Woolf had little to guide them and were really creating films out of the void. John Maxwell's British International Pictures made films for shareholders with an occasional plunge into the unknown. A policy of prudent expenditure paid off while other companies were moving into the red, but it did not make for memorable work or a great name.

Still, if Maxwell made *A Little Bit of Fluff* or *Show a Leg* he also made Dr Robison's *The Informer* and several Alfred Hitchcock pictures. The first Bernard Shaw film, *How He Lied to Her Husband*, was an Elstree film, bad as it was. In a few years these and other films made the name of Elstree known all over the world; it became the symbol of British film production, notwithstanding a mediocrity which was not flattering.

For several years in the later 1920s Maxwell employed a former Fleet Street film critic, Walter Mycroft, as his production chief. Mycroft, a discriminating writer on films, was one of the founders of the London Film Society and he established at Elstree a school of script-writers unique in character.

He introduced a Germanic element into British International, partly to secure the German market and partly because he felt that the continental star had glamour, more glamour than the British star. Exotic players like Lil Dagover, Dolly Haas, Lya de Putti and Marlene Dietrich were creating a fashion in sophistication, wickedness and elegance which went down well with the British public and was a welcome change from the hearty British beef served up by our studios.

British International became Associated British in 1931 and under the generic title of Elstree produced over 200 full-length features up to the year 1939. Among those to be remembered are: *Under the Greenwood Tree*, *The Informer*, *Atlantic*, *Juno and the Paycock*, *Blackmail*, *Blossom Time*, *Rich and Strange* and *Murder*—four of them by Hitchcock. The remainder are such things as *Not Quite a Lady*, *His Night Out* and *Over She Goes*. Of these there are dozens, but in the post-war period we find *The Hasty Heart*, *The Devil's Disciple*, *Woman in a Dressing Gown* and *Look Back in Anger*. These are no guarantee of a studio's continued success, for in the mid-fifties Elstree is more or less at a standstill.

Ealing studies differ from their contemporaries in being more tightly knit and compact and in projecting, for much of their history, a personality. In 1929, as Associated Talking Pictures, the studio was under the direction of Basil Dean who produced films with George Formby and Gracie Fields. These films were easily sold on the immense popularity of these stars but were not otherwise interesting. *The Constant Nymph, Java Head* and *Lorna Doone*, made in the early thirties, represent a more fruitful contribution. With Balcon a decade later the studio acquired a name and character.

The personal factor is both the virtue and the vice of Denham studios which Alexander Korda set up in 1936. It was part of the glittering image of London Film Productions. Korda was persuaded that it would be a great deal cheaper to own studios than to rent them, and with the backing of the Prudential Assurance Company he built the studios at Denham at a cost of £600,000. They were designed by an American, Jack Okey, and were said to be the last word in studio practice, but in fact they were inefficient and inconvenient to work in.

Yet in mere size, and in their peaceful green setting in Buckinghamshire they impressed, and became a great glamour factory spilling its glitter all over the countryside. Korda made some stunningly beautiful films in these studios, *Rembrandt* being the first. Here too, with help from other studios, he made *The Scarlet Pimpernel, The Ghost Goes West, Elephant Boy, The Thief of Baghdad, Catherine the Great,* and H. G. Wells's *Shape of Things to Come.* The elaborate staging and trick work for the Wellsian fantasy had to be done at Worton Hall, Isleworth. At Worton Hall too Korda directed Paulette Goddard and Burgess Meredith in *An Ideal Husband.*

Unfortunately while he was creating a studio on the international plan and making expensive but indifferent films such as *Knight Without Armour* and *Anna Karenina* he was getting deeper and deeper into the red and eventually was forced to hand over the studios to Arthur Rank.

With Charles Boot, a brick manufacturer as partner, Rank built Pinewood studios, also in Buckinghamshire, on a private estate known as Heathendon Hall. The owner, we are told, shot grouse and pheasant there and 'led an agreeable life, both public and private'. Such was the life Mr Boot desired to secure for the stars who worked there and he gave them elegant dressing-rooms and bathrooms and hair-dressing departments such as were never contemplated by Mrs Siddons or Sarah Bernhardt. The atmosphere of the country house was preserved and the art of the film made as painless as possible for the artists.

With the ceremonial opening of Pinewood in 1936 another stone was added to the pyramid known as the Rank Organisation. The first to make a film there was Herbert Wilcox with *London Melody*, the second was Carol Reed with *A Man With Your Voice*. Peter Rogers produced the prototype of his celebrated *Carry On* comedies there for £73,000. During the war Pinewood was used for stock-piling food and by the Royal Mint for making coins. In all that makes for filming it is as good as anything to be found in Hollywood.

Shepperton Studios are an outgrowth from a smaller building known in the 1930s as Sound City, developed like Pinewood from an old country house and controlled in the years before the war by an accountant, Norman Loudon. Quickies were made there at thirty shillings a foot. When British Lion took them over in 1963 they had already been greatly expanded and modernised and were used by American as well as British companies.

Though constantly active and stimulated by the presence of British Lion, Shepperton had little personal identity until, in the 1960s, the Boultings are associated there in management with Gilliat and Launder.

Shepperton, like other big studios, has also turned to television, but its reputation rests on such notable productions as *The African Queen*, *A Man for All Seasons*, *The Angry Silence*, *Dr Strangelove*, *I'm All Right Jack*, *Room at the Top* and *Oliver!* With the rise and fall of the economic temperature, it has gone through many fluctuations of fortune.

MGM Studios at Boreham Wood hold the ambivalent position of things which are British and not British. Owned by the parent MGM company in America and now linked to EMI, it has put the MGM polish on scores of big productions and given employment to many hundreds of players and technicians. *A Yank at Oxford, Ivanhoe, Moby Dick* and other expensive luxuries were made here, but of course other companies used them for their technical facilities.

What we notice in all these production centres, though in a lesser degree at Ealing because it is outside the combines, is the fantastic cost of maintaining them and the stultifying burden of overheads placed on the producer. This is the price paid for success in the international market. It is not until 1969, under heavy economic pressure, that a lead is given for more prudent policies at Elstree under Bryan Forbes. By then it has become a world problem. Shooting on location with live backgrounds, the economies that can be made in the film of ideas rather than with sets and stars, have from time to time diminished the studio's importance. But a film is a delicate and complex growth, it needs care and protection, and this is usually found between walls and in a place capable of silence. A new kind of film may change all this (there are many signs of it) but until that happens the conditions of filming remain the same.

Part III

The Film Matures

Chapter 12

Alfred Hitchcock and Anthony Asquith

When Hitchcock and Asquith began their careers in the early 1920s the film was silent and it was scarcely to be imagined that it would ever break into sound. Yet no sooner had the silent film settled down than the sound film came in with the force of a hurricane, overturned an industry, and compelled a reassessment of all values and plans. Directors of the calibre of Alfred Hitchcock and Anthony Asquith had not merely to formulate their own ideas of film but to educate the industry that employed them, an industry, as Bernard Shaw said, of 'very peculiar people'.

Naturally, film-makers were loath to adopt a technique which deprived them at a stroke of the freedom of movement they had enjoyed on the silent screen. They were alarmed, too, at the cost. Exhibitors felt the same. Critics, weighing the aesthetics of the matter, were prone to sit on the fence— it might all come to nothing. Others, a minority, declared outright that this was the end of film as an art.

Yet such was the power of the new medium, however deadly to the vision, it overcame all resistance. Audiences were still theatre-minded and cheerfully accepted what they were given. They were ravished by the voice of Clive Brook, Barbara Stanwyck or Herbert Marshall and the extraordinary things sound could do on the screen.

Alfred Hitchcock had already made a reputation by 1926 when at the age of 27 he directed *The Lodger*. He is one of the first to emerge with a recognisable personal style and with the ability to adapt to new forms and processes.

Alfred Joseph Hitchcock was born in 1899 at Leytonstone, London, of Catholic parents and was educated at a Jesuit boarding-school where he had a strict religious upbringing. The Jesuits instilled into him ideas of sin and guilt and the disciplines of religion, but they also sharpened his practical sense and he considers that he owes much in his career to their training.

After studying as an engineer he went to London University and applied himself to the arts, and at the age of 20, through an actor friend, he found a job in the art department of Famous-Players-Lasky in their Islington studios and began writing titles for them.

He wrote these for *The Great Day*, *Princess of New York*, and *Three Live Ghosts*. While thus engaged he tried his hand at directing a comedy, *Number Thirteen*, but the money ran out and he went back to titling.

Shortly after this the director of a Seymour Hicks film *Always Tell Your Wife*, fell ill and he was invited by Hicks to co-direct it with him. He was 24 then and had learned a great deal from working on the studio floor and from titling. His talent however does not get full recognition until Michael Balcon, who took over the studios from Famous Players, appointed Hitchcock assistant director to Graham Cutts, on *Woman to Woman* (1922)[1] and several other films. He took on a variety of jobs such as art director, script writer, and assistant on a number of subjects: *The Prude's Fall*, *The White Shadow* (both in 1923), *The Passionate Adventure* (1924) and *The Blackguard* (1925).

These were important films at the time, but for Hitchcock they were apprentice work. Michael Balcon had meanwhile formed Gainsborough Pictures and confirmed his belief in Hitchcock by giving him first *The Pleasure Garden* (1925), then *The Mountain Eagle* (1926) to direct. They were both produced in Germany.[2] Balcon could not get backing for Hitchcock in England, so went to Germany, and the symbolism and sombre treatment of the German school appear to have had a marked influence on the director. Hitchcock himself attaches little importance to these films. He had ideas of his own and was only awaiting the opportunity to express them. He found what he needed in *The Lodger* (1926), the key film in the Hitchcock canon.

In Francois Truffaut's *Le Cinema Selon Hitchcock*, we learn the director's own view of the matter. 'The Lodger *a été le premier film dans lequel j'ai tiré profit de ce que j'avais appris en Allemagne. Dans ce film, toute mon approche a été réellement instinctive, c'est la première fois que j'ai exercé mon style propre. En verité, on peut considérer que* The Lodger *est mon premier film.*'

Numerically it was his tenth, and it was then that he married his script-writer, Alma Reville, whom he had met at Famous Players in Islington and who worked with him henceforth on all his productions.

Few careers in British films are so well documented as Alfred Hitchcock's. No other director has suffered such a spate of intellectual analysis and reverential gush and emerged from it undamaged. While some critics compare him with Shakespeare and talk of masterpieces, others will denounce him for 'sheerest rubbish', as *Sight and Sound* did when *Psycho* was shown. *Cahiers du Cinéma* celebrate him with the highest honours. Like Noel Coward, he is soon enthroned as The Master.

Hitchcock planned his career from the days when he lived in a flat in Cromwell Road in his 20s to his present affluence at Bel Air, Hollywood, where the grass is green, the days are fruitful and the films multiply.

He is something of a hermit there, that is to say, he is no party-goer. He lives privately and is pleased with his kitchen and his symbolic collection of kitchen knives. He is not given to sounding off in the pages of *Variety* or to generalisations about the state of the film industry. A born showman, he pays as much attention to publicity as to the pictures he makes. He invented the slogan 'The Birds Is Coming', for his film *The Birds*. He insisted that film critics should not be admitted to the press show of *Psycho* after it had started. One or two were late. It caused a rumpus from which the film benefited.

His habit of signing himself with a sketch of his own profile and giving it to waiters and critics alike is well

119

known. In short, to use a cant phrase, he has created his own myth. His first independent film, *The Lodger*, was a Jack the Ripper story adapted by himself and Eliot Stannard from a novel by Mrs Belloc Lowndes. Alma Reville was the assistant director and Ivor Montagu wrote the titles.

The story is about a homicidal maniac known as 'The Avenger' who terrorises London with a series of brutal murders. His victims are always girls with golden hair.

The film opens with a close up of a woman screaming, a dim figure running downstairs out of a house and into the darkness. A crowd gathers, the police arrive, and a newspaper heading announces 'the seventh golden-haired victim'. A scrap of paper left behind by the murderer has the words 'The Avenger' scrawled on it.

The subdued lighting and the heavily dramatised treatment of the stranger, played by Ivor Novello, show Hitchcock's skill in building up an atmosphere of mystery and tension and his susceptibility to German influence. It is repeated in the famous shot of Novello pacing up and down his room, photographed from below through glass. There is the trembling of the chandelier, the rapid cutting to news head-lines, the scurrying of cats from dustbins, the documentary realism of the BBC announcer. Hitchcock's visual effects have always been his most powerful weapon in creating suspense and horror.

'You have to remember', he said in a television interview, 'that this process of frightening is done by means of a given medium, the medium of pure cinema. The putting together of pieces of film', he declared, 'is the essential part of my job', just as the painter puts certain colours together on the canvas. In *The Lodger* he reveals himself as an entertainer in the sense Graham Greene has defined for some of his novels. He is quite content to entertain millions and this after all is his great achievement.

After *The Lodger* he made half-a-dozen films which are chiefly remarkable for showing his versatility but are not specially distinguished—*Downhill*, *The Ring* (from a story of his own), *The Farmer's Wife*, *Easy Virtue*, *Champagne* and *The Manxman*, all for British International Pictures. It was

120

a period in his career in which he was not free to choose any subject he pleased and it would be difficult to infer his consuming interest in the mystery thriller from these examples.

But with *Blackmail* (1929) an entirely new situation confronts him, the transition from silence to sound. *Blackmail* was from a play by Charles Bennett and from a script by Hitchcock, Benn Levy and the playwright. The fiancée of a young detective kills an artist who tries to seduce her. She stabs him with a bread-knife. A stranger has seen the incident and tries to blackmail the girl, but the detective, convinced of her innocence, turns the tables on the stranger and returns blackmail for blackmail. Pursued by the police, the blackmailer escapes to the roof of the British Museum where he falls through a skylight and is killed. The case is considered closed, but the girl afterwards goes to Scotland Yard and confesses that she was, in fact, the murderer. The clerk thereupon hands her over to the young detective (the fiancé), an ending contrary to Hitchcock's intention.

Blackmail, with Anny Ondra, Sara Allgood and John Longden in the leading parts, had been planned as a silent film, but Hitchcock was given permission by John Maxwell, head of British International, to re-shoot a large part of it, which he did under great difficulties. Besides the unsolved problems of sound, he had to cope with a star, Anny Ondra, who could not speak English and her lines had to be given to a double, Joan Barry.

After *Blackmail* came Sean O'Casey's *Juno and the Paycock* (1929), chiefly of interest for Sara Allgood's performance as Juno, informed as it was with the tragic Irish passion. But Hitchcock did not think the play proper material for a film, though O'Casey himself thought highly of it and so did James Agate. Nor was Hitchcock happy about his film of Noel Coward's *Easy Virtue*.

In *Murder* (1930), adapted from a novel by Clemence Dane and Helen Simpson, he again found a congenial subject. In it Herbert Marshall played the part of a famous actor-manager serving on a jury who reconstructs the details of a murder committed by a young actress whom he is convinced is innocent of the charge.

The actor is in love with her, there is an unsolved mystery attaching to the case, and the film promises the kind of melodrama for which the director had a particular liking. To Herbert Marshall's voice, of importance at that time to the sound film, he joined the talents of Edward Chapman, Esmé Percy, Donald Calthrop and Norah Baring, who played the part of the heroine. He uses interior monologue for a scene in the actor's character to elucidate his thoughts, not, he has explained, as a particular device in sound.

More interesting than any technical gimmicks is Hitchcock's awareness of dissolving ethical standards, of the whole atmosphere of moral and psychological change. He confronts homosexual and other issues in a manner considered bold at the time.

His murderer is portrayed as a transvestite performing a trapeze act in a circus. The abnormal and the erotic were to play an ever larger part in the make-up of his films, he is fascinated by the devious moral aspects of his characters—but not as a moralist, only for what they bring in character, mystery or excitement to the story. This attitude is developed further in such films as *Rope* and *Psycho* which he made much later.

Murder, which he directed in German and English, was one of Hitchcock's successes. *The Times* critic observed of the film that 'Mr Hitchcock has never been more skilful in revealing the inner lives of his characters and the strangeness of the scene which enfolds them'. It was 'a brilliant exercise in mystery melodrama'.[4] Undoubtedly this picture, with *Rich and Strange*, to which Rohmer and Chabrol add *The Thirty Nine Steps*, was among the most distinguished of the period. It put Hitchcock first among British directors and challenged anything of the kind produced in Hollywood. It reflects both the irony and the folly of the film business that his career suffered a reverse at the precise moment that it should have gone forward.

He followed *Murder* with *The Skin Game* (1931), from John Galsworthy's play, but there was a lack of rapport between the director and his author. 'It wasn't a subject I chose and there is nothing to be said about it', he told Francois Truffaut.

Hitchcock's next picture, *Rich and Strange* (1932), was in his own view the most satisfying he had made in England, but it had a bad press and was not widely shown.

It concerned a young married couple who are left a sum of money and decide to go on a world cruise. The film contains a rare specimen of Hitchcock's most macabre manner. The couple eat with obvious relish a meal which they subsequently find was made from the entrails of a dead cat. After the meal they see the skin nailed to a wall to dry. This black humour in Hitchcock has often been criticised and has antagonised some people. No doubt the criticism is justified, but it is what distinguishes (or at that time distinguished) Hitchcock from other directors.

He then directed two films in which he had no particular interest, *Number Seventeen* (1932), his last film for British International, and *Waltzes from Vienna* (1933), a musical about the Strausses which he made independently for Tom Arnold, the theatre impresario.

His fortunes were now at a low ebb, he had made some bad films and he was passing through a crucial phase of doubt and self-questioning. What should he make next?

The answer was unexpected. While he was working on *Waltzes from Vienna* he met Michael Balcon again, and Balcon was willing to make another picture with him. Hitchcock unearthed the script of *The Man Who Knew Too Much* (1934) which had lain neglected in the British International files for some time. He bought it from John Maxwell and sold it to Balcon, who was then production head at Gaumont-British, and so the old partnership was renewed.

Hitchcock said of the English version that it was made by an amateur; of the American that it was made by a professional, a remark which could be taken to sum up his view of the difference in attitude to films of the two countries at that time.

He completed six films before deciding to leave England and try his luck in America. These six, between 1935 and 1939, were *The Thirty Nine Steps*, *The Secret Agent*, *Sabotage*,

123

Young and Innocent, The Lady Vanishes and *Jamaica Inn.*
We need consider here only two of them which draw attention to his versatility as a maker of thrillers. All these films
were equal if not superior to anything being made by his
contemporaries in the same field.

The Thirty Nine Steps (1935) was from a story by John
Buchan adapted by Charles Bennett and Ian Hay. It differed
very considerably from the original, for it was the director's
habit to take one look at a story and then make it his own.

It concerned a young Canadian caught up in a spy
intrigue. Vital secrets of the British Air Force were to be
sold to the enemy and we are taken through the back streets
of London, into music halls, onto the Scottish express and
across the moors to a political meeting, as the story unfolds.
The Canadian, bent on tracking down spies, leaves London
for Scotland after a woman he has put up in his flat has
been stabbed to death.

The film has a double action, and a double suspense; the
hero is out to kill and he expects to be killed; he is the
hunter and the hunted. There is a characteristic surprise
ending, with the death of a music-hall artist known as Mr
Memory whose act is involved with the capture of the stolen
plans. In the plans themselves and the explanations of what
happened Hitchcock is never really interested.

The film is not merely technically accomplished, it had the
qualities of ironic comment and visual ingenuity distinguishing a Hitchcock film—the piquant sequence, for example,
in which the stars—Robert Donat and Madeleine Carroll—
are handcuffed together and have to cope with the situation
of going to bed. There is the hero's escape from a train on
the Forth Bridge; the more unusual and inaccessible the
place the sooner it will be found in a Hitchcock film. There
is the disruption of a political meeting where the hero is
suddenly forced to make a speech.

The physical action is well salted with wit; if not with wit
then with sadism or sensationalism, anything that will attract
attention and create shock. And these elements he developed
with even greater resource as he gained mastery over them.

The Thirty Nine Steps was well received, especially in

America. The cliché 'it took critics and the public by storm' was the truth, and it did much to give British films prestige.

We take as a final example of his films in England *The Lady Vanishes* (1938) produced at the Islington studios and demonstrating that he could move as easily into comedy as into melodrama. Indeed, one feels that he might have excelled in it, for although his dramatic instinct is always dominant, his cast of thought is always that of ironic comedy. He never goes deeper; he never contemplates tragedy of the classic order.

The Lady Vanishes (1938) also concerns itself with spies, foreign powers and government secrets. A girl coming back from a Balkan holiday by train makes friends with an old lady who mysteriously disappears. Nobody believes the girl when she tells her story, but with the help of a friendly musician she discovers that her companion was a British agent who has been kidnapped because of the secrets she held.

When the train in which the girl is travelling is attacked by spies the old lady suddenly reappears but manages to get away and deliver her information to Scotland Yard. All it consists of is a few bars of song.

Hitchcock called this film a fantasy. His treatment of it is seen in the casting of Basil Radford and Naunton Wayne for two of the principal roles, hearty extrovert Britons who are only interested in cricket or in saying and doing incomparably silly things. Thus it blended the excitement of the spy story with occasional outbursts of the comic spirit, and this proved much to the taste of filmgoers. The film was based on a novel by Ethel Lina White and scripted by Sidney Gilliat and Frank Launder, who afterwards went into production themselves.

While making *The Lady Vanishes* Hitchcock had an offer from David Selznick to direct in America which he accepted, but his services were not needed until the following year and he filled in the time directing Charles Laughton in *Jamaica Inn* (1939), the Daphne du Maurier story. This picture, made in association with Erich Pommer, the German producer, was one of those misfires which occur in the best

125

regulated careers. It is mainly interesting for what went wrong than for what went right, for Charles Laughton was then at the height of his powers as an actor and his association with Pommer, which looked so promising, proved to be a sad miscalculation.

Jamaica Inn was the last film Hitchcock made in England until he returned in 1950 to make *Stage Fright* and in 1971 to make *Frenzy*. This survey excludes consideration of his American films, but it would give an altogether false impression of his career not to place his Hollywood films on record, for these brought him his greatest measure of fame.

Following *Rebecca* (1939), he directed some twenty-seven films of varied character and merit. Public taste in film and attitudes to film were undergoing bewildering changes, but Hitchcock more than survived the storm. *Psycho* (1960), the most startling, was well in the van of popular taste though its reception by the critics was far from unanimous. Nevertheless *Psycho* goes on record as one of his great triumphs, and it was made for 810,000 dollars when other directors were being less successful on budgets of two or three million.[5]

Suspicion (1941), *Shadow of a Doubt* (1943), *Strangers on a Train* (1951), *Rear Window* (1954), *The Trouble with Harry* (1955) and *Marnie* (1964), were among the most liked, if not always the most commended of his Hollywood productions. To these we must add *Topaz* (1969). In the 1960s he also directed or produced a series of television thrillers. In 1967 Francois Truffaut's celebrated book on Hitchcock appeared, a landmark in the literature of the cinema.

With Anthony Asquith (1902–1968) we are leagues removed from the Hitchcock private world. Asquith was that rarity in films, an aesthete (a word he would surely have disowned) who strayed from the academic groves into the gladiatorial combats of the studio. Lord David Cecil, his closest friend, said of him in a tribute after his death that 'his most precious and significant experiences were aesthetic.[6]

He was perhaps more of an artist than Hitchcock and less of a showman, and to this may be attributed the fact that he was less of a success. An unorthodox recruit from the Liberal statesman's family, Asquith entered films about the same time as Hitchcock and lost no time in establishing himself as a serious film-maker. After leaving Oxford he went to Hollywood to study production at first hand and he also familiarised himself with European developments.

His first assignments in the industry were with Bruce Woolfe, head of British Instructional Films, and were of a comparatively menial order. He took on whatever came to hand and was transport manager, assistant make-up artist and odd-job man, then rose to the position of script writer and personal assistant to Sinclair Hill on *Boadicea* (1926). We are still in the heyday of silent films.

Bruce Woolfe was impressed by Asquith's talents and by a script he had sent him, *Shooting Stars*. He put it into production with Asquith as assistant to the more experienced director, A. V. Bramble.

It was a story of life in a film studio, with its love affairs, illusions and intrigues and had elements of satire and invention which showed a fresh mind at work, highly individual and uncommitted. For this film he assembled a number of players who were constantly to be found in the films of the 1920s—Annette Benson, Brian Aherne, Donald Calthrop, Chili Bouchier and Wally Patch. *Shooting Stars* (1927) made it abundantly clear that Asquith had a natural grasp of the film medium. Critics considered it of equal merit with Hitchcock's *The Lodger*.

Underground (1928) did not have as great a success as *Shooting Stars*. The love affair of electricians and porters on railway trains lacked truth of observation, possibly because they found no correspondence in the director's own experience of life. At all events, this film misfired and was criticised for its mournful German lighting. The best things in it were its backgrounds of trains and power houses, which dramatise themselves.

An Anglo-German film, *The Runaway Princess* (1928), from a novel by Elizabeth Russell, did little to advance Asquith's reputation and he turned to a subject closer to his idea of what a film should be, *A Cottage on Dartmoor*.

Asquith had a deep feeling for the English scene and it is lovingly revealed in his treatment of the Devonshire countryside where the film is laid.

A Cottage on Dartmoor (1929) concerns a young hairdresser, Joe, who falls in love with Sally, a manicurist. She is unable to return his love and when she becomes engaged to a young farmer Joe attacks him with a razor and is sent to Dartmoor. He escapes to the farm where Sally is living, but is shot down by the police and dies in Sally's arms.

A sufficiently trite story redeemed nevertheless by the director's treatment of it. Asquith was praised for his boldness in opening the story with a flashback without any indication to the audience that it was one. He aroused comment by his subjective use of the camera, in which, for example during a scene in a barber's shop, it becomes the seeing eye of the spectator. The barber's razor poised above the farmer's face produces a high degree of trauma in the Hitchcock manner.

While one critic declared that this film 'consolidated Asquith's reputation', another felt he had missed his mark with a commonplace story. Paul Rotha, though generally appreciative, thought all his work 'unbalanced and erratic'. He had a feeling for cinema but had studied the Russian and German techniques without searching deep enough.[7]

A Cottage on Dartmoor (1930) was a silent film with one brief sequence of dialogue. Asquith was thus at a disadvantage compared with Hitchcock, who had redirected most of *Blackmail* in sound, and sound was what gave prestige to pictures at this moment of history. Comparisons of the two directors are constantly made by the critics, usually to Asquith's detriment. Acts of Parliament and the compulsory showing of British films did not help him.

Tell England (1930) from Ernest Raymond's novel, dealing with the experiences of two young officers in Gallipoli, was well timed for popular appeal and goes among the box-office successes. Its battle scenes (with which he had the help of Geoffrey Barkas) showed imagination and technical virtuosity, but the film was more impressive as a document than as fiction. Rotha praises it on these grounds but regrets

128

that such brilliantly produced scenes (as the Gallipoli land-ings) have to be mixed with so indifferent a story. '*Tell England* is a noble attempt which very nearly succeeds,' he declares.[8]

Dance Pretty Lady (1931) followed but failed at the box office, and Asquith then went under contract to Michael Balcon at Gainsborough Studios. He did not get very far, for he was at the end of the queue among half a dozen other directors, and he made only one film for the company, *Lucky Number* (1933) about a footballer and a lost sweep-stake ticket.

The films in which he is now involved represent aspects of Asquith's talent rather than its total expression and among them we may include the Anglo-German *Unfinished Sym-phony* (1934) based on the life of Schubert, and *Moscow Nights* (1935) which Graham Greene dismissed as completely bogus. 'The direction is puerile. No one can drop a tray or glass', he writes of this war-time romance, 'without Mr Asquith cutting to a shell-burst'.[9]

For the next two years he was embroiled in one of those crises of the film industry which injured or wasted so many careers. He was engaged by Max Schach, the German refugee producer who came to London from Berlin, who succeeded in becoming head of Capitol Films, and after a brief reign, went bankrupt. Asquith made no films for Schach but he worked on scripts for him, on one of which the present writer collaborated. This was a characteristic Asquith witticism about two old ladies in Bond Street who ran an employment agency as a front for the liquidation of unwanted persons. It had something in common with Capra's *Lady for a Day*.

It was not until 1938 that success of the resounding kind came to Asquith with his direction of Shaw's *Pygmalion*, which he made for Gabriel Pascal. This was a subject which engaged all his powers, and this film, more than any other, established him as a director of distinction. Leslie Howard, who received co-director's credit, played Professor Higgins, Wendy Hiller was Eliza and David Lean was the editor, a fact to which the production owed a great deal.

E   129

Pygmalion was more than a good adaptation of Shaw, it was acted with eloquence by a cast who perfectly understood how Shavian lines should be spoken. To the two principals were added Wilfred Lawson, Marie Lohr, Violet Vanbrugh, Jean Cadell, Esmé Percy, Cathleen Nesbitt, O. B. Clarence and Iris Hoey, a rare commingling of talents.

There could be no question of purely visual cinema here. After all that Shaw had put up with at the hands of British film producers, he was determined on the play undiluted, with every word intact. Asquith was very adroit in producing as filmic a version as could be expected from such densely-packed dialogue. Gabriel Pascal, moreover, did succeed in persuading Shaw to write three entirely new sequences for him, a sign that Shaw, though distrustful, was keenly aware of the film's potentialities.

Up to this point Asquith may be described as striving to find himself and to bring fully into play his divergent artistic gifts, particularly those of music and ballet; but as we approach his later work we begin to doubt whether he will ever do so.

Pygmalion was followed by *French Without Tears* (1939), from Terence Rattigan's play. This particular subject was witty in an English way, it appealed to Asquith's satirical eye, and on this occasion Grahame Greene described the film as a triumph. But it did not add much to Asquith's reputation.

Chapter 13

Victor Saville, Herbert Wilcox and Others

Among directors of the 1920s and 1930s Victor Saville holds an important place. These years represent only the first half of his career. Like other British directors, Saville is surprisingly neglected in the textbooks, yet he produced or directed more than fifty major films, twenty-nine of them in England. He cultivated an aggressive showmanship of the American sort and his pictures not only evoke an age, they declare the box-office qualities that went with it. They remind us how much films depended on film stars—how the whole concept of a film was based on star values—Robert Donat, Clive Brook, Greer Garson, George Arliss, Jack Hulbert, Jessie Matthews, Madeleine Carroll, Conrad Veidt, and many others.

Saville came from Birmingham where he was born in 1897. In 1916, after serving in the war and being wounded at the Battle of Loos, he entered the film industry in the distributing branch. He sold films on the road, and soon caught the fumes of popular taste. In 1927 he formed the partnership with Michael Balcon to which we have already referred and acquired a mastery of studio methods which enabled him, like Mervyn Leroy or Henry Hathaway in America, to handle almost any subject and make it attractive to vast numbers of people.

Saville has himself given an account of film-making conditions in the 1920s when he was working for British International Pictures at Elstree. 'My own period at the studio', he says, 'coincided with the switch-over from silent to talking pictures. When I started there in late 1927, making *Tesha* with Maria Corda, two companies could work at once on one of those huge barn-like stages we used. In the silent days it didn't bother us. I had my company working at one end of the stage, while the boy wonder, Alfred Hitchcock, was putting another through its paces at the other end.

'Elstree was the scene of my all-talking debut. The film was *The W Plan* produced in 1929 with a young ex-school teacher making one of her first appearances before the camera—Madeleine Carroll.

'Those were momentous days indeed and ushered in a completely new and exciting era in this business. But I sometimes wonder whether they weren't also perhaps the closing of another era, in some ways even more exciting. You wrote the picture yourself, cast it—did everything—and you lived the whole thing, and with it the thrill that comes with pioneering. . . . Now, because of the vastly increased technical complexities of film production, film-making has become a matter of intricate team work.'[1]

Saville turned out an extraordinary assortment of films—musicals, histories, dramas, farces, nearly always as director, sometimes as producer. They include such disparate works as *The Iron Duke*, *South Riding* and *Storm in a Teacup*, and it is difficult to discern any specific trend. There was a time in the 1930s when he made a series of musicals with Jessie Matthews, *Evergreen* and *Friday the Thirteenth* among them, and it was evidently the intention of these studios to establish the British musical as a genre of its own. But this never materialised.

We may take as representative of Saville's work *The Good Companions* (1932), *The Citadel* (1938, producer), *South Riding* (1938) and *Goodbye, Mr Chips* (1939, producer). There was one film that suggested a breakthrough—*Sunshine Susie* (1931), based on a German musical and starring a German actress, Renate Muller, with Jack Hulbert. German musicals were very much the thing in the early 1940s—William Thiele's *Three Men at a Petrol Station* and Erich Pommer's *Congress Dances* with Lilian Harvey.

Sunshine Susie was not in the same class, but it made

good use of sound, if in ways which now seem obvious—in the office typing sequences, for instance. It had the perfect nonsensical story for a musical comedy, that of a young secretary's love affairs in a Viennese bank, and it successfully matched the English comedy tradition with continental ideas. Renate Muller, unhappily, got into trouble with the Nazi party and was liquidated by Goebbels.

The Good Companions, made in the following year, was solid British film-making based on a solid J. B. Priestley best-seller and could not fail. *The Observer* went so far as to compare it with the novels of Fielding.

'The whole of the film is good', it declared, '. . . a tremendous personal triumph for Jessie Matthews who plays Susie."[2]

Evergreen (1934) which showed the same skill and showmanship, was written originally as a stage production by Benn Levy and then adapted for the screen by Emlyn Williams. It was described as one of the best musicals Britain had ever made, a doubtful compliment since Britain never made good musicals. But it had a certain magic deriving from the C. B. Cochran original and was designed to magnify the talents of Jessie Matthews. In this it succeeded, for as singer and dancer the film gave her opportuntities to express a tender youthfulness and grace, and sing some delightful numbers, indeed she would scarcely have been beneath the notice of Gautier and his portraits of ballet dancers. Yet this musical, popular though it was, did not advance the cause of British musicals. The history of the British film is full of these strange discontinuities where we succeed with a special talent but never follow it up, as 20th Century-Fox or Warner's would have done.

The Iron Duke brought a rebuke from C. A. Lejeune, on the ground that £40,000 had been paid to George Arliss for an indifferent performance as Wellington.[3] But Sydney Carroll in the *Sunday Times* considered it 'as fine a film as any British studio has yet presented . . . its history', said Carroll, 'must not be judged too severely.'[4]

Punch said of the Duke, 'he certainly is not ferruginous. . . . A nice old gentleman for a tea-party', and awarded the

133

honours to Gladys Cooper as the Duchess of Angouleme
and to Allan Aynesworth as Louis XVIII.[5] By international
standards, of course, these films hardly matched up to some
of the Oscar-seeking works of the 1930s, Frank Capra's *It
Happened One Night*, Julian Duvivier's *Poil de Carotte*,
Lubitsch's *Trouble in Paradise*, and Renoir's *La Bête
Humaine*.

The Citadel, made in 1938, shows a greater seriousness
and maturity, and was described by Basil Wright as 'the first
studio film of social or civic tendency to be made in this
country'.[6] Saville produced it but gave the direction to
King Vidor.

The Citadel was good box-office and even more so was
Goodbye, Mr Chips which Saville made for MGM British
in 1939. He was again the producer and an American, Sam
Wood, the director. James Hilton's novel had caught the
public school atmosphere with uncanny rightness, and in
the hands of Robert Donat and Greer Garson, it was a
triumph for the box-office and the old school tie. Even
Graham Greene, from whom it is hard to gain the approving
nod, somewhat unbends. 'Some of us may feel unsympathetic
to Mr Chips', he writes, 'and the rosy sentimental view of
an English public school, but there can be no doubt at all
of the skill of this production. The whole picture has an
assurance, it bears the glow of popularity like the face of a
successful candidate on election day.'[7]

Next came Winifred Holtby's novel *South Riding* in 1938,
which Saville directed for Alexander Korda, with Edna Best,
Ralph Richardson, John Clements and Milton Rosmer. It
was a return to the film of social comment, dealing with
local politics and corrupt housing schemes. *South Riding*
showed once again that its director could handle serious
subjects with imagination and insight and his reputation
might have been greater if he had concentrated on them more
often. This was not easy, nor was it his special aim, which was
to make successful films as they came to hand, and this he
did, adding much to the gaiety of the 1930s and the continuity of the film industry.

In 1940 Victor Saville went to America and his films

there do not concern us except to note that he produced some characteristic Hollywood cinema with Hollywood stars—*Dr Jekyll and Mr Hyde* with Spencer Tracy and Ingrid Bergman, *White Cargo* with Joan Crawford and Clark Gable and *Kiss Me Deadly* (1955). In 1959 he returned to England to direct *The Conspirator* with Elizabeth Taylor and Robert Taylor, and a number of other films which call for no special notice except perhaps for *The Greengage Summer* (1961) which had a good deal of sunny, scenic charm and brought a film career to Susannah York. His best films were made in England.

Herbert Wilcox covers roughly the same period. An Irishman, born in Cork in 1892, he was a partner with his brother Charles in Graham-Wilcox Productions.[8] He entered films as a salesman after the 1914 war and made his first film, *The Wonderful Story*, with Graham Cutts. It failed at the box-office but was well received by the press, and this enabled him to continue as a producer. By 1926 he had become production chief at Elstree studios and from 1927 he was in charge of British and Dominions Films, one of the many companies linked up with the Rank interests.

Iris Barry has pointed out that Herbert Wilcox 'made some awful pictures when he began', but allows that 'he soon advanced in technical skill' and 'got over his stage-like treatment of the screen'. Miss Barry describes his production of *Nell Gwyn* as 'not merely a very creditable British film, but an enjoyable, lively picture.'

Among his early productions were *Chu Chin Chow* (1923) and *Decameron Nights* (1924) stagey spectacles photographed for all they were worth and manifestly to the taste of the public. No film at that time could be negligible with Werner Krauss and Lionel Barrymore in the cast, and with Ivy Duke, a creamy postcard beauty as the feminine element. These were the stars of *Decameron Nights*.

Nell Gwyn (1926) introduced Dorothy Gish to England, an astute act of showmanship which opened up a market for the film in America. After this much-talked-of success Wilcox made *Dawn* with Sybil Thorndike as Edith Cavell,

135

the nurse shot by the Germans in Belgium during the 1914 war. Most of Wilcox's films have a certain shock value. He would take large dramatic subjects, an historic figure or a story from the headlines, cast them boldly, and set up a loud vibration in the press. He proved as others did that publicity is often half the picture, sometimes all of it. We notice this in film after film, from *The Only Way* (1926) to *Victoria the Great* (1937).

The Queen Victoria film did so well that Wilcox followed it in 1938 with *Sixty Glorious Years*, a kind of Victoria the Greater, again with Anna Neagle. These historical films were made with great attention to period detail and had a pleasing elegance, though they showed little distinction in the writing and usually had a conventional approach. Perhaps it was this treatment which made them so popular.

Sixty Glorious Years, which was given an award at the Venice Film Festival, brought great prestige to Anna Neagle, already well known as a star personality. She had begun as a chorus girl at the London Hippodrome, she was to appear in nearly all Wilcox's films, and in 1943 she married him.

Wilcox belongs to that group of film-makers for whom the show is always the thing and every film an occasion for dramatic exploitation. We shall see this later in his war-time and post-war films. At present he figures as a highly successful producer-director, shrewd in his judgement but always prepared to gamble. A story he tells in his autobiography is characteristic. According to this, he handed Terence Rattigan a cheque for £100,000 for the rights to his play, *Ross*, dealing with the career of T. E. Lawrence. Not long afterwards he discovered that Korda, through some entanglement of the rights, had a prior claim, leaving Wilcox without a film and without £100,000. Clearly, those were the good old days. Wilcox tells the story with relish.

Walter Forde, born in 1898, antedates both Saville and Wilcox, for he appeared in films as a slapstick comedian in 1920. One of his silent films, *Would You Believe It*, ran at the Tivoli Cinema in the Strand for twenty-two weeks.

136

During the 1930s he made the musical comedies with Jack Hulbert to which we have referred, among them *Jack's the Boy* and *Jack Ahoy!*, etc. He made *Cardboard Cavalier* with the gifted comedian Sid Field, a promising idea which proved a disaster.

But the film which brought him most *réclame* was *Rome Express* (1932), a story of crime and murder on the Blue Train told with great technical expertise and offering admirable parts to Conrad Veidt and Esther Ralston. *Rome Express* was one of the prestige films of the 1930s. Forde directed a well-constructed story with flair, making the most of the long claustrophic sequences on the train and giving the film a polish which surprised Hollywood.

His versatility was part of his character but was at that time required equipment for a competent film director. He would undertake a musical with Jimmie Durante such as *Land Without Music* (1936) and, making every variety of film in between, arrive at a full-blooded melodrama such as *The Master of Bankdam* (1947). He was best in lighter subjects; into comedy he was born and in comedy he was a master. Indeed, he was so good at so many things that he tends to be taken for granted and hence to be under-rated. It is significant that Forde left England and retired to America while still in demand as a director. He viewed the industry with amused indifference.

Monty Banks (1897–1950), whose real name was Mario Bianchi, was in the same comedy tradition as Forde. In the 1920s he had worked for Mack Sennett in Hollywood, and it was Fatty Arbuckle who discovered him and insisted he must change his name.[9] He then made a number of comedies for the Warner Brothers, but left about the time sound pictures were coming in. 'He had a voice', said Jack Warner, 'that could not handle the ruthless demands of sound.'

Monty Banks had the chubby face, toothbrush moustache and bouncing temperament which bespeak the lunatic performer. He was the first of the Americans to work in Britain and he brought over Thelma Todd, the Hollywood star, to appear with him in *You Made Me Love You*, a daring stroke

137

of showmanship in 1938. Denis Gifford lists forty-two films which Monty either directed or appeared in between 1928 and 1939. He was featured in numerous silent two-reelers, in one of which he shaves on a bicycle while riding to the office.

For most of his screen career he was under contract to British International Pictures at Elstree, for whom he appeared in *Atlantic, Almost a Honeymoon, Tonight's The Night, Weekend Wives,* and many more.

He stayed at Elstree until 1935 when he went to Ealing to direct the George Formby pictures and it was there that he met Gracie Fields whom he married in 1940. He directed her in *Keep Smiling* and *Shipyard Sally.* Like his contemporary, Lupino Lane, his brilliant moments never coalesced into lasting fame. His real talent was obscured by the obtuseness of the press, which insisted on classifying him as the husband of Gracie Fields and was not interested in his career as an actor and director. But he was in fact a valuable 'property', for whom Robert Clark, then of Associated British Pictures, negotiated a two-year contract with 20th Century-Fox worth £150,000.[10]

Basil Dean, born in 1888, does not fit into any of the familiar categories. A producer of high distinction in the theatre, it seemed likely at one time that he would be as great an influence in the cinema. In 1929 he formed Associated Talking Pictures at Ealing. It was a soundly-based studio and Dean made films there for nearly ten years, scoring heavily with his two bright stars, Gracie Fields and George Formby.

He made Margaret Kennedy's *The Constant Nymph* (1927), Galsworthy's *Escape* (1930) and *Loyalties* (1933), A. P. Herbert's *Water Gypsies* (1932), Dodie Smith's *Autumn Crocus* (1934) and J. B. Priestley's *Laburnum Grove* (1936), but only the Gracie Fields and George Formby films, it seems, made money. In 1938 he abandoned pictures and returned to the theatre.

As we have seen, it is the big name that determines the style and content of the film, and to Formby and Fields we must add Will Hay (1888–1949), the famous music-hall comedian, and his stage partners Moore Marriott and

138

Graham Moffat. They were very popular in burlesques of schools and schoolmasters, convicts, policemen, lawyers. They appeared in *Where There's A Will* (1935), *My Learned Friend* and the already mentioned *Oh, Mr Porter!* (1938), mildly amusing shows never departing from accepted formulae of slapstick and pantomime, and clearly inspired by prevailing modes from America. Buster Keaton is said to have influenced both Walter Forde and Will Hay.

Jack Raymond (1886–1953) contributed to the seemingly endless series of ephemeral comedies, from *French Leave* (1930) and *Tilly of Bloomsbury* to *Up for the Cup* (1950). He directed Ruth Chatterton and Pierre Blanchard in *A Royal Divorce* (1938) and Jack Buchanan in *When Knights Were Bold* (1936).

Jack Buchanan (1891–1957), who started in Lubitsch's *Monte Carlo* in 1930 and Arthur Freed's *The Band Wagon* in 1953, never reached as a film actor the dominating position he held on the London stage. However, this is not the opinion of the French encyclopaedists, René Jeanne and Charles Ford, who take a precisely opposite view.[12] His last Hollywood film, *Les Girls* (1957) gave no chances to his sophisticated English style.

For some years before the war, Robert Stevenson, born in 1905, made a reputation as a director, especially with the ornately pleasing historical film, *Tudor Rose* (1936), with Nova Pilbeam and Cedric Hardwicke, and the more spectacular *King Solomon's Mines* (1937), also with Hardwicke, Roland Young, and Stevenson's wife, Anna Lee. A conscientious objector, Stevenson could not take part in war, and in 1939, when he was 34, he left England for Hollywood and found a wider scope for his talents, culminating in the most successful film in Hollywood for many a year, *Mary Poppins* (1964).

To have acted as co-director on the huge misbegotten *Caesar and Cleopatra* (1945) would confer upon anyone a kind of celebrity. Brian Desmond Hurst undertook this task at a critical moment in the production and succeeded within the limits of his brief. But his reputation rests on more solid ground. An Irishman, born in 1900, assistant at one time to John Ford, he had an early *succés d'estime* with Edgar Allan Poe's *Tell-tale Heart* (1934). He followed his up with Synge's *Riders to the Sea* (1935), and *Prison Without Bars* (1939), and he showed a gift for psychological drama in his brilliant handling of *On the Night of the Fire* (1935), which gave Ralph Richardson opportunities for a moving study in remorse. Hurst made many more films of which perhaps the documentary *Men of Arnhem* (1944) is most satisfying. *Dangerous Moonlight* (1941), about a Polish pilot who fought the Germans, also brought him an extraordinary success, attributed as much to the music as to the film itself. It inspired Richard Addinsell to write the *Warsaw Concerto* as the film's musical theme, which became an outstanding best-seller.

Adrian Brunel (1892–1958), educated at Harrow and for a time an actor, was among the most intelligent and witty of the younger men making films in the 1920s and he continued actively into the 1930s. His gift was for parody, by no means an advantage in those days. *A Typical Budget* (1925) aped the clichés and pomposities of Pathé's *Topical Budget*.

Brunel directed Ivor Novello in *The Man Without Desire* (1923) and in Noel Coward's *The Vortex* (1927), and for the silent version of *The Constant Nymph*, to which I have referred, he cast Mabel Poulton as Tessa, a fetching Cockney actress who did not survive the talkie upheaval because of her accent.* Brunel also took a hand in the direction of *Elstree Calling*, a revue about the studio which still has life in it, and he made a number of satires and comedies including a version of Anthony Kimmins' stage success, *While Parents Sleep* (1935).

As script writer, producer, director and author—he wrote an excellent little book on filmcraft—Brunel cut a considerable figure. Yet, as Michael Balcon observed, he never reached the peaks. He was an old Harrovian who never got accustomed to the playing fields of Elstree. Few British

* There were two further versions of Margaret Kennedy's novel and play—Basil Dean's sound version in 1933 with Victoria Hopper as Tessa, and an American version in 1944 with Charles Boyer and Joan Fontaine which Edmund Goulding directed.

directors had prestige then, they were occupied with testing their powers and retaining their independence, and success was long in coming.

We have mentioned *The Citadel* as an example of a film that explored the field of social realism, though this was a thought incidental to its choice as a best-seller. But we must note at least one undisguised attempt at social comment in the work of John Baxter (1897–   ). His film, *Doss House*, which he made in 1932 is an unpretentious story of life in the lower depths. It was well observed and directed and being almost the first of its kind had a merit of its own.

Yet the films of the 1930s refuse to lend themselves to labels or the broadly expressed theme. Producers are more concerned to keep the shop open and keep it busy, for they never know when it will close.

Chapter 14

Sense and the Censorship

As a further element of risk there is always the censor with his abhorred shears ready to amend or emasculate or reject a director's work. As the film gains in significance it is subject to closer scrutiny for lapses of taste, moral offence, danger to the State, affronts to religion.

The powers shaping the morality of the film in the 1920s and 1930s are the London County Council, the British Board of Film Censors and the innumerable local authorities scattered over the country. These authorities, of long tradition and independence, seldom agree either with one another or with the London County Council or with the British Board of Film Censors. The Board and the LCC, from frequent consultation and similarity of interest, more often share an identity of view. The unions and trade organisations are concerned and must be heard. Overshadowing them all is the Government, anxious as a rule to avoid entanglement but still more anxious to have the last word.

In 1921 the LCC, faced with a chaos of conflicting rules and decisions, called for a report from its Theatres and Music Halls Committee to try and bring greater sense and order into censorship. The recommendations of the committee were adopted and proved to be 'a well thought out . . . scheme based on the work of the British Board of Film Censors'.

Modifications are made to the general rule that films 'subverse of public morality' or lacking the Board's certificate must not be shown. Until then the A and U certificates were merely labels describing films for adults or children; they had no legal force. Now they were made mandatory.

142

Films with an A certificate could be attended only by adults, and by children under 16 only if accompanied by a parent or guardian. The trade resented the restriction, but in a year or two it was accepted.

There still remained the unresolved dilemma of propaganda films, those dealing with sex, prostitution and so on, which had no specific condition of exhibition attached to them. The Censor's office ignored them. The LCC considered each case on its merits. Some were highly respectable, some were put on for their sensation value.

In 1923 these films were brought into line. Children under 16 were not admitted, and to protect adults from moral danger exhibitors were compelled to display special notices making unmistakable the nature of the film shown. Later that year children were admitted if accompanied by a parent or guardian.

In 1924 the LCC again revised its rules and, notwithstanding the complication of Sunday opening which affected most cinemas, the system of censorship worked, and continued to work more or less satisfactorily into the 1930s, though a number of problems remained unsolved.

When, for example, in 1925, in defiance of the ruling, the London Film Society decided to show a number of uncensored Russian films, such as *October, The Battleship Potemkin* and *Mother*, the LCC relaxed its rules on the ground that the performances were private and were given only to a limited audience. Hunnings points out, however, that *Mother* was banned for film society showing in West Ham because membership cost only a shilling, so it virtually became a public performance. But West Ham Council reversed the decision and the film was shown. It was also put on by an Edinburgh film society.[2]

As a result of this administrative muddle the LCC, in 1930, abandoned its ruling. Films not certified by the censor, it declared, could henceforth be shown by film societies on certain conditions, among them the condition that no children under 16 be admitted and that no subscription be under ten shillings.[3]

During the 1930s a further development occurred which

143

was to have much wider consequences for the film industry; the invention of the non-inflammable film, though as a matter of fact it had been known and in use for some time. Non-inflammable film was not controlled by the 1909 Act. Its growing adoption by commercial companies, and by educational and other interests, and the certainty that it would soon be in universal use, compelled the Home Office to consider how it could be brought within the law.

A committee was appointed in 1939 under Lord Stonehaven to report on the matter and confirmed the known fact that non-inflammable film stood outside the Cinematograph Act.[4] It could not be censored and needed no license. This was enough to justify a change in the law, but the outbreak of war made legislation impossible.

Newsreels, which were free from censorship, frequently came under attack on political grounds. Hunnings cites Herbert Morrison's objections in 1933 to pro-Fascist material in newsreels and objections by Ernest Bevin to a speech by Lloyd George accusing the Allies of bad faith towards Germany. (It was cut from the newsreel.)[5] The Government pleaded with the newsreel companies for restraint, and so things remained until the war.

Film censorship then came under the control of the Ministry of Information which shared the responsibility with the British Board of Film Censors and left censorship on a voluntary basis. A special security censorship was set up at the Ministry to deal with films that might endanger the war effort, and newsreels were brought under control for the first time.

Notwithstanding the Board's prestige we quite often hear of efforts being made by councils or other interested bodies to get rid of it altogether, the intention being to substitute either a government censorship or one of their own.

After the war there was a growing feeling of revulsion against the horror film, especially for its effects on children, and efforts to overthrow the Board were renewed. Pressure grew to such an extent that in 1947 the Government appointed another committee, headed by Professor K. C. Wheare, to report specifically on these matters. No action was taken on it.[6]

The report advocated the introduction of an X certificate that would totally exclude children from that category and suggestions for other categories that would admit them. The A certificate admitting children with adults was found unworkable, the X would replace it and absorb the H (for horror) certificate that had been introduced in 1933.

These proposals had a chilly reception from the film trade which feared that the X certificate would destroy the family audience, and this was probably the beginning of that process. The Rank Organisation and ABC refused to book X films for a time. A growing volume of protest and the need to take action over non-inflammable film compelled the Government to bring in new legislation, the Cinematograph Act of 1952.

It was virtually a new bill, for it dropped the safety measures of the 1909 Act, omitted all reference to inflammable film, and brought Scottish licensing into line with English. It revised the regulations regarding children.

Censorship was left, as before, in the hands of the BBFC and the local authorities. Films whether on 35 mm or on sub-standard stock would henceforth be controlled for the commercial cinema but freed for the non-commercial, so that film societies, which were becoming influential outposts of liberal opinion, were exempt from censorship. Thus the recommendations of the Wheare Committee, previously passed over, came effectively into force.

We have referred to the complication of Sunday opening. Some councils insisted on a special kind of film being shown on that day and imposed their own ban on films of a criminal or immoral tendency, even though passed by the Censor's office.[7] They had had this authority since 1927 but in 1931 Sunday opening was made illegal. In 1932, following a case in which the LCC was involved, the position was reversed and Sunday opening restored with the passing of the Sunday Entertainment Act. Again a confused situation was clarified and cinema owners retained the right to show or not to show on the Sabbath.

The passing of the Act was an important step on other grounds, for a condition of films on Sundays was that 5 per cent of the takings should be given to charity and this led to the financing from these funds of the British Film Institute.

The slow and protracted steps by which a more rational censorship developed can be traced to these embattled days. It was no longer conceivable that such innocuous films as Sutton Vane's *Outward Bound,* dealing with the after-life, could be banned (it was re-instated by three county councils), or the same treatment applied to Herbert Wilcox's *Dawn,* about Edith Cavell. This was held up following protests from the German embassy. Perhaps the most notable gain was in the political field, the great Russian films no longer being suppressed for their revolutionary content, nor those from any other country. At every stage the cinema's fight for freedom is mirrored in the attitudes and actions of the censorship.

Chapter 15

Alexander Korda and the 1930s

Production during the 1930s is largely identified with the work of Alexander Korda who may be said to have created or re-created the image of British films during that decade. The extraordinary success of *The Private Life of Henry VIII*, when other films were failing, gave him an almost mystical prestige. It was always a conceit of the great producers to establish their own myth, invest themselves with the purple, and enthrone themselves before their subjects. Korda was not free of this superstition; he understood it and made use of it.

Can we separate the man from the myth? Korda has an artist's obsession with the medium. With this he combines a highly professional technique, a certain flamboyance of manner, and a preference for intelligent themes. The manner was Hollywood but the matter was European, and this meant a programme whose values comprehended *The Thief of Baghdad* at one end and a Wellsian fantasy at the other. With these went panache, glamour, stardom, all heavily laid on, the safe and the experimental went together. As for the cost, that had little to do with it. Korda conceived the film as a process controlled at every stage by a single individual and he built the studios at Denham as a means to this end. Lubitsch demanded only time and space for a picture; Korda added the resources of the Prudential Assurance Company and the British Treasury.

The blue books of the period, commenting later on this design, summed it up in a single word: extravagance. Sir John Clements described Korda's methods as a waste of

147

time and a waste of money.¹ No doubt the comment was justified, but extravagance in Korda's mind was simply the cost of making a good film, it was essential to success at the box office.

His success, as with all the tribe of film producers, was one of personality as well as professional expertise. In appearance he was totally unlike the booming extrovert of the popular imagination posing for the publicity picture. There was something professorial about him. He was, in fact, a well-read man of affairs with a cultivated taste in the arts. He spoke several languages. He had rare conversational gifts and a compelling charm which not only got him into the best company but out of the worst situations.

Korda's views were particularly striking when set against the current practice of British producers. British studios were not only intellectually sterile, they had a fixation about money, they could not feel really happy about spending it, and when in rare moments of abandon they made a splash, they spent it on the wrong thing—*London Town*, *Caesar and Cleopatra*, *or Jew Suss*.

Korda had his failures. Like his successes they were on the grand scale, *Bonnie Prince Charlie*, for example. But *The Private Life of Henry VIII* and other films of equal or greater merit, secured his reputation.

A general view of British films at the time would discover a steady flow of subjects from Shepherd's Bush, where Gaumont-British were trying to break into the American market, and a similar outpouring from Elstree, whose principal claim to distinction was the work of Alfred Hitchcock and E. A. Dupont. These alternated with such things as *Bulldog Drummond* and *Blossom Time*.

J. Arthur Rank was moving on a parallel course and building Pinewood Studios. He and Korda had the same simple and worthy aim: production of British films for the world market. No two men could have differed more widely in temperament or method, Korda being a producer by instinct and training, Rank a financier who engaged producers. In the end they both lost money, but it is to be noted that the status of the director improved and so did that of the writer. The character of the British film broke out of its provincialism and timidity and showed greater courage and intelligence.

Alexander Korda (1893–1956) was born in Hungary and began life as a journalist. His reputation in England has tended to obscure his early career and the sixteen laborious years he spent making films in Germany, France and America. His best-known film in Hollywood was *The Private Life of Helen of Troy* (1927), but the atmosphere of Hollywood was repugnant to him, he soon found he was not appreciated there and he returned to Europe.[2] It was his association with Paramount that led him to settle in England, where the American company invited him to undertake quota films in England for their British subsidiary.

For Paramount he made *Service for Ladies* (1931), *Wedding Rehearsal* (1932), and *The Girl from Maxim's* (1933). They breathe a wit and sophistication learned in the cafés of Europe. The first two, moreover, show an unusual understanding of the English character, that of a detached observer who saw more of England than Englishmen.

This is particularly true of *The Private Life of Henry VIII*, now given a much lower rating than in 1933. Its gusty and irreverent treatment from a script by Lajos Biro and Arthur Wimperis brought delight to filmgoers but protests from historians, who challenged its accuracy. Nobody could deny its success or that it radically altered the climate of film-making and was a turning-point in British cinema. Yet in 1933 Korda had as great a difficulty in getting the film launched as any of his contemporaries. No one in Wardour Street was prepared to back it and he went on the floor not knowing whether he would have enough money to finish it. Members of the cast were put on deferred payments. It was not a very costly production, Korda's own estimate was £59,000[3]—a small price to pay for a film which opened the way to a production boom and made a deep impression on the American film industry.

Korda formed London Film Productions in 1932, with Lajos Biro, the Hungarian playwright, as his story editor and his brothers Vincent and Zoltan as active partners.

Vincent had a reputation in Paris as a painter and came in as art director. Zoltan supervised production until he engaged in direction. It was characteristic of Korda that he avoided Wardour Street and settled in Mayfair and late in the war moved to the even more exalted air of 144 Piccadilly, *'un enclave hongroise au coeur du cinema'*. It was an address which combined several natural elements of publicity. From this irreproachable height he could look down on bankers and film stars and on the two royal princesses, Elizabeth and Margaret, still children, living next door. Here, as they played on the lawn, Korda gave press receptions which were like garden parties, just as he employed debutantes in his films as extras; it added to the legend and it got into the headlines.

In a very few years he had set up an organisation which enabled him to make films of a strikingly individual character, using the most celebrated stars in the world. He was able to compete on equal terms with the tycoons of Hollywood. He controlled a major studio. He was on the board of Odeon Cinemas. His connections with America were strong, especially that with Douglas Fairbanks, senior, and the remaining members of United Artists, Chaplin, Pickford and Goldwyn.

Fairbanks joined Korda's board of directors. Sir Connop Guthrie of the Prudential already represented London Films on the United Artists board. All these strands came together and it was not long before Alexander Korda, in 1937, also became a director, indeed an owner-member of United Artists. This secured him a release for his films in America. Odeon secured their release in Great Britain. He thus completed the process of making, selling and exhibiting his films at home and abroad in ways most favourable to himself. In doing so he widened the scope of British films as a whole and freed them from attitudes that were often narrow and constricting. In 1941 he received a knighthood.

Korda did not direct many films himself nor was he outstanding in that role. He rejoiced in star values and he favoured a soft, decorative photography, especially when he could put Georges Perinal behind the camera, which he

150

frequently did. His films are often weak on narrative—
hence, possibly, the failure of *Rembrandt* (1937), which
Korda himself preferred to all others. It had a star performance from Charles Laughton, and Vincent Korda's
sets were a splendour in themselves. The majority of critics
liked the film, Richard Winnington excepted, but it did not
do well, and Korda did not direct another until *Lady
Hamilton* in 1941.

For the thirty or so subjects bringing us to 1939 he acts
only as producer, in which his genius is so clearly displayed.
Many of these productions are of the spectacular kind. He
employs Jacques Feyder (*Knight Without Armour*), René
Clair (*The Ghost Goes West*), Paul Czinner (*Catherine the
Great*), Robert Flaherty (*Elephant Boy*), with Zoltan Korda
co-directing, and this two-handed ploy, as it happened, did
no good to Flaherty.

Catherine the Great (1934), which co-starred Elizabeth
Bergner and Douglas Fairbanks, junior, 'is in the same class
as Henry VIII', said Campbell Dixon, 'indeed, to my mind,
rather better . . .'[4] Elizabeth Bergner's Catherine he finds
'too flower-like and spiritual for the brilliant, dominating
German sensualist', but he is impressed by Bergner's 'keen
intelligence and vivid, engaging personality'. '. . . almost
everything in the film seems the work of an intelligent
mind', said *The Times* critic, 'the varied and extremely
sensitive acting of Miss Bergner makes Catherine a real and
fascinating person'.[5]

When the film was shown in Germany it was banned
because Elizabeth Bergner was a Jewish subject. Its release
there corresponded with organised riots.

Korda does little better when he leaves biography for
science-fiction. The reception given to *Things To Come*, while
not one of unqualified praise, brought praise enough, and
prestige. But it did not do well at the box office. 'As visually
exciting a film as ever came out of a British or any other
studio', said Alistair Cooke, but he damns the dialogue as
Drury Lane fustian of the 1880s.[6]

I, Claudius (1937), based on the novel by Robert Graves,
was one of the sublimer ideas that came to nothing. Joseph

151

von Sternberg was engaged to direct it. Charles Laughton was cast as Claudius with Merle Oberon as Messalina and Emlyn Williams as Caligula, and to these were added any number of brilliant supporting players. Merle Oberon suffered a car accident and could not continue. Sternberg did not get on with Laughton and Laughton did not get on with Korda. There were scenes behind the scenes. Rumour and strife rent the film and after a few weeks it was abandoned. But the fragments which BBC television showed in 1965 were melancholy proof of how much, artistically speaking, was lost in this affair. A vision of first-century Rome had for a moment been splendidly realised but was destroyed by human frailty and temperament.

The cost of this and of Korda's whole programme was immense, and by 1937 production everywhere was failing. By 1939 London Films were heavily in debt and Korda was forced to hand back the studios to the Prudential. In 1940, unable to raise further finance, he went to America, and there he made *Lady Hamilton*.

Lady Hamilton (1941) compels the eye with one of those great star displays Korda favoured—in this case Laurence Olivier as Nelson and Vivien Leigh as Lady Hamilton. The film was criticised for its inaccuracy and faulty characterisation but as a screen subject it had a certain Englishness and topicality to recommend it. The film was about Nelson and Britain at bay and was irreproachably patriotic. It was about Lady Hamilton and therefore romantic. Hence it answered the needs of the moment for war-time entertainment and was put on with a lavishness of scene and largeness of emotion which audiences relished.

As *Lady Hamilton* was Sir Winston Churchill's favourite film—a point industriously circulated—it scarcely mattered that C. A. Lejeune did not approve it (or the fact of Korda's being in America at that critical time), nor was it of much consequence that the *New Statesman* thought it 'too untruthful to be bearable. Yet Lady Hamilton isn't so bad and Laurence Olivier's Nelson is striking'.[7]

James Agate, in a later consideration of Lady Hamilton, asks: 'What about Vivien Leigh? Well, what about her?

She's heavenly to look at and is an exquisite, charming, delightful, witty, entrancing little actress. She is indeed everything but what I would call a good actress and can be played off the screen any time by any number of actresses with a tenth of her good looks, exquisiteness, charm, delightfulness, etc.'

He concludes: 'Vivien lacked equally Emma's charm and Emma's vulgarity. Her Lady Hamilton was an ultra-refined young woman who, on Nelson's demise, must inevitably decline to weeds, barouche, and memorials.'[8] But Agate is an untrustworthy film critic. Shaw, at any rate, felt that the 'ultra-refined young woman' was good enough to play Cleopatra in the film of *Caesar and Cleopatra*.

It will be seen that in these years Korda produced or directed a dozen or so major productions and a score of lesser ones, such as *The Squeaker, Paradise for Two, The Divorce of Lady X, Spy in Black, The Drum*. Between 1933 and 1940 he is responsible for forty-two films. To have carried out a programme on such a scale was probably beyond the thinking, and certainly the achievement, of any other British studio at this time.

It has to be admitted, of course, that many of the films Korda announced were never begun or never finished—they simply served to keep him in the public eye—the *Jubilee* film on which Churchill worked, *Cyrano de Bergerac, The General*, from Daphne du Maurier's novel and that half-made production so nearly a triumph—*I, Claudius*.

Chapter 16

More Directors of the 1930s

The conditions of film-making when Korda entered the field were not encouraging. Films, it is true, were being produced but their directors too often share an unhappy relationship with the distributors and an absurdly complicated ritual of borrowing and lending is required to get a film off the ground. The position of the director is well stated by Michael Powell in an article he wrote concerning *The Edge of the World* (1936):

The Edge of the World was made . . . at a time when the fortune of British films was at a low ebb. It was not a question at that time of a scarcity of British films of a world-wide reputation: there were very few good films at all. Those that existed were due to the activities of a few men like Hitchcock, Saville, Korda, and Ted Black. (Black was in charge of the Shepherd's Bush studios for a time.)

'The reason was quite simple. Hardly any film was being made because the makers of the film wanted to make them. They were being made for a dozen reasons, mostly political or financial, but seldom for the reason that a particular film was one which the director and his associates wanted to make more than any other. This belief . . . is the only formula for making good films.'

It was in this context that Robert Flaherty, Carol Reed and a number of other directors made their first important contributions to cinema. There was no fixed creative centre for them to work in; they filmed where they could. As Pinewood Studios grew and flourished they worked for

154

Rank. When conditions did not favour them there they moved over to Korda at Denham or to some other studio. Carol Reed, Powell and Pressburger, John and Roy Boulting, Thorold Dickinson, Gilliat and Launder all came into prominence in the 1930s, some early, some late. Michael Balcon, who had left Gaumont-British in 1936, was now at MGM's British studios at Denham as production chief. Producers had no security of tenure, neither had directors.

Nevertheless, their presence marks an upward curve in the scale of values, an advance in the battle with the money men. We consider here only the films they produced up to the outbreak of war in 1939, Flaherty's career we follow to its conclusion. He exercises a greater influence than any of his contemporaries, but although he is accepted as the apostle of the documentary creed he is finally rejected for betraying it.

Carol Reed, born in London in 1906, was, in his young days an actor and appeared in several of Edgar Wallace's plays. He also directed plays for him, and in 1930 produced *On the Spot* in New York. His interest in films was awakened in 1932 when Basil Dean asked him to act as dialogue director at Ealing Studios. In 1934 he impressed the critics with his first film, *Midshipman Easy*, followed by *Laburnum Grove, Talk of the Devil* (a story of his own), and *Who's Your Lady Friend?* With *Bank Holiday* (1938) he showed a narrative skill and a gift in the handling of crowds and individuals which confirmed talents of an unusual order. His declared aim was simple: to excel in the art of telling a story.

Bank Holiday, about a hospital nurse, is an improbable melodrama but it has moments of truth and a feeling for life which make its faults unimportant. The American criticism of our films had always been that they had nothing to do with life; they had no roots in reality. *Bank Holiday* went some way to answer this criticism.

His next film, *The Stars Look Down*, made in 1939 but not shown till 1940, was a more testing affair, a real challenge to a director's powers. A. J. Cronin's novel (filmed

155

with Michael Redgrave, Margaret Lockwood and Emlyn Williams), had strong political overtones and a scale and depth which gave a director the widest scope for interpretation. Its story of miners on a Teeside coalfield who clash with the management and refuse to go on duty because of the risk of flood, is of the classic order and J. B. Williams, a neglected figure in British films, produced an excellent script.

At its centre is Joe Gowlem, a spiv of boundless ambition and vulgarity whose love affairs and lust for power give the film its dramatic centre. The wider issue is a plea for the nationalisation of the coal mines.

The *Spectator*, favourable to Cronin's novel, said: 'I doubt whether in England we have ever produced a better film.' (It was Graham Greene.) Commercially the film was an immense success and owed much to its element of realism.

Realism of another order is found in Michael Powell's documentary film, *The Edge of the World*, already referred to. Frustrating studio conditions made it impossible for him to get backing for it, and in the end it was an American producer, Joe Rock, who supported him and offered him his studios at Elstree when other sources failed. 'All the men and women who worked on the film', said Powell, 'had learned their profession on little films which were mostly cheap and generally nasty.'[2]

The Edge of the World is a study of the struggle for existence of the people of Foula, an island in the Outer Hebrides. It describes the harshness of their lives and their eviction from homes painfully won and deeply cherished, when poverty and adversity leave them with nothing to live on and nowhere to go.

Like *Man of Aran*, with which it is sometimes compared, it applies the documentary method to the theme of people struggling in a hostile environment and at the mercy of forces beyond them.

Shortly after making *The Edge of the World* Powell formed his own company, *The Archers*, with Emeric Pressburger, a Hungarian writer who came to England in 1935. They produced a series of films with a marked personal style of their own which frequently led to controversy. So,

156

too, did the Boulting brothers, directors of Charter Films, which they formed in 1937.

John and Roy Boulting, twins born in 1913, formed a writer-director-producing team whose work showed a predilection for the socially-angled theme. To this they joined a habit of dashing into public controversy and tilting at the establishment. *Consider Your Verdict* (1937) was followed in 1939 by *Pastor Hall*, though this was not shown till 1940.

Pastor Hall, from Ernst Toller's play, was based on the life of Pastor Niemoller. The priest, stirred by insults and barbarities in which his own daughter is involved, denounces the Nazis from the pulpit and is sent to a concentration camp. He escapes, but is shot dead at the door of his own church. It was an unpretentious but effective film, 'the first really successful anti-Nazi film', and it was praised for its courage and qualities of restraint.

Thorold Dickinson having learned much with Pearson, re-enters the field at this time, a gifted director whose films have a clearly recognisable style. A left-winger anxious to promote the causes in which he was interested, he devoted a good deal of his early career to political films. In 1937 he made *The High Command,* and in 1938 when, as he frankly explains, there was a slump in production, he produced a documentary of the Spanish civil war, *Spanish A.B.C.*

In 1939 he returned to feature production with a version of Patrick Hamilton's play *Gaslight,* with Anton Walbrook and Diana Wynward in the leading parts. It was not shown, however, until 1940.

Gaslight was a pyschological thriller about a woman sharing her life with a man in ignorance of the fact that he is a murderer, and of the agonising mental conflict she suffers when she is dragged into investigations by the police. The macabre direction, the Victorian gloom are admirably keyed to the mood of the story.

The merits of *Gaslight* did not go unnoticed but could not save it from oblivion. Metro-Goldwyn-Mayer bought the film and then suppressed it in order to make a version of their own called *Murder In Thornton Square.* It was one

157

of those bleak incidents which deface the record from time to time and show it at its commercial worst. Leslie Halliwell points out that although the negative was destroyed, prints of the original version remained, and the film has been shown in America under the title *Angel Street*.[3]

Thorold Dickinson made several other films of a highly individual character, to be considered in their place.

Robert Flaherty (1884–1951),* most highly regarded of the documentary makers of the 1930s, came to England in 1931 after several disillusioning years in the American film industry where, however, some of his best work was done. Though, strictly speaking, only his British films should be considered here, some reference must be made to his work in America, for Flaherty's films are a single, indivisible creation.

He belongs by instinct and background to the silent cinema. Self-centred and independent, he has no allies, no partner but his wife Frances, who saw him through the unending storm and stress which plague the creative life in the film industry. In all his film adventures—and they are more in the nature of adventures than productions—she was his constant companion and professional guide, of the same persistent breed, and she did not withdraw from the turmoil except occasionally when the needs of the family had to be given priority.

In 1920–2 he made *Nanook of the North*, a documentary about Eskimos which was at once recognised as the work of a master, penetrating deeply into the life and character of a remote people and bringing a new poetic experience to the screen. Flaherty's involvement in the scene, his understanding of men and his wonderful visual sense give a special quality of interest and excitement to *Nanook*. He is the advocate of pure cinema, but a cinema based on strict, imaginative truth.

In this film and in its successor, *Moana*, Flaherty gave

* I am indebted to Arthur Calder Marshall's *The Innocent Eye* for some of the details of Flaherty's career in this chapter. The rest is from personal knowledge.

first expression to the documentary idea. Nature had been observed in a thousand films, but it was left to Flaherty to give it the force of a personal vision. Nor was it some esoteric exercise, above the heads of ordinary people; these films were immensely popular and made a deep impression in America and Europe.

Although Flaherty was sought after by the major American production companies, they did not offer him the conditions which enabled him to work and which had made possible so great a triumph as *Nanook of the North*. When he came to make *Moana* (1926) for Paramount, they expected a film as successful as *Nanook* and Flaherty spent two years in Samoa absorbing the lives and manners of the inhabitants, bringing back material of an extraordinary and exhilarating beauty.

Moana was a great disappointment to Paramount who had expected Flaherty to provide hula-hula girls and all the traditional mumbo-jumbo of the South Seas. When the film was released it was exploited as 'the love story of a South Seas siren'. Flaherty, like Filippo del Giudice a generation later, realised that his films were being sold like goods at a grocer's shop, and he made great efforts to persuade the distributors to change their tactics, but in vain.

Metro then invited him to join W. S. Van Dyke in the direction of *White Shadows of the South Seas* (1926), but this again turned out to be the usual hocus-pocus, and Flaherty withdrew. In a further effort to find a congenial subject he linked up with the German director, F. W. Murnau, in the production of *Tabu* (1931), again in the South Seas, but this didn't work either; their methods were opposed and they parted before the film was completed.

Thus Flaherty was engaged in the same struggle for personal identity and artistic freedom that inspired his contemporaries in England, and it was to England he came. He was welcomed by John Grierson and Paul Rotha, leaders of the documentary school and their colleagues. After collaborating with Grierson on *Industrial Britain*, a film 'which finally reached the sereen as a co-operative work of several hands',[4] he conceived the idea of a subject dealing with the islanders of Aran off the Irish coast and won

159

Michael Balcon's support to make it. In the austere lives of the people of Aran scraping an existence from sea and earth he found the epic story he needed. He spent three years on Aran, cut off from all communication with the studio, and a number of disciples followed him there to study his methods at first hand.

Man of Aran (1932–4) had a mixed press and was criticised by the leaders of the documentary movement as a departure from principles. It favoured aestheticism at the expense of actuality, they declared, and was a betrayal of the documentary faith unsuited to a time of depression in England and of war neurosis in Europe. That it was being praised abroad by German Nazis and Italian Fascists made matters worse. 'In that mood', says Richard Griffith, coming to the defence, 'Flaherty's preoccupation with the classic beauties and braveries of existence seemed to them (the documentary leaders) irrelevant if not actually evasive or dishonest. . . . But no considerations of group unity, social realism or propaganda could explain or justify the outburst of denigration that followed the appearance of *Man of Aran* in Britain. After that', says Griffith, 'Flaherty stood alone, though in the midst of a flourishing movement based largely on the method he had himself founded.'[5]

Both Grierson and Rotha, while sticking to their point of view, acknowledged Flaherty's services to the film and the uniqueness of his achievement. 'Acknowledge our deep obligations to his pioneer spirit', Rotha wrote, 'his battles to break down commercial stupidity. . . . But realise . . . that his understanding of actuality is a sentimental reaction towards the past, an escape into a world that has little contemporary significance.'[6]

Grierson added: 'One may not—whatever one's difference in theory, be disrespectful of a great artist and a great teacher.'

C. A. Lejeune, while affirming that anything of Flaherty's was worth seeing, attacked *Man of Aran* for its lack of content. In her view, he had not told the real story.[7]

Graham Greene complained that photography alone could not make a poetic film. 'By itself it can only make arty cinema. *Man of Aran* was a glaring example of this: how affected and wearisome were those figures against the skyline, how meaningless that magnificent photography of storm after storm. *Man of Aran* did not even attempt to describe truthfully a way of life'.[8] This was the film, by the way, which bored James Joyce, as he mentions in his letters.

Flaherty, distressed by these attacks, and particularly by that of the documentary film-makers, did nothing for a year or two. He was a man for taking his ease, for eating and drinking and telling stories, and Arthur Calder-Marshall reminds us that at this time 'he entertained all and sundry at the Café Royal. He no longer patronised Grierson's documentary pubs.' His drinking friends were now Augustus John, James Agate, Liam O'Flaherty and Epstein, a group which indicates the depth of the breach between himself and his former colleagues. But he felt out of it. To those who knew him Flaherty seemed incapable of making an enemy, but he was of such sensitivity that almost anyone could make an enemy of him.

However, in the film trade the important thing is not the personal equation but the next picture, and we find Flaherty assigned by Alexander Korda to the making of *Elephant Boy* (1937), from a story by Rudyard Kipling. Sabu, discovered by Flaherty in India, was the star.

But now it had got abroad that Flaherty was difficult, dilatory and extravagant, and he was not permitted the independence which was the breath of life to him. *Elephant Boy* was made in India and at Denham Studios, with Lajos Biro as script-writer, followed at a later stage by John Collier. Monta Bell, an American director, and Zoltan Korda kept an eye on the direction. Produced under this wounding supervision, it had the expected scenes of elephants and jungles and India, but no real story and it was not well received. Flaherty's heart was not in it. Graham Greene attacked him, John Grierson defended him, and this was the end for the man who thought he would find freedom and fulfilment in England.

In 1939, when he was 55, he went back to America and made *The Land* (1941) for Pare Lorenz and the US Govern-

F   161

ment, of which Arthur Calder-Marshall gives so lively and compassionate an account. Delivered too late to be of value, it had no proper release. Paul Rotha and Basil Wright were both deeply impressed by it. For a brief period during the war he worked for Frank Capra's *State of the Nation* newsreel, but was not a success there and the project was abandoned. In 1944 the Standard Oil Company commissioned him to make *Louisiana Story*, a film about the problems of extracting oil from the earth, with Helen van Dongen as editor (from all accounts a bit of a genius herself), and this was completed in 1948. It proved to be his finest achievement, with no detractors, though Flaherty did not do too well out of it financially.

This was his last work, that of a man set somewhat apart from others, of the same integrity and innocence as W. H. Hudson or Henry Thoreau. His half-a-dozen films raised the cinema to new heights. He came back to Europe to watch over the release of *Louisiana Story* and went on a goodwill tour of Germany with some of his films for the US State Department, though what he had hoped to do was to make a film of Ceylon. There were other unfulfilled projects. But while he was in Germany he caught pneumonia and as soon as he was able he returned to America, where he received the degree of Doctor of Fine Arts. The Cinerama company invited him to direct a film for them which consisted of a sixty-minute newsreel of General MacArthur's return from Korea. This, with misgivings, he did. Again he caught pneumonia, probably an aggravation of his previous attack, and in July 1951 he died at the farm he and Frances owned at Brattleboro, Vermont. He was 67.

Chapter 17

Brief Encounters: Filippo del Giudice and Gabriel Pascal

Amid the ill-organised and crowded events of the 1930s when so much film history is being made it is not easy to isolate, still less to assess the careers of two men, both expatriates, who made a considerable impact on the film industry: Filippo del Giudice and Gabriel Pascal. They stand alone, odd fish in deep waters. Their work covers a comparatively brief period and is discontinuous. Neither stays long enough to put down roots. Del Giudice's name is known but not spoken of as one might speak of Korda or Goldwyn.

Yet he made *In Which We Serve, Odd Man Out, Hamlet, Blithe Spirit, Henry V*. Pascal is recalled if at all for his notoriety rather than his achievement. Each made a contribution to the film in Britain; del Giudice a more substantial one than Pascal; each had high aspirations and displayed an imagination and audacity lacking in others. They overcame some of the built-in prejudices of our studios and they rejected the advice of salesmen and accountants. They enter the industry unsung and they leave it unhonoured. Films are very much a personal equation but they also pursue a logic of their own, determined in the last resort by accountants, and this brought their downfall.

Filippo del Giudice (1892–1961) was for eight years Rank's senior producer. An Italian lawyer and refugee from Fascism, he came to London from Rome in the mid-thirties and earned a living by giving Italian lessons. His legal advice was sought in a case which Bette Davis brought against Warner Brothers and this stirred his interest in the cinema

163

and persuaded him that he could play an important part in it.

In 1937 with money raised from friends, one of whom was the Italian financier Toeplitz de Grand Ry, he formed Two Cities Films and in 1939 made his first picture, *French Without Tears*. A year or two later against the advice and without the help of Wardour Street he persuaded Noel Coward to co-direct and star in *In Which We Serve*. It was an immediate success and Wardour Street welcomed him into the club. The Ministry of Information, sensitive to the film's value as propaganda, put money into it and brought the producer an envied prestige.

Following this success del Giudice produced nearly a score of films, mostly for the Rank Organisation, and Two Cities became its leading production unit. Rank was his staunch supporter and established him in grandeur in Park Lane and on an estate in Buckinghamshire known as Sheepcote. To these insignia of greatness, del Giudice added a yacht which never set sail from the waters of the Thames. At Sheepcote he outlined a scheme for building studios, and here and on his yacht he entertained Sir Stafford Cripps, then President of the Board of Trade, Ernest Bevin and other men of money and power.

As time went on and films such as *The Way Ahead*, *Blithe Spirit* and others appeared under the Two Cities banner, del Giudice found himself increasingly critical of Rank's distribution policy. He maintained that the Rank sales force treated all films alike, irrespective of their quality and so deprived them of their proper standing in the market. He described this process as selling Cartier jewels as Woolworth paste. He was in fact the sworn enemy of the distributor or middleman who took a handsome percentage of the film's profit with no risk to himself, and he looked forward to a time when film production would be divorced from salesmanship and each film given proper value and audience. Audiences should be chosen for films, films should not be flung indiscriminately to audiences.

At the various studios where he worked del Giudice was valued by the directors he engaged for his ready assumption

164

of all the administrative burdens, in particular the financial and other pressures weighing on the studio. He left his directors free to concentrate on the creative problem.

James Agee, noting how he raised £465,000 for Laurence Olivier's *Henry V*, adds: 'He did something more remarkable; he never interfered with Olivier's work; he never let him know there were money difficulties.'[1]

Why then, if del Giudice was so competent and produced such brilliant films, did he fail? Was he indeed a failure? Was there a plot, as some alleged at the time, to ruin him?

His retirement from the scene arose from his disagreements with Mr Rank. He not only rejected Rank's ideas on production but by the time *Hamlet* was made was said to have lost him £600,000.

Del Giudice never admitted this but entered into an interminable correspondence with Rank. If indeed such losses could be proved, they would be repaid, he declared, out of the success of *Hamlet* and *Henry V*. But he does not come well out of this correspondence, whereas Rank, in spite of these losses, is still prepared to back him.

In 1947 they parted and del Giudice formed his own company, Pilgrim Pictures, the title being suggested by Sir Stafford Cripps. But now the situation was changed. No longer could he play host at Sheepcote or negotiate deals in Park Lane which were backed by a great organisation. Nor could he raise the substantial finance which had always been available to him as head of Two Cities. And indeed when for a moment the power again lay within his reach he lost it through sheer indiscretion.

He had been offered on conditions of absolute secrecy a large sum of money by Sir John Ellerman, the shipping magnate, but so far from keeping faith with his benefactor he could not resist giving the story to the press. Ellerman abhorred publicity and the offer was withdrawn.

This left him more or less penniless; he retired from the precincts of Park Lane to an office in Hanover Square. There for a time he languished until the Boulting brothers discovered a backer from the Midlands, brought him to London and put out the story that he was a millionaire who did not

165

wish his name to be disclosed. As the newcomer had served on one of Churchill's committees for cutting down expenses during the war, he seemed the ideal candidate for a similar role in Wardour Street. For a time, guided and supported by the Boultings and by the millionaire who was not in fact a millionaire but a prosperous glass manufacturer in the Midlands, del Giudice was able to return to production.

He produced *The Guinea Pig* and *Private Angelo* but these could not stave off accumulating losses and in desperation he went to America to seek new allies. But the word had got around that the great producer was in difficulties and this was enough to destroy him.

In 1952, having spent fifteen more or less active years in the industry, he retired to a monastery in Rome. After a time he reappeared with the idea of producing films in Dublin for the Catholic interest but this too, came to nothing. We hear of an eye operation and after several years of obscurity, of his death in 1962.

Gabriel Pascal (1894–1954), the Hungarian producer and director, embarked on a career no less erratic and less prolific of good works. He had all the qualities of the impresario channelled into a single obsession, that of persuading Bernard Shaw to permit the screening of his plays. The story of how he did so is well known, but has a fabled air, like so many of his exploits.*

Shaw had never heard of Pascal. He arrived one day in 1935 at Shaw's flat without an appointment but convinced by the words of a fortune-teller that the visit would be lucky.

Of this incident Miss Patch, Shaw's secretary, writes: 'Gabriel Pascal was Gabby, concerning whom a legend has arisen about his irruption into the life of G.B.S. He arrived at Whitehall Court in a taxi, just after the King George V's Jubilee celebrations in 1935. The story that Shaw paid for the taxi is a myth. Gabby paid for it himself out of the few

---

* His life and his partnership with Bernard Shaw are described in *The Devil and his Disciple*, by the Hungarian actress, Valerie Tibor, who became Pascal's wife. It contains some good Shaw letters but is written in a high-flown novelettish style.

shillings he had in his pocket, a circumstance which did not depress him. Money . . . or the lack of it never meant much to Gabriel Pascal.'

'What Gabby did', Miss Patch added, 'was to persuade Shaw to make the plays presentable in the new medium. He had swept ahead of all established bidders for a licence to film *Pygmalion*.'[2]

In 1935 when British films could not claim much intellectual substance this was surely an achievement. After Shaw's rejection of innumerable more rewarding offers it seemed inconceivable that he would relent. Pascal, moreover, was nearly everything that Shaw was not, sharing only his conceit and effervescence.

Pascal had worked diligently on the plays. He knew every line and undertook to film every word without a cut. He had a child-like love of Shaw. He fascinated him with stories about himself and his gallantries in the great celluloid cities and by expressing himself in atrocious English he gained a kind of reputation as a noble savage to whom proper honours were due. Shaw wrote: 'The man is a genius: that is all I have to say about him.'[3]

Though he achieved this extraordinary rapport with Shaw he was a good deal less successful at the studio level. His extravagance and bombast irritated the unions and he frequently clashed with them. His flamboyant style might have suited a de Mille or Mike Todd in the lush days, but not in the fourth year of war, and in the end it brought him down.

Pascal had impressed the critics with his production of *Pygmalion* in 1938. In 1940 he produced and directed *Major Barbara* with a cast of exceptional talents—Rex Harrison, Wendy Hiller, Sybil Thorndike, Deborah Kerr, Robert Newton and Emlyn Williams.

Major Barbara was a great success in England but not in America,[4] where there was little interest in a play which dealt with the Salvation Army; and even the genius of Shaw and Pascal conjoined could not avert disaster for *Caesar and Cleopatra* (1945), the film which worried and infuriated Shaw in his last years.

The sets of this fantastic production spread all over the

lot at Denham studios. Palaces and banqueting halls were set down in the middle of Buckinghamshire and amazed the passer-by. The interior sets were no less splendid. Rumour, scandal, gossip flew about. Every player not acting on the West End stage was said to be in the picture, which soon cost so much it could only be saved by still greater infusions of capital.

Shaw himself visited the set, peered into every detail, commanding and correcting, and giving instructions, for example, as to the kind of shoes Stewart Granger should wear as Apollodorus. Shaw was 89 then. He strode about the studio and skipped up ladders with vigour. He seems to have been conscience-stricken about the money Rank was pouring out, but Pascal reassured him.

The sum sanctioned by custom on an enterprise of this kind and encouraged by agents show how crushing the burden can be even before a film takes the floor. To take but one example: Vivien Leigh, as Cleopatra, was at that time under contract to David Selznick who is said to have received £50,000 for his share of her services and was entitled to a further share in the American film rights. The star herself received £25,000 for sixteen weeks' work and Claude Rains £15,000 free of tax, with dire penalties if he was not returned to America by a certain date. £12,000 was paid to Brian Desmond Hurst as co-producer. As production drew to a close he and Pascal were not on speaking terms and Pascal completed the film himself.

There was the bombing and the bad weather. Pascal and his staff had some narrow escapes. Perhaps the worst misfortune of all was Vivien Leigh's illness, due to a miscarriage, which held up filming for six weeks. There were innumerable feuds and unscripted scenes and the unions, which were not doing badly, complained of the extravagance and wanted Pascal banned.

After eight months the production was taken to Egypt for exterior scenes on the Sphinx, for the march to Alexandria, for the Lighthouse and galley scenes. The Sphinx used at Denham was the principal property exported to Egypt.

Marjorie Deans, script-writer on the film, explains why it

was necessary to take it there.[5] 'The Sphinx where Cleopatra and Caesar met', she writes, 'was never intended to be the Great Sphinx, but a quite different and smaller member of the same species. Besides, the two principal characters on the actual Sphinx would have been so far apart as to make any thought of conversation between them entirely out of the question.'

At one time difficulties of production were so great and morale so low it seemed that the whole film might have to be abandoned. Miss Deans, who pays understandable homage to Shaw and to Pascal, points out that if the film was not abandoned it was 'due entirely to the faith and determination of two people: Arthur Rank and Gabriel Pascal'. She re-affirms Rank's belief that if the film industry was to survive 'it was essential to have a few first-class productions aimed not merely at our own, but the world market'.

But it did not work out that way. America was not interested in the survival of British films and except for war films, made no effort to show them. If *Caesar and Cleopatra* had been even a moderate success over there, to say nothing of Britain, the money and the talent poured out on it would have been well spent. Unhappily this was not so. It was badly received by the critics and made an indifferent impression on release.

A year or two later Rank made a second film, *London Town* (1948), at a cost of £800,000, most of which was lost, and convinced the City once again that the makers of British films were not to be trusted with money or genius.

In the meantime *Caesar and Cleopatra* was described by the critics as 'a luxuriance of dullness', 'wasteful extravagance', while Richard Winnington complained that it was 'more than a disappointment . . . a dismal ordeal'.

James Agee is a notable dissentient. After remarking that the massive sets 'cloy one's attention and thus slow up the mind and the dialogue', he adds: 'But even as it stands, the show is exceedingly good at the core, if you enjoy Shaw.' He fails to see why it was 'generally panned' in England.

The film remains a curiosity for the student and a

melancholy entry in the books of the industry. Even 20th
Century-Fox's *Cleopatra* made years later at many times the
cost was a less boring piece of work and it was bad in the
right way; its vulgarities held the attention and helped to
restore the fortunes of Fox.

Pascal planned to produce one more film, *The Snow Goose*,
for which Rank, with astounding generosity, put up
£30,000, but it never materialised and they parted. Pascal
then went to Hollywood where he filmed Shaw's *Androcles
and the Lion* which passed almost unnoticed. This was his
last work.

Both Pascal and Filippo del Giudice had qualities the film
industry needed, with large ideas and powers of organisation
and a belief that great things could be done. Del Giudice
practised what he preached and believed in those qualitative
standards that are found in most of the films he made. He
deplored a shoddy piece of work being lumped together by
the distributors with works of distinction. He could make a
little English anecdote like *Tawny Pipit* (about an army
diverted to save a bird's nest) and he could make *Hamlet*.
Forced in the end to think in more modest terms, he intended
to film Donagh MacDonagh's Irish verse play, *Happy as
Larry* which had been a success in London and which he
bought for £2,000. This might have launched him on a less
glorious career or at least saved him from extinction, but it
never came to pass. Del Giudice's record, then, is of his
many productions at Two Cities Films. Among them are a
number of outstandingly good films for which he deserves
to be remembered.

Pascal's conquest of Shaw gives him a kind of immortality
but the industry could not forgive him the fiasco of *Caesar*
and *Cleopatra* and would not have him back on any terms.
'We must admit', says Sainte Beuve, 'that it is a rare gift
and a proof of genius too, to be able . . . to tame a genius.'

Pascal tamed his genius but the cost was too high.

Part IV

Documents and War Films

Chapter 18

The Documentary Movement, 1929–1940

In its origins and development the documentary film is in a category of its own differing radically from the commerce of the studios. Not without strife in its early days it provides one of the most fruitful and brilliant chapters in British film history. It was a struggle. It met with opposition. For as Lindsay Anderson has said of those trying to do something in films, 'to be British was and is to start with a handicap'[1]—as it also proved to be Scottish. For without the energy and persistence of its Scottish founder, John Grierson, and the group of film-makers he recruited, the documentary movement could never have become the force it was.

The film which marks its beginnings and led to government-sponsored film production on a large scale is Grierson's *Drifters*, describing the work of the Scottish herring fleet, first shown in 1929.

The sound film had just made its appearance. Alfred Hitchcock was making *Blackmail* and Ernst Lubitsch *The Love Parade*. Films were possessed by a single thought—to entertain.

For Grierson they had a wider significance. They had in a unique degree 'the power of making things known which need to be known',[2] and he went a good deal beyond this to challenge the whole concept of film-making. Documentary was in fact a revolutionary movement, the first important example of creative experiment in British films guided and inspired by a single individual to the end.

173

The conditions which enabled Grierson to carry this out were, first, his perception of the need for a new form of cinema, secondly his tenacity and organising skill in getting it off the ground, and thirdly his independence of the film industry.

We have seen that with few exceptions films were produced for entertainment and recreation. But now, after thousands of such films and years of exposure to the British or American dream, a handful of artists and technicians find that something has been omitted—the world of fact.

Documentary was an attempt to give expression to the factual world; it was 'the creative interpretation of reality'; a strictly practical movement though not without subtler overtones. The end was not entertainment in the accepted sense but educational in the broadest sense; it was 'a new idea in public education'.[3] Ruttman's *Berlin: Symphony of a City* (1926) and Cavalcanti's *Rien Que les Heures* (1926) had brought a documentary technique to the recording of daily events and these had received enthusiastic approval from critics and *cinéastes* alike. Grierson and Paul Rotha, with others of like mind, were responsible for developing and furthering and persistently writing about documentary, and demonstrating its worth in films of their own.

As the idea was new it was of course resisted, nobody wanted to hear about it or encourage it, it had to be justified by faith and works. This it succeeded in doing. By the 1930s it was already clear that the documentary film had created a school, perhaps the only one, to be traced in the development of British cinema.

How was this new kind of cinema to be defined? Grierson himself invented the word as long ago as 1926, deriving it from the French word *documentaire*, applied to travel films. 'If I remember rightly', he says, 'documentary was first used to describe the art of Mr Flaherty's *Moana* in a hurried article for a New York paper, and Mr Flaherty's art it represented for many a day. It stood for those theories of "action on the move", "the spontaneous on the screen", "the drama in the living fact" which he first initiated and in which some of us were trained.[4] If we did not then use the word "realism", it was for the good reason that, whatever Mr Flaherty might be in idyll and romance, he was never, in the academic sense, a realist. The realism came later and particularly in England.' Documentary was created 'to fill a need', and the need, which was social, was 'not only real but wide'.

The film of entertainment, as we have seen, emerged at the bidding of the machine. There was the machine, something of profit must be put into it. This was the doctrine that had given the cinema commercial mastery from the beginning. Now the situation was reversed. The machine was no longer the master but the servant, and could be turned to social ends unconnected with the profit motive. Grierson's cinema was of this order.

He was born at Deanston in Scotland in 1898, entered the Royal Navy in the 1914 war and went mine-sweeping in the North Sea. In 1919 he renewed his studies at Glasgow University which the war had interrupted, and in 1923 took a philosophy degree. The following year he went to the United States on a Rockefeller Research Fellowship in social science and studied the arts of communication. In 1929 he returned to England and joined the Empire Marketing Board under Sir Stephen Tallents. There he shared for a time the job of Films Officer with Walter Creighton. The Board existed to promote the sale of Empire foods and services in Britain and used all possible means of propaganda. Grierson, encouraged by Tallents, set up his own film unit there, the first to be sponsored by a government department; thus documentary acquired a habitation and a name. Until then it had been used to describe any kind of factual record from newsreels to scientific and medical films.

In 1932 the Empire Marketing Board came to an end and the film unit was transferred to the Public Relations Department of the General Post Office, again under Sir Stephen Tallents. Film was used to tell people about the Post Office services, to urge their wider use and to explain their advantages.

Public relations was then a new and developing technique, the beginning of the image-making which was to become

175

obsessive in later years. The value of the film, which had been forcefully demonstrated at the Empire Marketing Board, was soon recognised by other government departments and by commerce generally. The big business organisations, intent on more of this and that, commissioned documentaries to sell food, oil, machinery, sugar and so on. Shell, Cadbury, the Gas Board—these were the clients of the new race of persuaders, sometimes within, oftener outside the G.P.O. Some industries set up film units of their own and worked independently. Independence was the word, an air not breathed in studios.

Wardour Street, ever suspicious of developments which it could not control, did not take kindly to this one. The distributors ignored it. But it hardly mattered, for the documentary film flourished without them. Its audience was found outside the commercial cinema and within the industrial undertakings that sponsored it, that is to say, in the non-theatrical market of the factory, the school, the canteen, the camp. By 1939 the G.P.O. Film Unit had come to be accepted as the official film centre of the Government.[5]

During the war it was transferred to the Films Division of the Ministry of Information which, with the British Council, became 'the main war-time sponsors of the documentary film'.[6]

What sort of film was *Drifters* (1929) which 'laid the foundation for documentary in this country', and proved itself so inspired a model for the future? The subject of this film was the herring industry in the North Sea, an important interest to the Empire Marketing Board, but not particularly inspiring to the layman. It could have been an interesting film, leaving no mark.

Grierson had been an attentive student of the Russian film. He had worked on the version of *The Battleship Potemkin* (1925) which was later released in America, and he was profoundly influenced by the methods of Pudovkin and Eisenstein. Russian documentary had begun with the poet-director Dziga-Vertov's theory of Kino-Eye, 'the cinematography of actual incidents and objects of everyday life'

176

as if the human eye had followed them wherever they happened to be. The method is well described in Jey Leyda's study of the Russian cinema, *Kino*[6]: 'Vertov', he says, 'with his brother and chief cameraman, Mikhail Kaufman, lived in a Pioneer camp, visited markets with concealed cameras, rode with ambulances to accidents, spied on criminals from behind windows, haunted the doors of beer parlours, danced with rejoicing collective farmers—neglecting no technical device then known to camera work in order to transfer a sense of actual life on to a moving picture screen. Osip Brik, the Russian script writer, said: "It is necessary to get out of the limited circle of ordinary human vision; reality must be recorded not by imitating it, but by broadening the range ordinarily encompassed by the human eye." '[7]

The documentary film in Britain developed from this position. Grierson, in full sympathy with the method, discarded actors and studio effects and went straight to life. He did not report, he interpreted the facts before him and, in his own words, 'made a drama of the ordinary to set against the drama of the extraordinary'. Thus, in *Drifters* he observed all the actions of men at sea, of harbours, trawlers, fishing-nets, fish, the physical sweat and labour, and transformed them by his seeing eye and critical approach. The thing seen, to borrow a phrase from painting, is 'personally felt and rendered'.

To look at this four-reel work today is to be reminded that the silent film can perform miracles of statement and is a self-sufficient art. Here you are given the whole life of a Scottish trawlerman, his character, his job, what the labour and conditions of getting in the fish mean to him, and what they mean to the consumer. Time has overtaken the film and today critics are less kind to it.

Drifters is the only documentary Grierson directed himself, he acted henceforth as a producer and propagandist for his own ideas. There are divergences of view on what is technically proper to such films, and in particular on the value of the aesthetic element, which has been warmly debated.

To put his theories into practice Grierson assembled a group of directors, writers, artists and composers whose

177

approach to film was unhampered by conventional attitudes and who understood instinctively what he was getting at. Paul Rotha, Humphrey Jennings, Edgar Anstey, Arthur Elton, Cavalcanti, Basil Wright, Donald Taylor, Harry Watt, Marion Grierson—these are the makers of documentary film in the 1930s. Their task was defined as 'bringing alive the modern world'.

Up till now the factual film had been confined to the newsreel. Newsreels had been an important feature of the landscape since 1910 and the skill and enterprise of their producers, the most notable among them Castleton Knight of Gaumont-British, had made them immensely popular. They had ample resources and were sure of a wide distribution. But although they conveyed information they did not illuminate it. There was no thinking or probing behind the event, immediacy was all. The newsreel was not expected to have a point of view. The documentary, on the other hand, existed only for that purpose.

Earlier there had been some related efforts of an imaginative kind in the famous *Secrets of Nature* (1919–34) series initiated by Bruce Woolfe and Mary Field but these, which occupy a special place in British film-making, were objective studies; they did not use persuasion.

There were entertaining Hollywood documentaries, semi-fictional, diving into American history, or exploring remote corners of the earth, such as *Grass* (1925), *Chang* (1927), and *Bring 'Em Back Alive*.

Rotha mentions *The Covered Wagon* as an epic of national endeavour using natural backgrounds and 'having a greater purpose than mere fiction', and this was as long ago as 1924. Films like *The Covered Wagon* and *The Iron Horse* were conscious efforts to tell the American story in epic form, but they were cluttered up with stagey incident and did not see that the epic itself was enough. The newsreels remained an efficient and often sensational means of communication, but until American newsreel men revised their conception of reporting and Louis de Rochment produced *The March of Time* in 1934, there was little sign of genuine documentary impact.

178

Grierson continued at the G.P.O. the tradition he had established at the Empire Marketing Board. His group of film-makers, to whom W. H. Auden and Benjamin Britten lent their talents, saw in the propagandist film an opportunity to do meaningful work in film and at the same time free themselves from the pressures of the commercial studios.

Drifters was released commercially and did much to advance the documentary cause and combat prejudice. Clearly there was something in this new use of the medium which challenged the long-held assumptions of showmen and the rigid conventions of film-making.

During the mid-thirties, interest among industrialists was so great that some of the leading documentary men, Elton and Anstey among them, formed units of their own to meet the need, and this led in 1935 to the formation of the Association of Realist Film Producers.[8]

In 1937, Grierson left the G.P.O. Film Unit in the belief that he could be more useful outside it, and with Arthur Elton, Stuart Legg and J. P. R. Golightly established the London Film Centre to advise on documentary projects. It produced its own journal, the *Documentary News Letter*, and was often sharply critical of government film policy.

In 1938 Grierson was asked by the Canadian High Commissioner to produce a scheme for the development of film production in Canada and in that same year he began work. In 1939 he was appointed Film Commissioner to the Canadian National Film Board. With former colleagues he built up a government film industry, doing for Canada what he had already done for Britain. He produced, among other things, two celebrated series of films, *Canada Carries On*, dealing with the life and work of the Canadian people, and the influential *World in Action*, which surveyed world affairs and was exhibited in Canada, Britain and the United States.

When war broke out all these film-makers were well equipped for the task of propaganda . . . 'there was in Britain a pool of film-makers', writes Forsyth Hardy, 'trained in the use of film for informational and inspirational purposes'. The war-time record of British documentary from *Target for Tonight* to *Desert Victory* and the hundreds of small func-

179

tional films which taught us how to dig for victory and put out fire bombs, is a straight development from what had been created at the EMB and the G.P.O.

A Films Division had been set up at the Ministry of Information at the outbreak of war but did not make much progress owing to indecision at the top. The G.P.O. Film Unit was not invited to help. 'The pre-war part played by the documentary film in the public service was completely ignored,' says Rotha. A number of productions made by the Films Division itself were so bad they had to be shelved. With films for industry more or less at a standstill, the whole documentary movement stood in danger.

A Select Committee on National Expenditure strongly criticised the Films Division, but by the time its report was published, matters had improved. Jack Beddington, director of publicity at the Shell Organisation and known for his active interest in the arts, was appointed director of the Films Division—two others had already come and gone—and he at once called on the documentary group for its services.

In April 1940, the G.P.O. Film Unit became the Crown Film Unit under the wing of the Ministry. It had taken ten years to bring it into existence, for the hardest task was to break through the barbed wire of government departments and the brass fronts of Treasury officials. For the first two years the Crown Film Unit's campaign consisted of five-minute information films, issued every week, proffering exhortation and warning about salvage, food, orange juice for children, health hints and so on. There were films describing what the Services were doing and what our allies were doing. Many were made by independent producers, only a few by the Crown Film Unit itself, which was turning its guns on bigger targets.

Soon the Ministry was entering into full-scale film production. Its output during this period was prodigious, no subject escaped its vigilance, from the intimacies of Boiler Practice to the virtues of Oatmeal Porridge. Hundreds of films went out to village halls and factories, mostly on 16 mm, so that by the end of the war no man, woman or child could have been unaware of the long arm of documentation. Many more put the British point of view to the liberated countries of Europe.

These audiences were being educated in a new kind of film. No one paid anything to see them and the attendance figures were high. In 1940–1 2,240,000; in 1944–5 6,500,000.[9]

In 1945, having completed his task, Grierson resigned as Canadian Film Commissioner and moved to New York, where he founded International Film Associates to inform and increase the understanding of the world on current affairs and bring documentary into the international field.

As it happened, this scheme never matured and was the least fruitful period of Grierson's career. After the failure of his New York hopes he went, at the invitation of Julian Huxley, to Unesco, to become Director of Mass Communications, and here, in 1947, he was associated with Jean Benoit-Levy in making a number of internationally commissioned films. But this did not satisfy him either; he found the operations of Unesco slow and frustrating. 'It was easier to prepare plans', says Forsyth Hardy of this phase, 'than to see them fulfilled.' Grierson accordingly returned to Britain where we find him established as Controller of Films at the Central Office of Information, and so in charge of the Crown Film Unit on his old ground.

Not all the work of propaganda, of course, was planned by Ministries. We have to note the important part played by the British Council in promoting British interests through film. The Council's brief was capacious and ranged from architecture and history to biology and the English language. *Papworth Village* (1944), telling the story of the tuberculosis centre, is a good example of the kind of film produced; others dealt with the land, trade unions, Scotland Yard, machinery, crops, cotton, and so on. The British Council was, in fact, the principal official sponsor of the documentary film outside the Ministry of Information and sent its productions all over the world. Except as a supporter and spiritual ally of the documentary movement, it does not concern us here; its object was the entirely peaceful one of 'interpreting Britain in the widest sense'.

181

The documentary movement could not have succeeded but for its independence and singleness of purpose, two conditions conspicuously lacking in British production as a whole. Documentary producers did not have to consider profit motives. They were not concerned with circuit releases and box-office records but only with the most effective way of putting their vision of things on celluloid. 'The director (of a documentary film)', said Grierson, 'is free in his manner and method as no director outside the public service can hope to be.[10] His only limits are the limits of finance, the limits of his aesthetic conscience in dealing so exclusively with an art of persuasion, and the limits of his own ability'.

During the 1939 war this philosophy paid off handsomely, for some of the most popular films shown were *Target for Tonight*, *Desert Victory*, or films of fiction with a documentary gloss as, for example, *One of Our Aircraft is Missing*. They competed successfully with such strong Hollywood contenders as *The Philadelphia Story* and *The Maltese Falcon* and were a new experience for filmgoers. They marked a decisive change of direction away from the theatrical and the studio-bound concept towards realism and fresh air, and they opened people's minds to the power of the non-story film; to the fact that there were other kinds of film, more deeply satisfying and unconnected with the traditional patterns of entertainment.*

* John Grierson's final statement on the documentary movement, written in 1970, is given in Appendix I.

182

Chapter 19

War Films: Documentary, 1939–1945

Since 1937 the production side of the industry had been steadily disintegrating and there were no signs of a returning confidence. Rumours of war made things worse. But the war itself produced a sudden burst of creative activity which greatly enriched the cinema's material and aided its development. Deep emotions were stirred, a mood of crisis and dedication filled the studios which focused their energies on boosting the national morale.

The documentary movement had been from the first a purposive effort of propaganda and succeeded through its single-minded devotion to causes. Now this same spirit penetrated into the wider field of feature production and raised its energies and capacities to the highest level.

It has been said that the cinema 'merely provided a substitute for real life' and 'helped people to become watchers instead of doers'.[1] Céline described the cinema of the 1930s as 'that little clerk of our dreams that could be hired for an hour like a whore'. There was some truth in this, but the films of the war years could not be accused of it, for they gained in honesty and intelligence and made great advances in public esteem.

Of films produced during the war about half were propaganda and the other half fiction; those which did not directly aim at information or persuasion found an outlet in escapist themes such as *Kipps* or *Quiet Wedding* (both 1941), which allowed people to forget the war or reminded them of the values they were defending.

Considered as part of the war effort, British films were

deplorably slow in getting off the mark, though the fault was not theirs. As we have seen, the G.P.O. Film Unit was passed over. In Germany Goebbels did not make this mistake. He moved promptly and with blunter weapons. We were quite unprepared and had scarcely conceived of the film as a war-making instrument.

As the years went by, however, its value for psychological warfare became abundantly clear and more films were rushed into production. These were great years for British cinema and sometimes raised it to poetic heights. The films were reinforced by the BBC talks of J. B. Priestley and Quentin Reynolds, the American journalist, and by the *Music While You Work* programmes relayed to the factories, strong incentives to increased effort.

Early in 1939 when war seemed inevitable Alexander Korda produced *The Lion Has Wings*, a film directed by three different hands, Michael Powell, Brian Desmond Hurst and Adrian Brunel. It was a botched piece of work intended to show the strength of Britain's air defence. Two films directed by a brilliant young newcomer, Penrose Tennyson, deserve to be remembered, *There Ain't No Justice* (1939) and *Proud Valley* (1940). *Proud Valley* examines the position of a Negro seaman, Paul Robeson, who joins a mining community during the depression; it was followed by the more strictly documentary film, *Convoy* (1940). Pen Tennyson, a grandson of the poet, showed the highest promise as a director, but died in a flying accident while serving with the Fleet Air Arm. He was 26.

Anthony Asquith produced two documentaries, *Channel Incident* (1940) and *Rush Hour* (1941) as propaganda pieces, and then made the submarine story *We Dive At Dawn* (1943), full of humours and cheerful naval types.

All these early productions were by way of being experiments, They share a common technique of realism. No one knew how audiences would respond to them or what they wanted. *London Can Take It* (1940) directed by Harry Watt, a brilliant ten-minute short describing how the people stood up to the Battle of Britain, was a minor triumph and when

184

shown in America did much to sway opinion in our favour. But it is not until Watt's *Target for Tonight* (1941) that the documentary war film springs into a genuine popularity and challenges the best things in the commercial field.

Target for Tonight followed a basic narrative style which we find repeated in later war films. Men are briefed for a task, it is crucial for the war effort, there are failures and disasters, but after a period of suspense the mission is completed and the men return, or are found to be missing.

Harry Watt, who had worked with the G.P.O. Film Unit, was one of its most talented members and had, as we have seen, already made one or two strikingly effective documentaries, *Night Mail* (1936), with Basil Wright, to which he added *North Sea*. He was less influenced by theory than some of his colleagues and his interest in human relationships was more personal, hence his movement later into fiction.

Target for Tonight stands up well after more than thirty years. It is a close-up of a single action of war, rounded and complete, and concerns a Wellington bomber whose crew are ordered to Germany one night to destroy some oil storage tanks at Kiel. The crews are young and dashing and carelessly go into battle. The simple heroism of this story appealed to everyone and its success in Britain and America was immense. It stirred the Ministry into setting up a very much larger programme of feature films. *Nine Men* (1943) was among them, a tale of men besieged in a North African fort. This too was directed by Watt.

In a category of its own is Thorold Dickinson's *Next of Kin* (1942), alike for its merits as a document and the circumstances in which it was made. It was commissioned by the War Office as a warning to the Forces against careless talk, the leakage of information which could lead to heavy losses in action. It was not intended for commercial distribution and Michael Balcon, the producer, had been allotted the derisively small budget, for a full-length film, of £20,000. He persuaded the War Office to release the film to the ordinary cinemas and thus enable him to recover the £50,000 it had actually cost. In the event it made a small profit. But once again he had trouble with Churchill who felt that an incident in the picture foreshadowing the tragic Dieppe raid of 1942 might cause alarm and distress, and he ordered the film to be submitted to a military jury. The jury approved and the film got its release.[2]

Next of Kin (1942) has the close observation and tightly-knit construction we notice in other Thorold Dickinson films. C. A. Lejeune described it 'as the perfect spy story'. It had at its centre the harmless, seedy little man who was later to become the key figure in spy stories. Though classified as documentary by Richard Griffith, it contains strong elements of fiction.

The year 1942 is slow to move and is sparing with full-scale documentaries though it produces half a dozen films of the non-fictional kind. The strictly documentary ones follow the formal narrative pattern we have noted.

Then, a climactic moment, come the first battle pictures to be made in the firing line—*Wavell's 30,000*, a description of the campaign in Libya. It was a good workmanlike job and vividly brought home the realities of men fighting in a field of war too distant to comprehend, until factual exposition and shattering camera-work made them all too plain.

Jack Holmes, who had made *Merchant Seaman* in 1941, followed it with *Coastal Command* in 1942, an account of the work of the RAF sent out to protect Britain's coast line. It describes the monotonous vigils of the pilots defending our convoys in all weathers against German submarines and warships. Vaughan Williams composed the music for it.

Again we have the simplicity and heroism of a schoolboy yarn told in deadly earnest. Jonah Jones and F. Gamage are the photographers and there are three second unit directors, John Elton, Jack Lee and R. Q. McNaughton. The result is a film of rare quality which hit the popular taste and was widely shown at commercial cinemas.

There was never any shortage of subjects. One of the darkest and vilest episodes of the war was the planned destruction by the Germans of the Czechoslovakian village of Lidice in 1941, ordered as an act of vengeance for the assassination of Heydrich. Humphrey Jennings (1907–51) put this on to film in *The Silent Village* (1943). A director of highly individual style, by gift a painter, by nature a poet, he brought out the horror of the story by a chilling sobriety of statement and precision of detail.

In the same year he made *Fires Were Started* (1943), written by E. M. Forster and produced by Basil Wright, a truly remarkable work whose subject was the air raids on London in 1940–1 and how they were handled by the AFS (Auxiliary Fire Service). It is an impressionistic study put over with irony and humanity and showing a poetic insight into the lives of ordinary people caught in the full fury of war.

Daniel Millar makes the claim that *Fires Were Started* 'immeasurably surpasses every later British film in the intervening quarter century . . . an isolated masterpiece, even within Jennings' own work'.[3]

Gavin Lambert also maintains that *Fires Were Started* was 'one of his (Jennings') most ambitious films and his masterpiece'. *Family Portrait* (1950), the last film he made, was less artistically satisfying. It projected a series of reflections on his own philosophy of the British people. David Robinson concludes that 'the subjects he chose in the last years did not seem entirely to suit him or to stimulate his imagination. They are highly polished films in the best tradition of British documentary, but they lack the creative heat of his best work'.[4] Humphrey Jennings died while filming in Greece as a result of an accident. He was 43, he had made eighteen films, several of them greatly enriching the cinema for Britain.

Jack Lee's *Close Quarters* (1943) produced by Ian Dalrymple, an account of British submarines operating off Norway, gave more latitude to the creation of character though it used officers and men of the submarine service. A film which activates its own drama, it follows the usual story line of hazards overcome and success achieved.

But the high-water mark of 1943 is without doubt *Desert Victory*, one of the outstanding documents of the war. It received the not-easily-won praise of James Agee who

187

described it as 'the first completely admirable combat film'. To which he added: 'If only film makers and their bosses can learn the simple lessons it so vigorously teaches, its service to the immediate future and to history will be incalculably great.'[5]

Desert Victory (1943) recounted the grim early phases of the Egypt-Libya campaign when the British armour was dug in at El Alamein to halt Rommel's advance into Egypt. Churchill, Alexander and Montgomery are there, it is a crisis point in the war. After long preparation the attack is launched, it ploughs through Rommel's defences and is followed by the eighty-mile march to Tripoli.

The producers assembled the miles of footage shot by the newsmen and sound crews in the battle line and edited them into a profoundly moving drama. Some cameramen were killed in action or taken prisoner and the film is a memorial to their name. It is at pains to build up the human detail behind the battle, the men in their private thoughts, gathered in the canteen, writing home or on routine duties. Kipling's soldier is mechanised and the film shows ordinary men made great by great events.

Desert Victory was produced by David Macdonald and directed and edited by Roy Boulting. Summing it up, Agee said it was 'a stunning text book on how to make a non-fiction war film'. Most encouraging of all, it was exhibited at some 12,000 cinemas in America, an unprecedented Oscar for a British film.

This brings us to the last in the cycle of desert documentaries, *Tunisian Victory* (1944). Frank Capra joined with Roy Boulting and Hugh Stewart in this Anglo-American production. It gave a detailed survey of the North Africa campaign but was marred by excessive propaganda and sentiment, more noticeably in the scenes taken at Christmas. It was a more complex and tougher proposition than its predecessors; four technicians lost their lives in it.

More interesting perhaps for its treatment and beset with fewer difficulties of production was Pat Jackson's film of the Merchant Navy, *Western Approaches* (1944). Photographed in colour by Jack Cardiff, it has a majestic simplicity of

188

statement which the colour reinforces. It concerns the British crew of a lifeboat used as a decoy by the Germans to trap a rescue ship. It was acted by a non-professional cast whom Jackson handles with telling effect. He dispensed with written dialogue and took it from the mouths of the seamen themselves. A Crown Film Unit picture, more ambitious than *Ferry Pilot*, it unfortunately arrived too late and much of its impact was lost. Two documentaries widely shown in Britain must be referred to if this record is to be complete, for although American they were strictly relevant to the British war effort. The first was *The Battle of Britain*, the second was *Divide and Conquer* dealing with Hitler's plan for world conquest. They were both made by Frank Capra in 1943 in his *Why We Fight* series. The Americans learned the art of the documentary from Britain and they were quite ready to acknowledge it.

The year 1945 marks the final phase of the Ministry of Information's propaganda campaign with the making of *Burma Victory* and *Journey Together*. The second of these was a straightforward feature about the RAF as seen by its own men, and was directed by Roy Boulting from Terence Rattigan's script. It was a story based on the RAF's own records and it had the surprise and excitement of an experience genuinely felt and recorded.

Roy Boulting also directed *Burma Victory*, with David Macdonald again as his producer, a more formidable task expounding a complex politico-military background. But it is lucidly told and in its slogging way absorbing.

We have seen the waning of interest in documentary, not from any lessening of skill or failure of vision among its practitioners but from other causes. Audiences were becoming bored with war after five years of it but they did not mind looking back with a certain pride on what they had survived.

Carol Reed's *The True Glory* (1945), which he made with the American Garson Kanin, corresponded to this mood of recall. It surpasses in magnitude every film of war made up to that time and is the last act in the filmed drama of the war years.

The True Glory is the official record of Allied operations from 1939 until D Day and took a year to produce. It was given massive co-operation by the British and American governments. The great battles are fought again—Caen, Walcheren, the Bulge. Half-a-dozen countries sent in their combat cameramen to film them of whom more than thirty lost their lives and more than a hundred were said to have been wounded. General Eisenhower produced a foreword of his own and this sealed a consciously prestige effort. When completed it was found that a total of $6\frac{1}{2}$ million feet had been shot and this had to be edited down to 8,000.

Carol Reed's hand is abundantly clear in the atmosphere and the scrupulously built-up detail of the film, though it is needless to apportion responsibility between two such experienced directors. When, to detail and atmosphere, an equal skill is shown in the creation of character a satisfying unity is achieved, and to this William Aylwin's music contributed. The film is especially effective in viewing the war through the eyes of those who fought it and in recording it in their own words. No less than six writers worked on the script.[6] The blank verse narration, however, is generally considered a mistake; this was the majority view among critics, who mostly went out of their way to praise.

The *Manchester Guardian* spoke of 'the pretentious but indifferent blank verse' but acknowledged that much of the film was fine, true and moving.[7] Paul Rotha's view was that it 'set a new standard for actuality film-making'.

After the war the documentary declined.

Chapter 20

War Films: Fiction and Semi-Fiction

The propagandist themes of the documentary film were related strictly to government needs and presented their makers with clearly defined objectives. The choice for the producer of fiction or semi-fiction, however, was his own and a more speculative matter. His film was addressed not to pre-selected audiences gathered in army huts or village halls but to the ordinary commercial cinema, and this cinema was undergoing change. It had flourished on the stock materials of the screen for thirty years or more—drama, comedy, musicals, adventure. Now, the medium which had produced the entertainment had also to produce the message, and the emphasis shifts from the surface to deeper levels.

During the war years Rank moved ahead with his production plans at the expense of Alexander Korda, who was in America. He spent £450,000 on *Henry V*, more than a million on *Caesar and Cleopatra*. Some films of outstanding character were made and succeeded in their purpose of informing, moving and delighting. Glamour and heroism such as we found in the 1914 war have gone, they are replaced by an austere realism. The humour remains, of course, and as a record of the fortitude, manners and behaviour of a society living under bombardment, these films have an historic value. Yet there is no co-ordination, no consistent development of ideas, each film carried along by its own momentum, is sufficient unto itself.

The American studios faced none of the problems of British production; they did not gear themselves to the

191

subject of war until 1943. The year's best film in 1941, judged by the New York critics, was Orson Welles's *Citizen Kane*; the Academy Award went to Ford's *How Green Was My Valley*. Other pictures show that Hollywood was still living in a great star-building dream and making exceptionally good use of her talents—*The Maltese Falcon*, *The Little Foxes*, *King's Row*, *Dr Jekyll and Mr Hyde*, and Garbo in her last film, *Two-Faced Woman*. The year 1942 was given up to such frolics as *My Sister Eileen* and *Holiday Inn*, and to these we must add Orson Welles's *The Magnificent Ambersons* and Greer Garson's *Mrs Miniver*, a film which, with all its faults, did much to swing American opinion in our favour.

All these and many other productions were released in Britain and more or less monopolised the screen. Without them British exhibitors would have faced ruin, a thing, by the way, they were constantly facing and as constantly surviving. Moreover these brilliant American productions gave an undoubted moral boost to British audiences who could scarcely have existed on the handful of films coming from British studios.

France could send us none of those productions we found so inspiriting. Clair and Renoir were in Hollywood. Films were certainly being made, such as Marcel Carné's *Les Enfants du Paradis* (1943–1944), and Jean Delannoy's *L'Eternel Retour* (1943), but few of them were seen in England until after the war.

In 1941 Thorold Dickinson made *The Prime Minister*, with Sir John Gielgud as Disraeli, an efficient but not otherwise distinguished production. Carol Reed produced the mildly interesting *The Young Mr Pitt*, with Robert Donat. Korda's *Lady Hamilton* we have already discussed. Though so English in character, it did not qualify as a British film.

One or two small things made an unexpected impact. John Baxter, who had made *Doss House* in 1933, turned once again to the underworld with *Love on the Dole* (1940) from Walter Greenwood's stage play, and *The Common Touch* (1941). The area of the defeated and the futile to which Baxter went for his sources was so far unexplored

192

1. The Electric Theatre, 1901

2. The Plaza, 1934

3. *Trip to the Moon* (1902), technical effects far in advance of their time

4. Scene from *Voyage to the Impossible* (1902), prototype of a long list of imaginative fantasies

5. (*a*) Stewart Rome

(*b*) Florence Turner

(*c*) Chrissie White

(*d*) Alma Taylor

(*e*) Henry Edwards

(*f*) Violet Hopson

7. Betty Balfour as *Squibs* in the Welsh-Pearson film (1921)

6. Dorothy Gish in Herbert Wilcox's production of *Nell Gwyn* (1926).

8. Florence Turner and Henry Edwards in *East is East* (1917), which Henry Edwards produced

9. Estelle Brody and Marie Ault in *Hindle Wakes* (1927), directed by Maurice Elvey

10. *The Flag Lieutenant* (1926), 1920s super production, directed by Maurice Elvey with Dorothy Seacombe,

1. Sarah Allgood (far end), Charles Paton and Anny Ondra in Alfred Hitchcock's *Blackmail* (1929)

12. *Left to right:* John
    Longden, Anny Ondra
    and Donald Calthrop
    in Hitchcock's *Black-
    mail* (1929)

13. Trio of stars—Gordon
    Harker, Donald
    Calthrop and Conrad
    Veidt in *Rome Express*
    (1932), directed by
    Walter Forde

14. *Right to left:* Jessie
    Matthews visiting
    Conrad Veidt, Walter
    Forde, Cedric Hard-
    wicke and Eliot
    Makeham on the set of
    Rome Express (1932)

15. Charles Laughton in the banqueting scene in *The Private Life of Henry VIII* (1933), directed by Alexander Korda

16. Scene from Alexander Korda's *Rembrandt* (1937)

18. Laurence Olivier and Renée Ascherson in *Henry V* (1944)

19. The Agincourt scene in *Henry V*

20. Filippo del Giudice with some of his 'talents'. *Left to right:* Peter Ustinov, Filippo del Giudice, Laurence Olivier, Jill Craigie

21. Gabriel Pascal, George Bernard Shaw and Vivien Leigh meet to discuss the film version of Shaw's *Caesar and Cleopatra* (1945), produced by Pascal

22. *Fires Were Started* (1945), directed by Humphrey Jennings and produced by Ian Dalrymple for the Crown Film Unit with the co-operation of the Ministry of Home Security and the National Fire Service

23. Jennings' *The Silent Village* (1943), a Crown Film Unit production, made with the co-operation of the Czechoslovak Ministry of Foreign Affairs

24. Two scenes from *Hue and Cry* (1946)

25. *Passport to Pimlico* (1948)

26. *Whisky Galore* (1948). *Left to right* (omitting man with crock): Gordon Jackson, Joan Greenwood, Bruce Seton, Gabrielle Blunt

27. *Passport to Pimlico* (1949). News from the underground: Pimlico is in Burgundy. Barbara Murray and Stanley Holloway

28. Leonid Massine, Moira Shearer and Robert Helpmann in Michael Powell and Emeric Pressburger's *The Red Shoes* (1948)

29. *A Warning to Wantons* (1950), one of the Independent Frame films, produced by Donald Wilson with Anne Vernon, Sonia Holm, Harold Warrender and David Tomlinson

30. *Accident* (1967). Opening shot. Dirk Bogarde carries Jacqueline Sassard from the car after the accident

31. Eric Portman in Bryan Forbes' *Deadfall* (1968)

32. Eric Portman, Michael Caine and Giovanni Ralli in *Deadfall*

33. The wedding breakfast scene in *Ryan's Daughter* (1970). *Left to right:* Arthur O'Sullivan, Leo McKern, Sarah Miles and Robert Mitchum

34. Space and movement in *Ryan's Daughter*. Christopher Jones, the young officer, reconnoitres the Irish village

35. *The Railway Children* (1970). Jenny Agutter, Gary Warren and Sally Thomsett stage an emergency hold-up on the line

36. Jenny Agutter and Peter Bromilow

37. *The Go-Between* (1971). Alan Bates and Julie Christie, the secret lovers, in sentimental village sing-song

38. Julie Christie and Dominic Guard

and, moreover, was considered anti-box office. He needed some such unconventional figure such as Lady Yule to back him and so he made his films for British National on a meagre budget and without star names.

Love on the Dole, however, in which Deborah Kerr appeared (before she had really become a star) proved a genuine success and drew respectful critical attention. And this film, which is closely observed, and burns with the fire of bitter experience, remains even now a moving document. Greenwood's down-and-out characters, unsentimentalised, were a discovery. They anticipated the beats and the junkies of the 1950s, the angry young men looking for their souls between Saturday night and Sunday morning.

More significant, perhaps, than any single film is the increasing status of the director, his experience deepened by the war, his authority extended. Carol Reed, David Lean, Powell and Pressburger, are among those beginning to assert a much fuller control, though we do not see it in full operation until the post-war period.

Carol Reed's *Kipps* (1941) and Anthony Asquith's *Quiet Wedding* (1941) are random shots at an unpredictable mood, respectable entertainments. Asquith also made two other films in 1941, *Cottage To Let*, a spy film with a Scottish background, and *Freedom Radio*, concerned with the underground movement in Nazi Germany. Considering the trend of events in 1940, it is surprising that nothing more forceful was forthcoming. But this is characteristic of the British film industry which stood aside and let significant events pass over it.

Since the disaster of Dunkirk in June the danger from fifth columnists and from enemy propaganda caused great anxiety; our defeat in France was felt to be the certain prelude to invasion. Most menacing of the various forms of enemy propaganda was the series of broadcasts from Berlin by 'Lord Haw-Haw'. Haw-Haw was the name given by a London newspaper columnist to William Joyce, formerly one of Mosley's army of Fascists, and now in the pay of Dr Goebbels. His nickname derived from his absurdly exaggerated upper-class accent. Haw-Haw was a master of

G

the insidious phrase and unnerving rumour, varying his attacks on Churchill with warnings of the hideous fate which lay in store for those who followed him.

Some counterblast was needed to these attacks which were more successful than Whitehall admitted. But as far as the film studios are concerned, the British lion is still amiably wagging his tail and no major effort is seen until *Forty-Ninth Parallel* (1941) directed by Michael Powell. This is one of the first large-scale attempts at fictional propaganda. It was partly financed by the Government and was given top priority and a prestige send-off by Vincent Massey, High Commissioner for Canada, where the film was made. No other project of the war was so boosted. Money, publicity and stars were unstintingly forthcoming—Laurence Olivier, Eric Portman, Leslie Howard, Raymond Massey, Anton Walbrook and Elizabeth Bergner. Of the film's budget of £130,000, £40,000 was supplied by the taxpayer.

On location it soon ran into difficulties. Miss Bergner left the picture after a disagreement over the part she was playing. Efforts to persuade her to return were unsuccessful and she was replaced by Glynis Johns.

The film describes the adventures of six fanatical Nazis, survivors from a U-boat in the Gulf of St Lawrence, and their flight from the Arctic to Niagara Falls in an attempt to reach America. Those who oppose them by word or deed meet death or a savage beating-up. The film develops into an ideological tract, putting the case for the free nations against the dictators.

Sometimes the German in the film seems to be the better man; there is an immense persuasiveness in Eric Portman's performance as a fanatical Nazi putting to flight the apostles of freedom and light represented by Laurence Olivier, Raymond Massey and Leslie Howard. The balance is precarious and the film lacks shape, but these deficiencies did not harm the film, which did well at the box-office. 'An admirable piece of work from every point of view', said the BFI *Monthly Film Bulletin*.[1] Richard Griffith thought Powell's work with Emeric Pressburger 'second-hand Hollywood, plus a dubious social outlook of "the Churchill renaissance".' Powell was 'a very gifted technician . . . unable to make up his mind as to what he wants to say'.[2]

Powell's *One of Our Aircraft is Missing* (1942), a collaboration with Pressburger, was a straightforward story of a British bomber crew who attack Stuttgart and are forced to bail out in Holland. The Dutch Underground help them to get back to England; so the heroic qualities of bomber crews and the Dutch Resistance are equally acknowledged. Viewed simply on the level of entertainment it was an admirably made thriller, 'the best non-documentary film the war has inspired', said the *New Statesman* critic; but the war had not been long in progress.[3]

It is of interest that this film was edited by David Lean and photographed by Ronald Neame, and that its art director was David Rawnsley, creator of the Independent Frame method of production. Its cast included Godfrey Tearle, Eric Portman, Hugh Williams and Bernard Miles. *Pimpernel Smith* (1941), about a professor who helped Jews to escape from Germany, finds a place less on account of its intrinsic merits than its association with Leslie Howard (1893–1943).

Howard had started his career with Adrian Brunel in the 1920s. His real name was Leslie Stainer, and his good looks, intelligence and charm were exactly attuned to the American cinema of the 1930s. Those years brought him a phenomenal success. He starred with Norma Shearer in three Metro films—*A Free Soul, Smilin' Through* and in *Romeo and Juliet*. He was in *Secrets* with Mary Pickford in 1933. Two more films, *Pygmalion* and *Gone With The Wind* took him higher still; in all these he exhibited a gentle charm and characteristic English humour. Perhaps his best piece of portraiture and certainly his best war film was as Mitchell, the inventor of the Spitfire, whose character he created in *The First of the Few* (1942).

In this a more reflective mind was at work, a concern to express a point of view, and this can also be seen in *The Lamp Still Burns* (1943), which Howard produced and Maurice Elvey directed. Dealing with the experiences of a probationary nurse, its more biting candour was censored,

195

but the keen observation remained. It came from Monica Dickens' novel, *One Pair of Feet* and starred Stewart Granger and Rosamund John. This was Leslie Howard's last film. In 1943 he was shot down and killed while flying back to England from Spain.

But the studios could not confine themselves to the quality films of Leslie Howard. At the opposite extreme, conceived wholly in terms of the music hall, were the antics of Lucan and McShane in *Old Mother Riley*. The irascible Arthur Lucan and his pretty Irish partner, Kitty McShane, appeared and reappeared with unflagging vitality right through the war in a series of domestic or preposterously foreign adventures. Arthur Lucan had a spark of true music hall in him and his films were greatly relished by provincial audiences who cared nothing for London tastes, just as London cared nothing for Lancashire and the films of George Formby. Particularly in northern England, people were dismayed to see the variety show fading out as the cinema faded in, introducing a sophisticated type of comedy which they frankly despised.

In Which We Serve (1942), Filippo del Giudice's first big project, was written and produced by Noel Coward who starred in it and wrote the music for it. He shared the direction with David Lean. John Mills, Celia Johnson, Joyce Carey and Kay Walsh had leading parts. Not surprisingly, Coward was attacked by some critics for over-celebrating Noel Coward and under-celebrating the Royal Navy. A look at the film today scarcely justifies this view.

In a series of flashbacks *In Which We Serve* tells the story of H.M.S. *Torrin*, dive-bombed and sunk during the battle of Crete. Her commander and crew, struggling in the water, re-live the past. Each memory is a sequence—the commissioning of the ship, Christmas at sea, the ship torpedoed, the action at Dunkirk and so on. But finally the emphasis is on the ship and the men who serve in her.

In America the film was held up because sailors used the word 'bloody' in it. C. A. Lejeune compared its craftsmanship with John Ford's seafaring picture, *The Long Voyage*

Home. 'A good, nearly a very good film', said William Whitebait, who complained nevertheless, of too much Coward.[4]

Leslie Halliwell describes it as 'the first really important film about the Second World War'. Paul Rotha, unimpressed, classes it with *One of Our Aircraft Is Missing* and *San Demetrio, London*, as among the 'over-praised films . . . which reveal a crude and even amateur approach to the observation of reality'.[5]

Little credit is given to Filippo del Giudice who induced Coward to make *In Which We Serve*, but could raise no interest in Wardour Street for it. Yet the film made £300,000 in England and a great deal more in America and received an Academy Award.

The Foreman Went To France (1942), J. B. Priestley's story about factory workers, made freer use of the documentary method, and was directed by Charles Frend. Some of the best things in the film, made at Ealing, are the scenes on the workshop floor, the air raids in London, the sharp little dramas of the plane spotters. These impressionistic shots and the more ambitious refugee scenes in France are vivid and telling.

The story is of a man sent to France in 1940 to recover a piece of machinery essential to the war effort. Clifford Evans played this part; Tommy Trinder and Gordon Jackson two Tommies of the conventional wise-cracking kind, and Constance Cummings an American secretary.

The Boulting brothers' *Thunder Rock* (1942), adapted from the stage play of Robert Ardrey, foreshadows the more controversial themes they were to discuss or to satirise later. Its story of a man living in a lighthouse as an escape from reality was well chosen for the time and gave stimulating parts to Michael Redgrave and Barbara Mullen.

In 1942 life in Britain was harder and more subject to war strain. The words 'austerity' and 'utility' filled the air and, in particular, the phrase 'browned off' which represented a universal rejection of the human condition. This was the year of Pearl Harbour and of the sinking of two British

197

battleships off Malaya—*The Prince of Wales* and *The Repulse*, with a loss of 600 men. In this year Singapore fell.

Cavalcanti's film *Went The Day Well* (1942) has an ironic ring in this context, but was an attempt to create the mood of Britain invaded, and the manner in which a village and its inhabitants would react. Seen again, the film is rather like a charade and is too lightweight for its serious message.

In 1943 another Powell and Pressburger film, *The Life and Death of Colonel Blimp*, appears and runs into political censorship. Churchill (who attended the first night), disapproved and banned for a time its presentation abroad.

The film is based on the famous Low cartoon of the blustering British colonel, usually to be found in his bath, uttering platitudes on strategy and topics of the day. Blimp is the soul of muddle and incompetence. In the film he is a Home Guard colonel routed in an exercise by a young Army officer, and no doubt this scene and the film's satirical overtones caused offence.

Blimp is first shown as a young officer in the Boer War, Clive Candy V.C., who fights a duel with a Prussian officer following a café brawl. After the duel they become friends, but Candy loses the girl he loves to the Prussian officer. He finds her again (or her physical counterpart) in the 1914 war, and afterwards marries her. Thence we pass to the Second World War in which all Blimp's theories are shown to be fatally outmoded. The old prejudices stick, but a bond unites the two officers which defies time and war.

Powell's skill in projecting a wide canvas over several periods is abundantly shown, but the result is a curious mixture of sentiment and satire and seems an odd choice at such a time when the war was at its darkest. As in *49th Parallel*, the German is much shrewder, tougher, more intelligent than the Englishman. This plausible but perverse judgement opened the film to easy criticism. Ward Price, the war correspondent, attacked it in the *Daily Mail* as 'disastrously bad propaganda in time of war'. The American critic, Howard Barnes, however, found it 'a singularly pertinent and touching film'. Roger Livesey was cast to the life as Colonel Blimp, Anton Walbrook was the Prussian officer, and Deborah Kerr the beautiful chauffeuse whom they both loved.

Gilliat and Launder's *Millions Like Us* (1943), a far less ambitious production, came closer to the norm of documentary fiction. It told a story of women conscripted into war work in the factories. The directors also wrote the script, they had written many of the films for Gaumont-British, and had an uncommon skill in putting a comedy together. *Millions Like Us* abounds in small, telling incidents, and in those emotional states in which the tragic and the comic are inextricably mixed. Patricia Roc, Anne Crawford and Gordon Jackson were given reasonably life-like parts, and though propagandist, the machinery is well camouflaged.

Perhaps some reference should be made here to Frank Capra's 45-minute film of the Invasion, *Battle of Britain* (1943), which holds an important place in the contemporary record. Though directed by an American, it required a close collaboration with British newsreel cameramen. The striking material they had obtained was interwoven with revealing newsreels captured from the Germans. Dunkirk, the air battles over Southern England and the bombing of London are edited in brilliant documentary style.

The Man In Grey (1943), a costume piece directed by Leslie Arliss, is to be noticed chiefly because it is the first sign of a change in taste, audiences being sated by now with documentary realism and seeking relief in some form of escapism. A cloak-and-dagger story of Regency bucks and ravished maidens, it introduced the elements of sadism and sensuality which were to find such fulsome expression a generation later. Several films of the same kind were to follow—*The Wicked Lady* and *Madonna of the Seven Moons* (both 1945), and in the modern style, *Love Story* (1944) and *The Seventh Veil* (1946).

The popularity of *The Man In Grey* and others like it gave a pronounced stimulus to the careers of James Mason and Stewart Granger which ended in their leaving the country for greater rewards in Hollywood, a process constantly eroding or reversing the commercial success of British films. *The Man In Grey* gave good theatrical opportunities to

199

Margaret Lockwood and Phyllis Calvert and was immensely popular. In *The Wicked Lady* (1945) Miss Lockwood's part was felt to be dangerous to morals and demonstrated on what trivial grounds the censor could use his veto. The practical effect was to enhance her box-office popularity.

Perhaps the popularity of this kind of film decided Anthony Asquith to choose Michael Sadleir's novel *Fanny By Gaslight* (1944) as his next film, a Victorian melodrama which could have been made by any competent director. The Cabinet Minister in the centre moves melodramatically from low life in Pimlico to high life in Belgravia, to country mansions, London brothels, and Paris of the 1890s. Involved in scandal, he ends by throwing himself under a train.

This flamboyant piece pleased some of the most critical but not all. C. A. Lejeune questions the value of making the film at all and says: '*Fanny by Gaslight* adds up in the end to a long and fairly substantial chronicle of many worthless people in the Naughty Nineties.'[6] In the upshot, James Mason and Stewart Granger both advanced their reputations.

The Seventh Veil (1946), though strictly it is post-war, may be conveniently considered here as of the period. A psychological melodrama about a young girl pianist, portrayed with great intelligence by Ann Todd, it was the work of a new producer of many talents, Sydney Box, who made documentaries during the war. He is one of a film-making family which includes his former wife, Muriel, and his sister, Betty. Muriel and Betty directed films and Sydney produced. A journalist who turned to films, Sydney Box's ambition was always to write, but his fate was to produce. He had all the qualities of the impresario.

In the 1940s he was for a time production chief at Gaumont-British studios. There and at Islington he made many popular films. But he had other ambitions and one of his merits as a creative film-maker lay in the encouragement he gave to the short story in films and the care he took in making them.

Herbert Wilcox is unfailingly active during the war years, producing two films in America, *No, No, Nanette* and *Irene* (both in 1940), then returning to England to make *They*

Flew Alone (based on the Amy Johnson–Jim Mollison story (1942) and *Yellow Canary* (1943). His fondness for stories of fashion and sophistication is seen in the production of four 'society' films between 1943 and 1947—*I Live in Grosvenor Square, Piccadilly Incident, The Courtneys of Curzon Street* and *Spring in Park Lane*. In these films of lords and butlers and white ties (pre-war period pieces) he starred a newcomer, Michael Wilding, with Anna Neagle, then a good deal more celebrated than he was. With *Odette* (1951) and *Lady With a Lamp* (1952) Wilcox showed a more serious interest, but these films, though popular and conscientiously made, lacked some of the sacred fire and heroic scale.

Chapter 21

War Films: The Final Phase, 1943–1945

The tide of change in popular taste which began to flow in 1943 reached its height in the following year with Laurence Olivier's *Henry V*. In that year *The Way Ahead* and *The Way to the Stars* were also produced, but themes of war are clearly losing favour. To a nation nerving itself to the effort of invasion *Henry V* had an obvious relevance. Its interest for critics, however, lay in what Olivier would make of it and how he would overcome the problems of adaptation that had not been solved by others. He made no special claim for his own version and was criticised for too wordy a script; for his treatment of the Globe Theatre sequences; for too literary an approach, and so on. But as a whole he received more praise than blame.

Roger Manvell considered that *Henry V* 'achieved a certain cinematic quality in the prose scenes where Shakespeare's speech is at its most intimate, idiomatic and realistic, such as Mistress Quickly's story of the death of Falstaff and Henry's scene with the soldiers the night before Agincourt. Agincourt itself is excellent cinema'.[1]

It is the text that comes in for the roughest treatment as the most intractable of all the problems. James Agee said of Olivier's *Henry*: 'No attempt is made to develop a movie style which might in poetic energy and originality work as a cinematic counterpart to the verse.' He castigates the Globe Theatre sequences for their 'subtly patronising' manner, and the comic characters as not being 'honestly and generally amusing'. What he praises unreservedly is the Shakespearean line. 'The one great glory of the film is the language. The

202

greatest credit I can assign to those who made the film is that they loved and served the language so well.'²

Henry V, then, is an actor's film and an instance of the word taking precedence over the image. It reminds us that great differences of opinion exist on the subject of filmed Shakespeare, as for example that he writes ideal scripts, hence should be ideal film material, that he must be taken literally or irreverently or not at all. Orson Welles is uncertain in his view but feels that if Shakespeare is to be filmed, it should be done boldly and freely. Olivier's *Henry V* will no doubt rank among those films which do Shakespeare most honour and, judged by critical opinion at the time, it is superior to anything Shakespearean from Hollywood.

Carol Reed's *The Way Ahead* (1944) is an account of the making of a new army of British foot-sloggers from the raw material of clerks, shopwalkers and factory hands. It was originally made as a War Office instructional film under the title *The New Lot*, but was later developed into a full-length commercial feature at the suggestion of Filippo del Giudice. Reed's film penetrates the mind of the civilian unnaturally pressed into service and gives a true account of that painful process. Its truth remains valid nearly thirty years later.

Generally speaking, *The Way Ahead* had the kind of critical reception that goes with a major work by a favoured director. The British Film Institute Bulletin described it as 'an outstanding piece of film making', and most critics were impressed. Richard Griffith placed it in the highest class.

Our own feeling, after seeing it again is that the documentary method does not really suit a director like Reed; it imposes severe limitations of treatment and imagination and these limitations are finally the film's faults. David Niven, Raymond Huntley, William Hartnell and others were given fully-rounded characters, but they were in the end figures in a military exercise.

A semi-documentary which again was an attempt to explore the minds of men was Anthony Asquith's *The Way to the Stars* (1945). A story of British and American airmen brought together on the airfield during the Battle of Britain

203

and the strains and conflicts it produced was ideal material. The war was in its last phase; we could stand back and survey some of our achievements. Asquith and Rattigan were well-matched collaborators, and this is seen in the result, one of the best films Asquith made.

Richard Winnington, observing that we are 'better at this sort of thing than Hollywood and Russia combined', concludes with the words: 'A moving film, this, in its own flat and rather formless level of solid goodness, a film which somehow catches the rhythm of war and the baffled courage of men.'[3]

Signs of a new direction in taste are seen again in Noel Coward's three productions, *This Happy Breed* (1944), *Brief Encounter* (1945), and *Blithe Spirit* (1945). *This Happy Breed*, with Robert Newton and Celia Johnson in the principal roles, was David Lean's first independent job as a director, though his collaboration with Coward on the treatment must have been close. The play on which it was based was a narrative of suburban life between the wars, 1918–39, and records the matter-of-fact but occasionally dramatic lives of a working-class family against a background of the Wembley Exhibition, the General Strike, the Charleston, George V's funeral, and the Munich crisis. It is the *Cavalcade* formula repeated. 'In point of photography, direction and acting', says Winnington, 'few recent films from America—and I mean recent in terms of years—have approached it.'[4] Indeed, the critical response is almost wholly favourable. *The Times* critic considered it 'a brilliant piece of reporting—something observed and treasured from within'. C. A. Lejeune makes the point that 'Coward films are the nearest thing we have to a valid modern school in British cinema'.

Brief Encounter (1945), considered a failure though a worthy one by Lindsay Anderson,[5] nevertheless received as much praise as any British production during the war, and opinion was no less favourable when the film was televised a generation later. The realistic mood is invoked to describe an unhappy love affair between a young suburban housewife and a married doctor. The furtive meetings of the lovers, the dreary railway buffet where they meet, the days of boredom and loss in between—these were transmuted into a tragedy uncharacteristic of Coward, but wholly traditional: the tragedy of Puritanism and passion found in so much English writing. The film was fortunate in the partnership of Celia Johnson and Trevor Howard as the lovers and was an enormous success.

Blithe Spirit too (1945) was a decided triumph both for Coward and for David Lean, who translated a piece of purest theatre into acceptable cinema terms and varnished the whole thing in ravishing colours.

Powell and Pressburger were also casting about for some unwarlike theme and finally found inspiration in Chaucer. *A Canterbury Tale* (1944) was happier in thought than execution for it turned out to be 'an elaborate and often witty piece of muddle'.[6] Its merits of old Englishness, reflected in the fine Erwin Hillier photography, the march of the pilgrims, the Cathedral, the spiritual struggle of ordinary men, were obscured by mystification and sadism.

One can see the point of the American critic who accused Powell of not being able to make up his mind. The film, charged though it is with poetry and piety, tells of salvation. But it is incongruously linked with a story of detectives seeking a character known as the Glue Man. He pours glue on the hair of girls in the black-out, a streak of perversity found in other Powell films—*Colonel Blimp*, for example, and, a good many years later, in *Peeping Tom*.

'I carried away from *A Canterbury Tale* an enjoyment that I was loath to examine too closely', said one critic. Winnington found it confused and vaguely unpleasant. In short, its virtues of Englishness are diminished by its poor story content. No man could be plainer than Chaucer; it is odd that he should have inspired such 'a witty piece of muddle'.

Basil Dearden's less ambitious film *Halfway House* (1944), dealing with the problems of conscience and the tricks of time, was at least clear in its story and contained some admirable melodrama. Dearden does not mystify or sermonise, but he usually entertains.

205

J. B. Priestley's *They Came to a City* (1944), a kind of morality, had little more than good intentions to recommend it.

Tawny Pipit (1944), a Bernard Miles film, one of those oddities every country throws up from time to time, showed British tanks on army manoeuvres being re-routed to avoid crushing a bird's nest. It was immensely English, and if too much of an anecdote for full-length treatment, at least it gave an independent film-maker the chance to make a film of his choice. For this, Filippo del Giudice who sponsored it, must be given the credit.

A few other good things followed. Powell and Pressburger again appear with *I Know Where I'm Going* (1945) a charming Scottish parable of the simple life in which Wendy Hiller and Roger Livesy starred. Anthony Asquith directed the submarine thriller, *We Dive at Dawn* (1943). These were decidedly above the average of films being made at the time. Half the nation, or 25 to 30 million people a week were going to the pictures and almost anything would do. Most film directors rose above that level.

We must not fail to note the work of Sidney Gilliat and Frank Launder with such films as *I See A Dark Stranger* and *Waterloo Road*, both 1945. In the second of these the camera went out into the streets to get its effects and the film is most to be noted for that reason. The post-war cinema was to develop the technique into a movement of much wider significance.

Part V

End of The Great Days

Chapter 22

War-time Changes and the Monopoly Report

The war closed down cinemas for a time; it was impossible for the authorities to know when the bombing of cities would begin or what damage might come of it. Official bodies took no chances and put the danger at its worst. Some cinemas, like the Tivoli in the Strand (now a department store), were set aside for the storage of coffins in the expectation of enormous casualties. However, after a few days both cinemas and theatres were allowed to give performances on condition that they closed at six o'clock in the evening.

A shortage of films was immediately felt, and it was feared that the Government would black out studios altogether, leaving the supply entirely to the Americans. The prospect brought protests from the exhibitors. They recalled that the 1914 war had more or less put a stop to British film production and caused a set-back from which it never recovered. If studios were closed and the Quota Act suspended, which some seemed to think likely, it would make a bad situation infinitely worse.

Sidney Bernstein of the Granada circuit, appealed to the Government to keep the studios at work. 'The public has always wanted good British films', he said, 'not the million-pound "epics" which so often bore them, but the good honest unpretentious stories in which we have shown such promise . . . the records of everyday English life.'

In practice, film production met with great difficulties. The major studios were requisitioned by the Government—Denham, Pinewood, Elstree, Islington, Shepherd's Bush and

209

Sound City (Shepperton). Pinewood was mainly set aside for the use of the Crown Film Unit and more than half the available studio space was put out of commission. Shortage of manpower and construction materials made things even more frustrating. Clothes rationing decimated the wardrobe departments and dressmakers and their assistants vanished into factories.

The year 1939 had found film production in bad shape. It had not yet recovered from the crisis of 1937 which had so shaken the City. Production was tailing off and was represented by Korda's *The Four Feathers*, Victor Saville's *Goodbye, Mr Chips*, and Charles Laughton's and Erich Pommer's *Jamaica Inn*. Hollywood was in its usual good form with *Wuthering Heights*, *The Wizard of Oz*, and *Confessions of a Nazi Spy*, and was about to produce a whole series of anti-Nazi films.

France, depressed ever since the coming of sound, was in the doldrums, but produced Marcel Carné's *Le Jour se Lève*, and Renoir's *La Marseillaise*. In the heavily charged air of 1939 films suddenly ceased to be of importance.

Nevertheless, 103 films were produced in Britain that year and 108 in 1940. After that the yearly average stayed at about 60 until the end of the war, accounting for less than half our studio capacity.

In 1941 the deaths occurred of John Maxwell and of Oscar Deutsch. This left the way clear for Rank to extend his empire still further. He gained control of Gaumont-British for which Maxwell had made his unsuccessful bid, and this time there was no opposition from 20th Century-Fox. In a series of complicated moves he also gained possession of the Odeon circuit. The fruit of all these acquisitions was 'a film combine of enormous power' which by 1944 owned 619 cinemas and more than half the studios in Britain.

Warner Bros. also joined in this reshuffle from the opposite camp and bought a 25 per cent interest in the Associated British Corporation for just under a million pounds (£903,150). It put them in a position to influence Elstree production, but this was always firmly denied.

In 1943 C. M. Woolf died. Woolf was a key figure in production at Gaumont-British. He and Maxwell had been responsible for a great many films, and between them it is hardly too much to say that they had created a production industry. But they had not been able to stave off repeated crises and studio closures and notwithstanding their pride in the 100 per cent British film it is doubtful whether they projected an image abroad which did justice to Britain's artistic resources or could compare in energy and imagination with that of Hollywood. They were financiers and salesmen and they built good foundations.

After 1941 it was difficult to make films at all because of the air raids. When an alert sounded and the skies looked dangerous work had to stop, though it often continued in defiance of orders and there were casualties. Bombs were dropped on many studios. At Teddington, where Warner Bros. were making *Flight from Folly*, the studio manager, Doc Saloman and two of his assistants were killed. On a single day filming was interrupted by twenty-two air raid alerts.

The war, it might be supposed, was an opportunity for the independent film producer to step in and increase production. That had been the object of the Quota Act. But the big groups dedicated their remaining studio space to a few costly productions which took months to complete instead of calling on the independents for a larger output of good, medium-priced pictures. The expensive ones were planned on the off-chance that they would succeed in the American market which, in fact, they did not. There was a further reason for these extravagant ventures. They saved the producers Excess Profits Tax. The independent exhibitor, meanwhile, for want of the true-blue British article, could not meet his $12\frac{1}{2}$ per cent quota and he was frequently taken to court for it.

The big cinema circuits, on the other hand, did well. Gaumont-British, Odeon and Associated British between them owned 1,101 cinemas out of some four or five thousand, representing 20 per cent of the paying public. Production and distribution being dominated by these groups, who

211

dictated not only what films should be made but also what should be seen, it is not surprising that the cry of monopoly that had been raised in the earliest days of cinema was raised again and led to the setting up of a government inquiry in 1943. In this anti-monopoly campaign Michael Balcon, who was a member of the Films Council, played a leading part.

In 1944, while Britain was still engaged in a titanic struggle for survival, the report of the inquiry was published and made a resounding tinkle amid the universal gunfire. 'No action (on the report) was taken for many years', said Lord Grantley, 'nor were its recommendations ever carried out in their entirety.'

This report—*Tendencies to Monopoly in the Cinematograph Film Industry*—was the work of a committee appointed by the Films Council at the request of the Board of Trade. It is a classic among film documents and gives an admirably lucid account of how the industry works. It exposes a number of abuses and malpractices, it examines with an impartial eye the trade's methods of business, and it makes abundantly clear why the British film producer has no real independence.

The committee that produced this report had as its chairman Albert Palache, with Sir Walter Citrine, Professor Arnold Plant and Philip Guedalla (who retired later because of illness) as members. (The report is usually referred to as the Palache report.)

It views monopoly as 'a threat to the future prospects of an independent and unfettered British film industry'. 'By "independent"', the report declares, 'we have in mind both freedom from foreign domination and freedom from dominating British control' (i.e. Rank and Associated British). ' "Unfettered" means reasonable access both to means of production of film and to screen time.' To which is added freedom from restrictive practices by exhibitors or others.

The essence of this report is contained in this paragraph.

'A healthy British film industry', it states, 'can only be built up from the remnants existing at present on condition

212

that independent production remains in being and is properly safeguarded'.[1] Criticism was directed mainly at the following points:

1. The concentration of power in the combines.[2]
2. Unfair allocation of studio space.
3. Danger of American domination.
4. Uncertain finance.
5. Inordinate charges by distributors, leaving little or nothing to the producers.
6. Survival of British production, it declares, is dependent on two persons, the head of Gaumont-British-Odeon and the head of Associated British Pictures. Moreover, these two persons 'are or may ultimately be guided by American interests'.
7. The number of cinemas controlled by the big circuits should be limited by law.
8. The London release, which determines the success or failure of a film . . . is tantamount in an important degree to monopoly power.

The conclusion of the Palache Committee was that monopoly had been proved and that independent production had definitely suffered from it. The whole industry shared the guilt for 'undesirable practices in restraint of trade'— producers, distributors and exhibitors. Finally the Committee brought into the open 'the preponderating influence of American interests in this country (which) has been further accentuated both in distribution and exhibition'.

Recommendations are made to meet all or most of the charges, especially those relating to independent production. A larger number of medium-priced pictures should be produced and protection should be given to the documentary and the small feature—the first occasion on which an authoritative voice had spoken up for these sections of the industry.

Most valued of all the recommendations was that the independent film-maker should be guaranteed time on the screen and space in the studio. Exhibitors must be able to book films in a free market and block booking should be stopped. A tribunal would pronounce on studio space and film finance. A film finance corporation should be established. Failing other safeguards, the Board of Trade should introduce legislation to prevent domination of the British film industry by the United States. The Government was urged to discuss with America steps 'to increase the exhibition of British films in the United States'.

These entirely admirable proposals were chiefly of value in opening up the film industry to public scrutiny and exposing its various shades of iniquity and incompetence. They led to a number of minor reforms but not to that radical overhaul which had been overdue for so long.

What is significant in studying this report, and confirmed by the reading of other reports is the frequency with which the phrase is repeated—'Legislation should be introduced'— and the Board of Trade invited to take certain courses of action. Britain is once again making films by Act of Parliament.

Chapter 23

The Post-War Film Industry

Politically, the most significant event of the war had been the publication of the Palache report on Monopoly.[1] As we noticed, no action was taken at the time, yet from that moment the whole thinking of the film industry underwent a change.

The moral effect of the report was considerable. Little was known among ordinary people of the workings of the industry, and the abuses laid open came as a shock, especially when set down in the disapproving prose of the Civil Service. Wardour Street never imagined that the full glare of publicity would be turned on its own errors, still less that it would suffer a public rebuke from the Board of Trade. And it is interesting to note the recommendation that some kind of trustee arrangement should be made 'in order to allay the continuing apprehension in the country that the physical control of these combines may at some time be transferred to the United States', an idea which, the writers point out, would be 'absolutely repugnant to those at present exercising control'.[2]

Though the main recommendations of the report were pigeon-holed. the circuits had to give an undertaking not to acquire more cinemas, and more screen time was promised to the independent producer. Had this report appeared in 1941 it is unlikely that Warner Bros. would have been allowed to acquire a large share in the Associated British Picture Corporation in that year, for the report ruled specifically against any action which might compromise the corporation's independence. It was twenty-one years before a further inquiry was to appear in the Monopolies Commission's report, thus allowing a decent interval for further procrastination.

In 1946 Alexander Korda bought Shepperton Studios from the British Lion Film Corporation, a move that was to have important consequences.

In that year too, the first Royal Film Performance took place, with Michael Powell's *A Matter of Life and Death*. In 1947 the British Film Academy was formed to encourage the art of the film. Its director was Roger Manvell, critic and biographer, author of numerous works on the British, European and American cinema.

The British Film Academy came at a time when our feature films stood well in the estimation of the world and our educational and documentary films only added to that reputation. These high opinions favoured the creation of some kind of cultural body which would give formal recognition to the place of British cinema in the arts. Korda and Balcon took a leading part in this scheme which was in fact the idea of the film-makers themselves, David Lean being the Academy's first chairman with Carol Reed, Thorold Dickinson and Paul Rotha on the council. One of its most valued functions was to sponsor a series of annual awards as a counterblast to the Oscar ceremonies in America and so draw attention to the best cinema in Britain.

On the industrial front the post-war years are plagued with troubles; the independent producer, though he has gained in authority, is still in doubt about his future, and spends more time raising money than making films. In its financing methods the industry is as unbending as ever, affairs are always moving towards a crisis.

Before the war, Britain had been paying America an average of £7 million ($28 million) a year in film hire and there were no restrictions on the amount American distributors could send home.

But the need to safeguard our balance of payments when war broke out had forced the Government to impose restrictions, and in 1940 remittances to the United States were reduced to £4·8 million and in 1941 to £5·7 million.

In 1947 Britain is again in deep water and the Chancellor,

Hugh Dalton, introduced a Customs or *ad valorem* duty of 75 per cent on imported films.[3] The American industry, angered at what they considered a punitive tax, said they would stop all exports of films to Britain. They did not do so. Their leaders could not, or would not, see that for Britain the duty was an economic necessity, and they imputed all kinds of base motives to the Chancellor for his action. It was a tax to protect British film production, it was a reprisal for America's refusal to show British films, and so on.

The press made much of it and the trade itself predicted grave shortages and a further fall in attendances. But there were plenty of American films in stock, many, of course, reissues and the public was not seriously affected. Indeed, at the time of the Dalton duty, Britain was paying America $50 million a year for them.

In the following year (1948), an Anglo-American film agreement was signed, repealing the duty and allowing American companies to remit $17 million (about £3 million) annually of their British earnings.

It might have been supposed that these restrictions on U.S. imports provided an opportunity for Britain to cash in on the film shortage and speed up her film production. It was, but the opportunity was lost. Private capital to assist the industry could not be found and the Rank Organisation's production programme in 1948 brought a loss variously estimated at six to seven million pounds.[4] Korda also suffered heavy losses and these also could be counted in millions.

Mr Rank, while admitting failure, told his shareholders that the industry had not been consulted about the Anglo-American film agreement, so that a large number of held-up American films collided when released with his own, some of which were 'not of a quality to ensure even reasonable returns'. Some wrong decisions had been taken, plans were too ambitious (*London Town, Caesar and Cleopatra*) and too great a burden had been placed on the creative talents.

A solution had to be found to these recurring difficulties or a complete breakdown in film production seemed likely.

It was becoming increasingly clear that the Treasury was the only purse which could be opened to keep production flowing, and this argument was reinforced by the reports of no less than three committees.

The first was that of the Film Studio Committee (1948), the second that of the Working Party on Film Production Costs (1949), presided over by Sir George Gater. The third was the committee under Sir Arnold Plant (1949) which inquired into distribution and exhibition.

The first report set out to examine the possibilities of a studio 'owned and/or managed by the State', but discovered reasons for its outright rejection. Investigation showed that there was plenty of studio space, some of it not occupied.

Nevertheless, the committee finally sat on the fence and concluded that it would be better to 'delay action until the Film Finance Corporation has been at work for some time and the effect of its work upon the output of films can be estimated'.

As for the views that were canvassed in other sections of the industry, the British Film Producers' Association wanted a group of film-makers to get together in a co-operative effort. The independent producers demanded their rightful studio space and a fair deal in 'all the functions which go to make a film industry'.[5] The technicians, members of the left-wing ACTT put their faith in a State studio, an idea they had canvassed since 1941.[6]

The Gater report on production was to examine how costs could be reduced. The film economy was in bad shape, it declared, because too small a proportion of the box office receipts and of the Entertainments Duty went into production, and this is 'no new problem'. 'At no time since the substitution of sound for silent films', we are told, 'has the British film industry been on a satisfactory financial basis. Indeed it may truthfully be said that it is only in the last two years that (it) has become substantially organised.'[7]

Extravagance in production is again rebuked, so too are the high salaries of stars, totally inadequate planning, the excessive location costs, the demarcation hold-ups 'while the appropriate man is fetched to knock in a nail or change the

218

position of a potted plant'. Lack of confidence between management and workers is perhaps the most serious problem, for it affects the cost of every department of film-making. The managements lack the modern conciliatory outlook, and the workers think only of the past. As to cost, between 1946 and 1948 a feature film varied in scale from £100,000 or less to £350,000 or more. Control of wages as of salaries of stars was 'extremely difficult' and accounts for the generally uneconomic state of film production.

The report puts forward recommendations for speeding up production ('the vital factor'), and reducing costs. But the doubt still remains whether, under prevailing conditions, long-term planning is possible. The unions dissented from this view. Years of strife had made them traditionally hostile.

'Add to these motives', says *A Competitive Cinema*, 'strong Communist and extreme left-wing socialist influence in the upper echelons of the ACTT and it is not surprising that labour relations have long been acrimonious. . . . Both sides appear to agree that there is a head-on clash between management and labour, particularly at shop steward level'.[8]

The Plant report on distribution and exhibition covered ground already dealt with in the Monopoly report. Observing the rigid structure and unalterable habits of the industry, it demanded greater competition in the selling and distribution of films, so that the filmgoer got better value at the box office and the producer was left with a reasonable profit. The renter could look after himself—indeed he had usually done so at the expense of the industry.

'Our underlying aim', said the report, 'is that . . . the cinemas which have the greatest box-office potentiality shall be entitled to bid for the first release showing of any film . . . and that the distributor shall be under an obligation to accept the highest bid for each competitive district.' Thus, the best films would be immediately available to all and the box-office could not fail to benefit.[9]

The PEP report observed of this plan that 'the theory seems to be sounder than the practice', and that 'it is very difficult for legislative action to overcome powerful economic forces', that is to say, 'the power of the main circuits'.[10]

219

The Films Council was more or less of the same opinion. The decisive element in all these debates was that British films were bankrupt . . . 'apart from the Rank Group', says PEP, quoting Mr Wilson in Hansard, 'pretty well the whole of the rest of the industry is now facing a stoppage unless financial provision is made available'.

These were the conditions that led to the creation under Board of Trade sponsorship of the National Film Finance Corporation in October 1948, with power to grant loans to independent producers. The Corporation was given a provisional life of five years, by which time it was hoped that the production industry would be sufficiently strengthened to stand on its own feet. The Government contributed £5 million to the enterprise, for which a special Bill was enacted.

The circumstances surrounding the loans made by the Government to British producers at that time are not always easy to understand and offer some strange insights into film finance.

How did it come about that in the crisis of 1948, when Harold Wilson was President of the Board of Trade, a loan of £1 million (later increased to £3 million) was made to Alexander Korda and to no one else?

Filippo del Giudice, as producer of *In Which We Serve, Hamlet, Henry V,* and *Odd Man Out,* was perhaps as deserving of recognition, yet his claims were ignored, as were those of many less important producers.

The explanation seems to lie in Korda's political one-upmanship when the whole British production industry was speeding towards disaster. Korda invited Harold Wilson to a dinner party attended by all the leading directors and producers in the country and was as persuasive as usual.

The Korda charisma and the presence of so awe-inspiring an array of talent evidently triumphed, for it was not long before he received Treasury sanction for his million pounds.

On the proceeds of the loan and the £2 million which followed, Korda went on to produce a number of films and, notwithstanding their losses, left a large fortune. Del

Giudice, abandoned by the Government, declined in influence and was soon forgotten.

In 1950, the NFFC was again short of money and was forced to borrow a further £1 million. From these resources it helped to finance some important pictures, among them *The Magic Box, Morning Departure, Maytime in Mayfair.* By March 1951 it had spent £5,539,404 on 101 films. If it did not simplify the system of lending money, which was excessively cumbersome, it was always a certain source of finance, but for the independent producer it could still mean the raising of one or several thousand pounds of his own money. For an art to be confronted with so much business is a daunting prospect.

The corporation meanwhile put forward three schemes. It sponsored a new company called British Film Makers (1951) with a programme of films to be made at Pinewood by directors of repute. Some familiar names are connected with this enterprise—Roy Boulting, Betty Box, Thorold Dickinson, Ronald Neame, George Brown. It made a similar arrangement with Associated British for a number of films under the supervision of Robert Clark, chief executive at Elstree. Only two films came of this arrangement: *So Little Time* and *Angels One Five.*

But perhaps the most interesting of these projects was Group 3, which was designed to train new men and to encourage the small budget film and documentary, a recommendation which had appeared in the Palache report. The difficulty of making a film cheaply is a recurrent theme in British film production, as we have just seen. Group 3, formed under John Grierson and John Baxter at the small Southall studios, was a move in this direction, and turned out three films of which *Brandy for the Parson* was the most promising.

Yet none of these schemes survived for long, and both the known and the unknown names associated with them are soon engaged elsewhere.

In supporting the off-beat or non-box-office subject from time to time, the NFFC was taking an even greater risk than

221

Rank or ABC, who recognised no obligation to put money into anything of doubtful box-office value. The corporation, under the terms of its charter was not only expected to encourage new ideas, but urged to make a profit on them, or at least to avoid a loss. It had 'a statutory duty to endeavour to pay its way.' With its huge repayments on the British Lion loan, its advances at the end of the year looked too often like retreats. The £3 million loan was to cripple the efforts of the corporation for many years.

As part of the policy of retrenchment and reform the Rank Organisation carried out an interesting experiment, the Independent Frame method already referred to. This was a method of studio automation devised at Pinewood by David Rawnsley, an art director with the Rank Organisation. In 1946 strenuous efforts were being made to reduce costs. Rawnsley was convinced that this could be done by intensive pre-planning joined with the processes of automation. He saw that mechanical handling of equipment, new applications of photography, the building of sets away from the production area and other time-and-labour-saving devices could cut costs down radically.

Six films were made by this method by Donald Wilson, in later years to produce the BBC's *Forsyte Saga* on television. But then the scheme, for a number of reasons, was dropped. The unions were opposed to it, so were a number of directors. Yet all these films were brought in on a low budget and undoubtedly proved the effectiveness of the method. Many of Rawnsley's ideas were incorporated into television techniques a few years later. They were too advanced for the films of the late 1940s.

A consequence of the production losses at Denham and Pinewood (many Pinewood directors going over to Korda), was that only fifty-five feature films were made in 1947–8. Many studios were closed down. Shepherd's Bush was sold to the BBC. Islington, Highbury and Twickenham all went dark. That any production, at least of a major kind, continued, was either because a producer was already too

222

deeply committed to quit or because somewhere the light of faith still burned.

The film trade, sunk in gloom, knew that drastic measures were needed if film production was to survive, and it welcomed intervention by the Government, for it was powerless to act itself. How far government film-making could be called a success we shall see later.

Both France and Italy had some form of subsidy, France a tax on admissions and on the films themselves; Italy a subsidy based on a film's gross takings. The Government did some thinking on parallel lines, and in 1950 evolved the Eady Plan (named after Sir Wilfred Eady of the Treasury) or British Production Fund. The plan made reductions in entertainments tax and allowed increases in prices.

These concessions had to be paid for by a farthing drawn from the exhibitor on every seat he sold. (There were exceptions for the smallest cinemas.) The millions of farthings produced substantial finance and an ingenious new method of subsidising films was introduced.

Though the first year's working of the Eady Plan proved its usefulness, there were many problems, and negotiations continued between the industry and Hugh Gaitskell, the Chancellor. The producers, as usual, were not getting back their costs, the exhibitors too faced losses and efforts were made to expand the British Production Fund. Mr Gaitskell's Budget proposals in 1950, which again increased entertainments tax by a complicated system of grading and knocked a halfpenny off the admission price, were brusquely rejected by the trade.

Instead, the Eady Plan was expanded, a further series of price adjustments was introduced through the nimble farthing which increased prices and was expected to raise £12½ million a year. Half went to the Treasury, £2·3 million to producers and £3·7 million to the exhibitors. An annual grant was made to the Children's Film Foundation.

The 1952 PEP report comments on these developments: 'There can be no doubt that however indirect it may be, the present Fund is a form of subvention, but it is not permanent. Nevertheless it does offer producers a security which they

223

lacked previously, for whereas the original Eady Plan remained in force for one year, the present scheme is to continue until August 1954 (that is, for three years).'

The PEP report adds that although the circumstances are favourable, 'both the experience of the past and evidence of the present . . . point to the error of a forecast which believes that production will remain on a paying basis after that date (1954) without further assistance from the Government'.

This warning proved all too justified. Perhaps worth noting, too, is that in these many deliberations the voices of writers, artists, and the makers of films are seldom heard.

By now attendances at cinemas were slipping. In 1952 the Fund was already more than half a million pounds short of its target. Again unforeseen events compelled the NFFC to borrow a further £3 million to meet the case.

In that year the Crown Film Unit was brought to an end amid much protest and lament. The only favourable news we hear for producers is that David Lean's *Sound Barrier* has received an Academy Award.

In 1951 the British Board of Film Censors introduced the X certificate. Since the war films had been less inhibited and more outspoken, there was not only a greater sophistication, but a greater freedom in the discussion of controversial issues, whether of sex, race, religion or politics. All the mass media reflected this change. The X certificate was the response to it and was designed to cover films that were wholly adult in theme or treatment' or 'suitable for adults only'.

'The films placed in this category', said the BBFC 'may be either those whose subjects would normally qualify for an A certificate, but whose treatment is so frank, realistic, or sordid, as to place them in the X class, or those whose subject matter is unquestionably adult'. Children under 16 years of age were forbidden to see an X film whether an adult went with them or not. *A Streetcar named Desire*, *Death of a Salesman*, *Rashomon*, *Les Jeux Interdits*, and *La Ronde* were among the films put into the X category. In the early 1950s work of this order was reaching the screen for the first time.

During the post-war years films had been badly hit. Yet they were gaining in intelligence and artistry and reflected with deeper insight the life and spirit of the age. Television was to overshadow all these considerations and stir up a revolution of greater depth and consequence than the industry had yet known. The new medium reversed the trend of forty years and deprived films at a stroke of their sovereignty.

Chapter 24

TV Changes the Pattern

The havoc television could bring to the cinema was not seriously felt until the middle of the 1950s when the BBC and the commercial networks between them were seizing great tracts of the nation's leisure and taking the lead in mass entertainment. Television had been a BBC service since 1939 when it was sufficiently advanced to give demonstrations on a wide screen. Post-war developments had been rapid but they were not considered a real threat to films. Films were indestructible and rooted in the habits of two generations. But now the balance of power was shaken, old loyalties crumbled and traditions held sacred were overturned. Showmen could not believe that the great days of the commercial cinema were over, and that an ugly little contraption on a roof-top was to signal their fortunes away. Indeed, for many it had the reverse effect and brought them fortunes over again.

One of the attractions of the film for the majority had been that it took them out of their homes into the splendours of the picture palace. The little black box reversed this process and took them back again, usually into homes which were by then a good deal pleasanter to live in. Television, once it took root, surprised its audience into a submission as total as that produced by the cinema in its first days. If in one sense this was an invasion of the cinema, it was also a liberation, for television widened the horizon to areas the film had not explored and for which it was not adapted.

Long before the mid-fifties there were signs of disintegration in the fixed patterns of film-going. Audiences were shrinking all over the world. Television, though accepted as the main cause, was not the sole cause. The mind of Britain was changing. It was moving into the waterless deserts of technology and computerism; paperbacks brought knowledge and sophistication, new attitudes to work and leisure; a whole range of interests and habits were in dissolution, and among those habits which no longer took priority was the habit of going to the pictures.

During the five years between 1946 and 1951 cinema attendances fell by 5 million and this was merely the flickering of the red light warning of even greater disaster.[1] John Spraos points to 1955 as the year of 'dramatic expansion of television among the working class', and the fact that this class, a majority of all filmgoers, had formed the wealth and strength of the cinema in it palmiest days made its defection to television all the more damaging.

The provision of two television services instead of one did not, Spraos finds, make much difference. The principal causes of the decline were threefold: first, the convenience of having an entertainment in one's own home; second, the diversion of part of the weekly income from films to television, and third, the fact that the price of television is practically nothing compared with the price of a seat at the cinema. Wages were increasing; but they were being spent on refrigerators, on holidays and, to a lesser extent, on cars. Something had to go. It was the cinema.

There was, moreover, a great shortage of films, both British and American, and, most crippling of all was the successive closing down of cinemas since 1950, not in tens but in hundreds. The shortage of films diminished interest in films as a whole. This, and the closures, together proved fatal. Each closure of a cinema could mean the loss for good of the audience it created and every absentee filmgoer spread defection to others. The drift away from films, it was argued, may have been the cause of the closures, or the closures may have been the cause of the drift. However explained, the problem was the same for the industry: how to arrest the landslide. Between 1950 and 1960 nearly 1,500 cinemas vanished into thin air, a good third of the total, and no end could be seen to the process.

The Americans, facing similar losses, applied their wits to counter measures. They introduced a number of technical innovations in sight and sound. One of these was 3–D or three-dimensional films. This had to be viewed through polarised spectacles and produced a stereoscopic image of greater clarity and depth than the normal film. The idea won a certain popularity but soon faded out.

The principal weapon of attack was the panoramic screen pioneered by 20th Century-Fox as Cinemascope, with its concomitant aid, stereophonic sound. It introduced a screen about two-and-a-half times the conventional size with an aspect ratio of 2·55 : 1, and as a rescue bid it made more sense for it fostered a belief in a new kind of magic beyond the reach of the television camera. It had in fact been discussed twenty years earlier in Hollywood, but rejected on the ground of expense.[2]

Cinemascope was based on an optical device invented many years earlier by Henri Chretien and employed an anamorphic lens which contracted the image when photographed and expanded it when projected. Cinemascope accorded with the American concept that what was bigger must be better, and judged by the success of the first production, *The Robe*, shown in London in 1953, the Americans were right. Cinemascope did undoubtedly stave off further disaster. It had, of course, no aesthetic pretensions. On the contrary, it denied them, for it laid upon the director the necessity of conceiving his film exclusively in terms of size rather than content, and it produced numerous difficulties for technicians and actors.

Paramount followed with Vistavision and Warners with Warnerscope, and every company blossomed forth with ever more startling forms of width, depth and stereoscopic sound, winding up with Todd–AO and Cinerama, which seemingly offered the spectator flights to infinity.

While these efforts prevented a bad situation from getting worse, they also provoked one of those minor crises endemic to the industry. Exhibitors were already being severely milked for the cost of the new equipment, and when to this was added the cost of stereoscopic sound, which Fox regarded

228

as an integral part of the system, they rebelled. The disagreement was mainly between the Rank Organisation and Fox, already linked by commercial ties, and it created much ill-will. But exhibitors, whether singly or in battalions, were in no position to risk a livelihood already so deeply endangered. The Americans won their point and in a year or two nearly every cinema screen in the country was noticeably wider and spoke with a strong stereophonic accent.

The cold climate of television had chilled the bones of many a showman in the first days and set him brooding over his fate. Now a much colder blast awaited him for which he was wholly unprepared. This was the sale of old films to television. The Cinematograph Exhibitors' Association banned it at once, permitting only the use of trailers to advertise forthcoming productions, and these must not exceed five minutes in length.

To sell off their old films, said the exhibitors, was the extreme of folly, for it was to hand over the very bread of their existence to the enemy. Who would go to the cinema if he could see a film at home, even an old film or one shown late at night after the last performance? (This was a condition of the sale.)

Everyone saw the point but everyone evaded it, and found nothing wrong in disposing of valuable film rights to a rich new market. A number of Alexander Korda's films were the first to go, followed by RKO's and those of Michael Balcon from Ealing. Protests followed. The whole industry rose up in its wrath and vowed that it would boycott the films of any producer or renter who defied the anti-TV ruling.

But as some of the leading members of the film industry had recently, or were soon to become, leading members of the television industry—the Bernsteins, Lord Rank, Sir Philip Warter of Associated British—this was a threat of doubtful validity, and a way out had to be found.

The solution, put forward by Cecil Bernstein, was to create a fund something like the Eady Fund, imposing a farthing levy on every cinema seat sold, and by this means buy up old films and preserve them from the shame of the small screen.

To carry out the scheme the Film Industry Defence

229

Organisation (FIDO) was formed in 1958, and for a time it had a deterrent effect. But it was too much to expect that producers with valuable properties to sell would not sell them to the highest bidder. They did so—to the BBC, to ITV or to America—and in a few years FIDO was abandoned.

These developments, disturbing though they were, did not alter or make more flexible the character of the industry. The structure was as rigid as ever, as the Plant report had complained, and the success or failure of a film still depended on the fiat of two men who booked films for the two major circuits. A spirit of conservatism prevailed. Lord Rank and the heads of Associated British continued to hold the power and guide the future, subject only to the decrees of Parliament.

But they now added television to their interests, Rank with Southern Television and Associated British with ABC, which covered the Midlands. Granada created its own network in the North and many film companies and film directors applied for TV licences. The Rank Organisation later diversified into other fields—bingo, dancing, bowling, hotels, etc., but this did not affect the overall structure of the film industry.

Films continued to be made, sixty-three first features in 1952, but they were not making a profit. Rank threatened a total stoppage of film production unless conditions improved. Between 1950 and 1956 films cost more to produce than they made at the box-office, and this clearly bore some relation to the huge entertainments tax paid over roughly the same period—1950 to 1957—which reached the fantastic figure of £280 million—nearly three times as much as the public paid at the box-office in a single year.[3]

It required a prolonged anti-tax campaign conducted with great vigour and expertise by the Cinematograph Exhibitors' Association to remedy this situation. Over a period of ten years the Government made concessions which gradually eased the burden, and in 1960 the tax was abolished for good. It was an immense benefit and enabled a saner economy to prevail.

230

Great changes were overtaking the film industry, not merely in its outward forms, but in its inner life and creativeness. The lines of demarcation between film and television were becoming so blurred it was difficult to recognise them as separate entities. In the event, they stole brazenly from each other and so became thick as thieves. Viewed in this context, the fall of the cinema was quantitative, a decline of numbers merely. Qualitatively, films were to rise to higher levels than ever before and to gain immeasurably in status if not in popularity.

Chapter 25

Some Post-War Films, 1945–1950

The war had raised British films to their highest point of excellence and advanced their reputation all over the world. Individual triumphs there had been for twenty years or so, but it needed a consistent body of such work over a period to establish a case and destroy the myth that a truly British film did not exist, or if it did, it was by accident. We must remember that in 1945 four-fifths of our cinema programmes were American; they tended to obscure the view for the British film and reduce its importance.[1]

Now at last a film with conspicuously native roots was emerging from the war, revolutionary in character, more deeply concerned with truth, bringing a new life and dignity to film making. Most of the great productions of the war were documents, but documents written not with the austerity of a White Paper but with the fire of a crusade and a strong sense of purpose.

In France, no specific trend is discernible, her efforts are represented by René Clement's *La Bataille du Rail*, Cocteau's *La Belle et la Bête*, Sartre's *Les Jeux Sont Faits*, and Clair's *Le Silence est d'Or*.

It Italy, the neo-realist movement was re-creating a cinema reflecting the social unrest of the time, but the discontents of Italy and their mode of expression found no echo in the work of British film directors until the late 1950s, when the angry young men were making themselves heard. For the moment, a series of prestige features occupied our studios—*Great Expectations*, *Hamlet*, *A Matter of Life and Death*, *The Red Shoes*, and Carol Reed's trio, *The Third Man*,

232

The Fallen Idol and *Odd Man Out*. Some were described by sober-minded critics as masterpieces; others were considered too literary or theatrical. All had some special kind of merit. They were part of the achievement and they re-established the case for Britain.

But although these productions were a matter of pride there is nothing very adventurous in their choice of subject, no new fields are explored, nothing significant seems to have come out of the war, or into the post-war situation for comment or analysis. Perhaps the reason for this was the intense conservatism of the distributors, which still acted as a bar to the discussion of social or political ideas, or indeed to the presentation of any serious contemporary issue. For many years, too, exhibitors banned outright any film of political complexion. The ban became one of those clichés of the film industry such as 'racing films are dead', or religious themes are 'box-office poison'.

Hence in 1945 we are still confronting a star-struck screen, Directors had to find vehicles for stars, known or likely to be known, and while this was good for the box-office, we cannot fail to notice the inhibiting effect it had on ideas, and the stereotyped work it produced. Nevertheless, a change of policy was commercially unthinkable. Audiences went to the pictures to see their favourite stars. They had always done so. 'Who is in it?' was always the question asked. It was seldom 'What is in it?'

The films of these years, as in all previous years, excluding the war, are judged by this criterion. Stars dominate. Among them are Charles Laughton, Rex Harrison, Vivien Leigh, Dirk Bogarde, Trevor Howard, David Niven, Richard Attenborough, Robert Donat, Michael Wilding, James Mason, Anna Neagle, Virginia McKenna, Jack Hawkins, Kenneth More, Alec Guinness.

Maurice Elvey made two of his last productions about this time—*The Gentle Sex* (1934) and *Beware of Pity* (1946), but in 1953 he lost the sight of an eye and could not continue working. He did, however, successfully make the transition from silence to sound and was much respected in his time. *The Times* said of him: He had 'a certain liveliness and truth

233

of observation but was more remarkable for his commercial than his artistic qualities'.

Work of a more significant kind was on the way. The stress and grief of war, once it was over, called for something more meaningful than stars, though this point of view did not immediately find expression. The contemporary scene was long in coming to life.

David Robinson has noticed the cardinal deficiency of the cinema in the mid-1940s and after: 'What never seemed to appear on the screen', he writes, 'was the reality of post-war England—the England of the Labour Government and the return to Conservatism in the fifties, of the years after the 1944 Education Act; of the social changes in the country; of urban Britain, of industrial Britain, of working-class Britain, of provincial Britain.' He quotes Lindsay Anderson's belief that, not the low-brow but the middle-brow is 'the great danger to British cinema, for he is incapacitated by a dislike of reality'.[2]

Only in one direction, that of comedy, was the English scene more truly observed, and that was in the series of films made at Ealing studios between 1946 and 1958.

The transition to peace diminished the prospect for the documentary film. It no longer shared the responsibilities of war-time feature production with the commercial studies, nor did it have the same security of tenure from the State. The talents and labours of a whole group of documentary men returned to the less inspiring task of instruction and public relations in industry—coal, electricity, gas, railways, to programmes of science and education or to schemes of private enterprise.

Paul Rotha, Stuart Legg, Basil Wright and Humphrey Jennings continued with work of their own. Denis Forman recalls some of the best post-war documentary in Jennings' *Family Portrait* and Basil Wright's *Waters of Time*, the latter shown at the 1951 Festival of Britain. Edgar Anstey established a film unit at the British Transport Commission. Shell had always had a unit of its own and continued to operate one under Arthur Elton, but as a dedication to social causes the mainspring had **gone** from the movement.

234

Nor did the war-time successes do much for post-war documentary.

In the commercial cinema, the Rank Organisation sponsored a topical magazine, *This Modern Age* (1946), produced by Sergei Nolbandov, who had worked at Ealing Studios. It dealt objectively and in greater depth with current affairs and was a much needed counterblast to the conventional newsreel. It did well, but after four years was axed for economic reasons.

David Lean's *Great Expectations* (1946), partly photographed on the Essex flats and giving Alex Guinness his first part on the screen, is one of the few important works of fiction to re-animate the post-war scene. It was a Cineguild film by David Lean, Ronald Neame and Anthony Havelock-Allen, the adaptation is bold and uncompromising, clearing away the dense undergrowth of the novel yet remaining a wholly Dickensian creation. It also shows unmistakably the style of the director, with his power to evoke the Dickens scene, character, or moment, and his ability to sustain a strong narrative movement.

Lean has always been praised for his work as an editor, being pre-eminent in it, and his success has been largely attributed to that skill. But though this counts for much it does not count for everything. Without his painterly cye, his feeling for the poetic and, obvious though it may seem, for the dramatic, he might well have remained an editor and not a maker of films. Richard Winnington described *Great Expectations* as 'probably the best British film yet made'.

In America it was only a success in New York, it never appealed to the mass of the people. Our films of the mid-forties, according to Richard Griffith, are still 'an antiquarian's version of a national art'. They are pictures for the 'select few'.

Oliver Twist (1948) fell below *Great Expectations* as a film, in the same way as the novel falls below it as literature. But it is still a stylish achievement and drew a highly idiosyncratic piece of acting from Alec Guinness as Fagin. Again the Cineguild teamwork results in a finely polished

235

production, alive and full of atmosphere, if not perfect in casting. Denis Forman described John Howard Davies's Oliver as 'a Little Lord Fauntleroy who had strayed among the Dead End Kids'.³ Guy Green was the photographer, John Bryan the art director, and the music was by Arnold Bax.

Release of the film was held up in America on the ground that his interpretation of Fagin was anti-Semitic. It was a ludicrous claim, but the American industry had repeatedly shown its hostility to British films and could always find reasons for rejecting them.

The David Lean Dickens films were followed by the goodish but not altogether satisfactory adaptation of H. G. Wells's *The Passionate Friends* (1949) and by *Madeleine* (1950), a mid-Victorian melodrama based on the case of a Scotswoman accused of murdering her French lover.

Thorold Dickinson's most elaborate and stylish production belongs to this time, *The Queen of Spades* (1948), adapted from the Pushkin story. This darkly enthralling drama is directed with splendid theatricality. Dickinson concentrates all the arts of decor, lighting and costume on the majestically wicked figure of Edith Evans and gives us the shock and eccentricity and beauty of an authentically Russian composition.

Hamlet (1948), Laurence Olivier's second Shakespeare film, from a text prepared by Alan Dent and himself, was by no means universally approved. Critics praised the splendours of decor and design and Oliver's own performance but had reservations on other grounds.

Olivier has explained why he chose to make the film in black and white; he saw *Hamlet* as an engraving rather than a painting. Some years later when Grigori Kozintzev made his version of *Hamlet* in 1963, he said: 'For Hamlet I want the cool greys of the North'.

C. A. Lejeune found Olivier's production very much more mature than his *Henry V* but less exciting. She disapproves of his bleached hair 'which ages him considerably . . . it is disconcerting to watch a Hamlet who might be the father of his own mother'. Moreover there is nothing in the production to compare with the thrilling ten minutes of the French knights' charge at Agincourt in *Henry V*.

The long tracking shots and dolly shots downstairs, round pillars and along corridors are blamed by Campbell Dixon for slowing down the tempo but his view is generally favourable.

So too is that of Paul Dehn who writes of the 'prodigious pruning' Olivier has made. 'Rosencrantz and Guildenstern, Voltimand and Cornelius are cut, likewise Fortinbras, part of whose final speech is given to Horatio. . . . If there is much that scholars and sticklers find cause to blame', he adds, 'there is infinitely more for them and for us to praise.' *The Times* produced a clap of thunder with the words 'melodrama magnificently managed'.

Olivier has given his own views on the filming of Shakespeare which indicate alike the boldness and good sense of his approach. 'If you are going to cut a Shakespeare play', he argues, 'there is only one thing to do—lift out scenes. If you cut the lines down merely to keep all the characters in, you end up with a mass of short ends. This is one of the problems with *Richard III*'.

'*Hamlet* contains a good deal of spoken thought, but it is contemplative. On the other hand, Richard talks to the audience all the time (like Iago does). This is absolute audience approach, not meditation. When I do it in my film I talk to the camera, and take the camera into my confidence. I take it by the arm and walk it about with me as if I'd just come to town with it. I thought I'd just do this and see what happens. I treated the camera as a person without, I hope, embarrassing it.'[4]

Hamlet was considered indecent in America. Objection was taken to it by the Boston police and by the Catholic League of Decency which could not tolerate Hamlet's suggestive dialogue with Ophelia or his condemnation of his mother.

Powell and Pressburger's *A Matter of Life and Death* (1946) indulges in bizarre forms of cinema which challenge belief but are carried through with panache. The producers call on

237

all the resources of cameraman, art directors and trick men to sustain a fantastic notion—that of an airman's dream when he crashes to earth and, after a brain operation, meets with experiences in another world.

'Could any story be more vulgarly idiotic?' the critic of the *New Statesman* asked 'Yet . . . the film has astonishing merits. While nothing can retrieve so fatuous a plot, which seems worse the more one thinks of it, there are passages of genuine imagination . . . an impressive exploration of space, and this extra mundane theme is kept going by the trips to and from heaven, fog rolling over the Atlantic, sensations of going under an anaesthetic, etc. . . . Though by no stretch of critical kindness can *A Matter of Life and Death* be called a good film, yet it is not boring and it is not undramatic.'[5] The truth was, it was too metaphysical and failed to suspend disbelief. Nevertheless, it gave some well-written parts to David Niven, Roger Livesey and Kim Hunter.

Black Narcissus (1947), Powell and Pressburger's next film, set in a convent in the Himalayas made little impression, but *The Red Shoes* (1948) had the distinction which in one way or another is always present in the work of this team. It concerns the career of a ballet dancer and the conflicting claims of love and the stage in her life. This commonplace idea was merely a device to exploit the gorgeous trappings of the ballet.

Moira Shearer, who had just won a striking success as a youthful prima ballerina at Covent Garden, was partnered by Robert Helpmann; Beecham conducted the music; Massine devised the choreography. Anton Walbrook played the part of the impresario.

The line-up of talent was impressive. The hysteria, madness and beauty which attend the creation of a ballet were skilfully compounded and the film was a tribute to an art that had acquired an immense popularity during the war. With Brian Easdale's score and the dazzling sweep of Jack Cardiff's photography this was enough. All the same many critics thought this a bad film. As Gautier said: 'It is difficult to write for legs.'

238

Richard Griffith described Powell's collaboration with Pressburger in this kind of film as 'secondhand Hollywood'. It seems an unduly harsh judgement. What is certain is that the good and bad elements in their films tend to argue with each other and create a disunity, leaving a confused impression, and the occasional lapse of taste we have noted.

The Boulting brothers followed up their war films with a quartet of uneven productions between 1945 and 1950— *Fame is the Spur* (1946) based on Howard Spring's political novel; *Brighton Rock* (1947), early Graham Greene; *The Guinea Pig* (1949) from Chetham Strode's play; and *Seven Days to Noon* (1950) from a story by Paul Dehn and James Bernard.

Of these, the last was the most satisfying, a cleverly sustained thriller about a lunatic scientist threatening to drop an atomic bomb on London. *The Guinea Pig*, with Richard Attenborough in the leading part, discussed the situation of an elementary schoolboy confronting the snobberies of a public school. It mildly projected a theme of social discontent and is not the Boultings at their best.

Carol Reed, having in 1945 completed his term with the Army Kinematograph Service—he had been making training films—produced three features strikingly different in subject and treatment: *Odd Man Out, The Fallen Idol,* and *The Third Man.* Unsurpassed among British directors of the 1940s, he was now free to make whatever he chose, and his choice and his making were never done in a hurry.

Odd Man Out (1947) which he produced and directed, is based on F. L. Green's novel and was adapted by the author and R. C. Sherriff. The film opens up the whole spectrum of Reed's talents, the powerful narrative drive, the eye for detail, the searching illumination of character and place. We are drawn into the story from the moment when Johnny McQueen, the Irish revolutionary leader, plans the robbery at the flax mill to his death on the streets twenty-four hours later, a man wanted for murder.

The film is in the immemorial tradition of the chase, it is

a good run through the streets of Belfast, it peers into the faces of the men and women in pubs and tenements, drifting towards a tragedy they invite and cannot escape.

The pervasive sense of irony and waste is centred in the character of Shell, the betrayer, played with an inimitable cringeing humour by F. J. McCormick of the Abbey Theatre. James Mason's Johnny has few acting opportunities, it is the conspirators, Murphy, Pat, Dennis Nolan and the crowd of shiftless vagabonds observed with such fidelity who give truth to the scene. So too do the fine contrasts of Robert Krasker's black and white photography. *Odd Man Out* has lost none of its quality with the years. It remains the most deeply felt of the trio we are considering.

The Fallen Idol was chosen by the British Film Academy as the best British film of 1948. It was a story by Graham Greene about a boy, still a child, son of an ambassador, who fancies he sees a murder committed by the butler of the house whom he worships, and whom he strives later to defend. The success of this idea, of course, depends on the boy having an adult understanding of the criminal events in which he is involved, which is unlikely. Graham Greene's original story does not so deeply involve him. In the film the boy, Bobby Henrey, is made a compelling figure by Carol Reed's sympathetic direction and by the support of Ralph Richardson as the butler and Michele Morgan as his mistress. But his performance, says Denis Forman, remains 'a brilliant trick'.[6]

The Third Man (1949), again a collaboration between Carol Reed and Graham Greene, is probably Reed's most celebrated film, certainly among his greatest successes commercially. It is a romantic thriller set in post-war Vienna and peers into the corrupt little lives of the city and their devious occupations. Orson Welles, Joseph Cotten, Trevor Howard and Valli figure in a manhunt which begins quietly enough in the streets and ends violently in the sewers of the city.

In Greene's story the young American writer, Joseph Cotten, innocent of guile, who has come to the city to meet his friend, Orson Welles, learns that he has died in a street accident. Then he discovers that he is still alive but a murderer, and of a peculiarly repulsive type. The American is drawn into the web of corruption and intrigue. It is a characteristic Graham Greene investigation into the powers of evil.

The film has some Hitchcockian touches, and certainly in the scenes on the Big Wheel and in the sewers, the mental and physical tensions can be related to his work. But all seem agreed that *The Third Man* is quintessentially Carol Reed in its unity of style, in its evocation of the seedy but proud city and in the fine performances he draws from Orson Welles, Joseph Cotten and Trevor Howard, whose British major is for once worthy of this actor's skill.

The film then is entertainment in the Graham Greene sense of not pretending to be anything else. It lacks the nobility of *Odd Man Out*, there is no sense of awe, of the gods disposing, no tragic frailty, it is all calculation and self-interest.

By one of those curious quirks of show business the zither music composed for the film by Anton Karas—the Harry Lime theme—played a greater part in bringing the film its popularity than any of its more glittering elements.

It remains to consider a number of other productions which carry on the tradition of skill and craftsmanship of the post-war period and are marked in every case by a deep Englishness of spirit.

Scott of the Antarctic (1948) in which John Mills played the lead, is of this order and had some admirable sequences of action and suspense, but its conscientiousness often turned out to be dullness and as narrative it sagged.

There were tales of heroism without heroes and in this category we would place Jack Lee's *The Wooden Horse* (Wessex Films, 1950), one of the first and best stories of escape from enemy territories. This particular example was a tunnelling from Germany and produced the thrill of an authentic experience, and it led to a number of imitations which were soon to become stereotyped.

Peter Ustinov's furious invention produced three films for

this period. He wrote and directed *School for Secrets* (1946), a comedy of back-room boys in war-time, *Vice-Versa* (1948), from the Anstey farce, and *Private Angelo*, adapted from Eric Linklater's novel, in which Ustinov also played the leading part.

Of these the most successful is *Vice-Versa*, alike for its theatrical wit and its suitability to the director's style. Yet none of these productions have the root of cinema in them; the director's work is stagey and his talents divided.

Chapter 26

The Englishness of Ealing

The work of Ealing Studios is chiefly memorable for the series of comedies Balcon produced between 1946 and 1958, though these are part of a much larger output. They stand in a category of their own and have often been spoken of as the nearest thing to a school (if we exclude documentary) in British cinema. They broke away from the old tradition of film comedy, with its breeziness, vulgarity and snobbery, and re-created a freer and more realistic style which owed something to documentary.

To follow events in their proper order we must consider briefly what went before. Balcon's experience as production chief of MGM British was not a happy one. He came into conflict with Louis B. Mayer, and after producing *A Yank at Oxford* (1938) he was, according to his own version of the matter, quietly frozen out of the company.[1] In order to continue in active production he made independently a film of Edgar Wallace's *The Ringer* (1938) (renamed *The Gaunt Stranger*) which Walter Forde directed.

But the year 1938, as by a miracle, provided him with the opportunity he most desired. He was invited by Stephen Courtauld and Reggie Baker, directors of Ealing, to join the studios and thus began the most fruitful period of his career. Under his direction the studio enjoyed a visible independence. A single mind was in control and Ealing was its expression.

The films to which Balcon now turned, such as the George Formbys, are of no special interest and nothing of consequence appears until the war. Cavalcanti joined him in 1940 and so did Harry Watt, and while these talents were simmering

243

Will Hay and Tommy Trinder made box-office comedies—
The Ghost of St Michael's and *Sailors Three* (both 1940).

As we have noted, no one quite knew what film to make,
but a good star name was felt to be an insurance against
failure and soon it would not matter what anyone made, the
worst and the best were devoured equally by a war-time
public of no taste and tremendous appetite.

Some of the Ealing war films we have already considered.
Thirteen others of various kinds were produced between 1943
and 1948. These figures say no more than that Ealing was
busy and producing work of value—*Halfway House,
Johnny Frenchman* and *Painted Boats* (about life on the
canals).

But again, well before the end of the war, the studios
were running into difficulties and could not get an adequate
release for their films. Balcon, as a leading member of the
Films Council, had campaigned vigorously against monopoly
in the film industry and his films were more or less barred
by the Rank Organisation and Associated British. The
combines, moreover, like the Americans, did not want rival
films competing with their own, least of all those which were
good box office.

But soon, by one of those strange reversals of fortune
whereby all things are expedient, Balcon is back on friendly
terms with Rank and is promised better distribution and
complete autonomy at the studios and he is appointed to
the board of Rank's companies. Ealing returns to form.

The comedies that brought such an uncommon fame to
the studio were not so much a new direction as the redis-
covery of an old one. As Arnold Bennett may be said to
have rediscovered the Potteries and the Manchester dramatists
Lancashire, so Ealing rediscovered England, or rather, those
several and distinct areas of it known as suburbia, the
provinces and the countryside.

The Englishness of Ealing is apparent not only in the
comedies but in some much earlier non-Ealing productions
and in the studio's whole attitude to film-making. It guided
the creative process from the choice of subject right
through to its release.

244

Ealing's public pronouncements had none of the usual Wardour Street vulgarity but were factual or witty, the wit stemming from the studio's publicist, Monja Danischewsky, who later produced *Whisky Galore*.[2] Even the poster designs had a freshness and originality no other company could rival, which indeed the major companies rather despised as the work of uncommercial travellers. But they helped to create a style. They were reminders that artists were at work and could express themselves in all they undertook.

First of the group of comedies was *Hue and Cry* (1946) directed by Charles Crichton. It is English in the way we have suggested. The story, by T. E. B. Clarke, a Fleet Street journalist with a natural gift of comedy, is concerned with the activities of a gang of children on a bombed site in London. Its approach to character and scene is more realistic than the usual collection of British jokes which passed at that time for comedy.

It was a film, moreover, that understood children. The scene of loads of them arriving for battle in a taxi is as true as a page of *Huckleberry Finn*. London is filmed with affection, the streets are full of magic. Clair and Mack Sennett have been cited as influences on Ealing comedies, but they owe quite as much to their writers, having a true eye for character combined with an intuitive awareness of how funny the human race can be. Paul Dehn wrote of *Hue and Cry*: 'Here is the first British comedy I have seen to borrow the brilliance of French comedy and superimpose it impeccably on a purely London scene.'[3]

Passport to Pimlico (1948), again the work of T. E. B. Clarke, is based on the idea that Pimlico is really a part of Burgundy and that a passport is needed to enter it. This quirky fantasy was well received by the critics, though the direction of Henry Cornelius in his first film left something to be desired. Campbell Dixon described it as 'very English', and in a review headed 'British Burgundy' Dilys Powell applied her astringent wit to the witticism before her and, with some reservations, approved. She points out that, as in *Hue and Cry*, the film 'didn't simply have a good idea and leave it at that: the idea was worked out, every incident had

245

its own vitality and its share in the general vitality, a funny and fantastic picture was funny and fantastic in detail'.[4]

The Times Educational Supplement rejoiced on the ground that 'a film which holds up present-day Britain to intelligent laughter, and which is moreover wholly suitable for children, is a gift to educationists'.

Passport to Pimlico is in many ways the pattern of all the other comedies. Fantasy begets the theme, enabling the writer to draw the maximum amount of ridicule from people and institutions, but in the process not to stray too far from the truth.

For example, in *Passport to Pimlico*, the introduction of war-time laws about passports, rationing and essential services lead to ludicrous discussions between government departments and finally to Downing Street, and in all these we are presented with characters whom we feel to be real. London, as in *Hue and Cry*, adds to the Englishness of the scene. These are virtues and they are emphasised by the high professionalism of the cast—Stanley Holloway, Margaret Rutherford, Hermione Baddeley, and those admirable farceurs, Basil Radford and Naunton Wayne.

In *Whisky Galore* (1949), which Alexander Mackendrick directed, there is the same spirit of eccentricity and unlikelihood leading to lunatic conflicts between odd characters whom we yet recognise as real. There is the documentary detail, the oddity of clothes or accents.

We recognise too the experienced hand of Compton Mackenzie in the story, his collaborator being the equally experienced Angus MacPhail. Between them they tell a story about a cargo of whiskey from a wrecked ship in the Outer Hebrides and the uproarious fight for its possession. Richard Winnington compares its fresh spontaneous humour with 'the terrible affliction of self-consciousness' which all the post-war comedies suffer from, even (he thinks) *Passport to Pimlico*.

Kind Hearts and Coronets (1949), a caricature in the Max Beerbohm manner, is at the same time a reminder how much the reputation of Ealing is linked to the name of Alec Guinness, who appears in four other comedies—*A Run for*

Your Money, *The Lavender Hill Mob* (1951), *The Man in the White Suit* (1952) and *The Ladykillers* (1955).

His playing of eight parts in *Kind Hearts and Coronets*, each a distinct portrait, was a *tour de force* which naturally won attention, though we must not deny an equal credit to Robert Hamer both for the writing (in which he collaborates with John Dighton), and the direction. He produced a beautifully stuffy piece of Victoriana whose solid mahogany decor planted it firmly among the aspidistras.

The story is of a rejected member of an aristocratic family (Dennis Price) who murders his eight rivals to the title in order to secure it for himself.

The film had what may be called a prestige reception though it was not one of total acceptance. Campbell Dixon looks at it from the point of view of the Venice Festival of that year whose critics generally were unimpressed. 'Essentially literary in conception', he writes, 'its poker-faced fun can be appreciated only by people with a good working knowledge of the English language and the English people.'

Fred Majdalany, a critic too little regarded, thought the whole joke went on too long and 'became the victim of its own dryness and artificiality'. Nevertheless, *Kind Hearts and Coronets* wears better today than some of its rivals and the dialogue retains its point and elegance.

The success of this film, following *Whisky Galore*, did much to spread the fame of Ealing and of course of Alec Guinness, who is shortly afterwards committed to the flames of world stardom.

The Lavender Hill Mob (1951), again from a script by Tibby Clarke, has a characteristic opening. It presents Guinness as the innocent little bank official in bowler hat and spectacles undertaking the transport of gold bullion to and from the Bank of England. Against this immensely respectable background is a fantastic plot to seize the bullion, melt it down into paper-weights, and export it to France. Guinness and his gang will thus become millionaires.

The bank official hatches his scheme from his seedy hotel in Lavender Hill. Not only is the City dramatised with affection, but Paris and the Eiffel Tower, with a final chase

247

through London in true Mack Sennett fashion. Again, the performance of Alec Guinness impresses by its idiosyncratic style, the intense application to the matter in hand which divides acting from a display of personality.

C. A. Lejeune made the point that 'T. E. B. Clarke was the "author" of this film in a way that many more distinguished "authors" are not, in the sense that he takes as large a share in the final shaping of the picture as the director himself. The present director, Charles Crichton, knows his little ways and between them, in *The Lavender Hill Mob*, they scarcely miss a trick'.[5]

Alexander Mackendrick directed Guinness once again in *The Man in the White Suit* (1951), a story concerned with the invention of an indestructible material which makes clothes last for ever and triggers off instant rebellion in homes and factories.

The *Tribune* critic finds it pleasant enough but complains that 'the Ealing slapstick, with lots of chasing, sometimes gets twinges of *significance*' (*Tribune's* italics). It is four years before we see Guinness in another Ealing comedy, *The Ladykillers* (1955), with Peter Sellers in a small part. Guinness is the lodger in a suburban flat who conducts string quartets but is really a crook persuading an eccentric old lady from the stage (Katie Johnson) to a life of crime.

It is black comedy in the *Kind Hearts and Coronets* manner, no new thing, for we have met it in *Monsieur Verdoux*, *Arsenic and Old Lace*, and other examples of the black arts. Alexander Mackendrick again directs, and a talented new script-writer, William Rose, provides the story, an American who is soon being naturalised by Ealing. (He is today a British citizen.)

By now professional attitudes are becoming more critical. Derek Granger in the *Sunday Times* can rise to no higher praise of *The Ladykillers* than 'engaging stuff' and William Whitebait is scarcely more pleased. 'A film with all the talents that began by over-impressing has proved stylish but a bit of a bore', he declares. 'Of course, the incidental pleasures, the execution . . . raise it high above the run of screen comedies.' So the reaction is setting in, as always it does. The *Ladykillers* brings us to the last of the comedies in the series.

Michael Balcon did of course produce a number of other films during this period, notably *The Blue Lamp* (1950), an immensely popular police melodrama, with Jack Warner and Dirk Bogarde, and two other productions by Harry Watt— *Where No Vultures Fly* (1951) and *West of Zanzibar* (1953). These show a side of Ealing seldom canvassed, the feeling for the outdoor life and the vigour of young people in new territories, the point perhaps where 'English' merges into 'British'. To this phase also belongs *Sammy Going South* (1962), produced in Africa, with Edward G. Robinson, who was seriously ill while making it. This, however was made with Bryanston-Seven Arts.

How do the comedies stand in relation to cinema as a whole? Contemporary opinion gives them a high place even if hindsight waters it down. The Ealing comedies had intelligence and style and that greater rarity, wit, and they marked an advance in the conventions applying to them. Some of them, like *Kind Hearts and Coronets*, have become classics, they are compared with some of the best French cinema. They made not the slightest attempt to match the star-clustered comedies of Hollywood, the Marilyn Monroes and Cary Grants, they were originals, the things that cannot be repeated, unpretentious, of a certain excellence, and they were in the happiest sense English.

The year 1955 brought yet another crisis to Ealing's fortunes and compelled Balcon to sell the studios to the BBC. Pinewood was offered as an alternative but as the arrangement did not give him the independence he needed, the plan fell through. After one more film, *The Long Arm*, Rank and Balcon parted company.

Ealing came to an end. Balcon and his team had worked there for eighteen years, a family of talents some of whom, like Robert Hamer, Harry Watt and Sandy Mackendrick, he had brought to success. He had created a studio of character and single-mindedness, the kind nearest to the heart of the

249

film-maker and most favourable to his development. At a certain cost to the more ambitious type of film he had achieved an independence which other producers, burdened with greatness, found difficult, if not impossible, to sustain.

In the end the price of independence had been too high, as it had proved with Korda and a number of others, and as the annual reports of the NFFC showed even more conclusively. Some new enterprise had to be sought to meet the new situation, for Ealing could not be revived.

In the meantime commercial television had brought not merely another crisis but a revolution in the audio-visual arts and the most serious threat so far to the cinema's survival. Desperate remedies were being sought and applied, particularly in America, to meet this situation.

Whatever the crisis, films had to be made. Balcon visited New York, and renewed a previous acquaintance with Arthur Loew, the king-pin of Loew's Incorporated (parent company of Metro), and a contract was signed for the production of half-a-dozen pictures at MGM's Boreham Wood studios. Thus he resumed the partnership with MGM which had ended so disastrously in pre-war days.[6] Of the series of productions made under this contract, the best was probably *The Shiralee* (1956) with Peter Finch, followed by *The Man in the Sky* (1956) with Jack Hawkins. The least successful and the most ambitious was *Dunkirk* (1958). None of these films, being made for another company, had the character, the charm, the singularity of the Ealing days.

Conditions were getting worse, box-office takings dived fearfully, cinemas closed down by the score. Exhibitors strove to protect their interests by boycotting anyone who sold his films to television. Balcon sold them. So did John Woolf. The industry hummed and ha'd and was split down the middle. It was less than ever a time when producers could look ahead with confidence.

Deprived of his studios, Balcon filmed at Boreham Wood or at Elstree, and made *The Long and the Short and the Tall* (1961) from the play by Willis Hall. According to his own account, he was not satisfied with the casting of this film, but being associated with the American distributor, Walter

250

Reade, he was not free to make his own decisions and choose his own cast.

The Long and the Short and the Tall was made by a new company, but in 1959 this became the basis for Bryanston Films, which brought together a number of independent producers on a co-operative basis.[7] (Its first release was *Battle of the Sexes* with Peter Sellers.) Some big names were connected with Bryanston, among them John Osborne and Tony Richardson of Woodfall Films.

Bryanston Films were distributed by British Lion, a producer-distributor company of small beginnings but increasing importance since 1946 when Korda acquired it and Sir Arthur Jarratt became managing director. By 1955 it was generally viewed as a third force to balance the power of the combines, hence its special importance to the economy of the industry.

Part VI

Transition Stage

Chapter 27

The Lion's Tail Twisted

It is perhaps worth recalling that there was a British Lion Film Company (not connected with the present one) in 1919. It was formed by an ex-army man, David Falcke and his partner Cyril Hicks from Belfast and its producer was A. V. Bramble. It made several pictures at the Ideal Company's studios at Elstree but after a year or two went bankrupt. This did not prevent the Ideal Company from taking over and expanding the company to renting as well as producing and it continued a lively existence into the 1920s.

When we endeavour to trace the course of the British Lion company of today we are confronted with a history of baffling complexity, of which, as it were, we give here only the headlines.

In 1949 it was saddled with the £3 million debt left by Korda, and this debt was inherited by the National Film Finance corporation when the Government set it up.

In 1954 it was found that the company was insolvent and a receiver and manager was installed. In 1955 we hear of a new company, British Lion Films Ltd. A lively trade in films continues, some produced at Shepperton studios but most of it by other companies. During this time the Lion is gradually changing its skin and in the process it contrives, between 1955 and 1970, to release nearly a hundred films, among them *Orders to Kill, I'm Allright Jack, The Angry Silence, Morgan, A Suitable Case for Treatment, Ulysses,* and *Saturday Night and Sunday Morning.*

In 1958 David Kingsley, the former managing director of the NFFC becomes the new managing director of British Lion. John and Roy Boulting, Sidney Gilliat and Frank

255

Launder, with John Woolf, join the board. (Woolf later resigned.)

Bryanston Films is closely linked to these operations and for the four years of its existence became the main source of supply for British Lion. Some of these films such as Woodfall's *Saturday Night and Sunday Morning* and *A Taste of Honey* were successes of a high order.

But Bryanston too, in this distracted time, had its difficulties. As on former occasions, the company's films were not being give a fair release, they took too long to recover their money, interest rates were high and repayment of loans ruinous. When, therefore, in 1963 Associated Rediffusion made an offer for the Bryanston assets, it was accepted.

There ensued shortly after one of those tribal wars for the possession of British Lion which make such diverting headlines in the press. The NFFC were empowered to buy the management shares and sell the company to anyone who had sufficient temerity and cash to acquire it.

Balcon entered the lists against several influential bidders, including Sydney Box, and acquired the company with a bid of £1,600,000. He thus became the new British Lion chairman though he did not intend to hold that office for long.

And, as it turned out, he had been in office only a year or two when he was out again. 'I realised', he says, 'that my principal colleagues were not with me in my determination to stimulate and increase production . . . they were falling back on the old belief that we would not be able to get our films into the circuits and that therefore the risks inherent in producing as many films as we had envisaged were too great.' He resigned and Lord Goodman took his place.

British Lion were set on a different course.

In the account of British Lion given in *A Competitive Cinema*[1] the authors parcel out about equal measure of praise and blame, commending the company for being run by producers rather than accountants. This was no doubt an admirable policy, but in 1963 the company ran into trouble on another front. A batch of British films they were putting out, among them *Lord of the Flies, The Leather*

256

Boys and *A Place to Go*, was held up by the major circuits.[2] Eighteen films of mixed vintage were involved, some of them dealing with serious contemporary themes. Few were what John Davis of the Rank Organisation would have called, 'good entertainment'. The film of ideas, it would seem, emptied his cinemas.

The case of the 'missing' British Lion films was taken up by the press and this had a pronounced effect. There were several views of the matter. One held that the company was indulging in anti-monopoly propaganda, for it was the monopolists who were rejecting the films. Another view was that the films were ahead of their time or, again, were behind it; they were not up to standard as entertainment.

These strictures contrast with the optimism of producers like Harry Saltzman, the Canadian who made *The Battle of Britain* and declared that the British film industry was 'fat and rich and it's got wrinkles in its belly'. Many of these wrinkles, however, were directly the result of too heavy a dollar diet.

British Lion anyway had more than enough resilience to survive a crisis which, one way and another, year after year, hit all independents alike. Hollywood films were taking second place in the affections of audiences and this was in the independent's favour. British films were taking at that time more money in the London area than the American ones. Many of these British films, however, were more American than British.

The Boulting brothers had no American affiliations. As Charter Films they made a trio of comedies for British Lion—*Brothers-in-law* (1956), *Lucky Jim* (1957), and *I'm All Right, Jack* (1959). They were sailing evenly into the 1960s and building up a sounder and more thrusting image for the company; but these did not save British Lion from further changes of fortune and identity.

We must now turn to the wider situation of the NFFC and its relation to film-making generally. The corporation's reports offer a more valuable insight into the state of British film production than any other source outside the Department of Trade and Industry.

I

Film companies do not usually disclose in detail their production costs. But the NFFC is compelled, as a state institution, to provide more information both statistically and by way of comment than is offered by private enterprise, and its accounts are therefore a more dependable guide to production expenditure in the industry generally. In these balance sheets British films can be *seen* to be in debt. Hence their interest for the student, who is also the tax-payer, and must pay not only for the good films but for the losses on the bad ones. Few ordinary citizens comprehend that by law they are shareholders in the film business.

In March 1957, after eight years in office, the NFFC showed a deficit of £3,598,086, but of this amount £2,665,531 related to the British Lion loan, leaving £932,555 as a deficit on other loans.[3]

During the period 1950–7 only three years yielded a profit. Losses of over £1 million are shown in 1954 and 1955. Over the whole eight years a sum of £14,255,529 accounts for 378 feature films and 85 shorts.

Compared with the amount spent on production by Associated British and Rank over a slightly longer period, the NFFC, handicapped by debts, makes a relatively good showing, though it is an absolute loss.

Between 1956 and 1965 Associated British financed sixty-seven films at a cost of £6,764,700. Over a similar period, 1955–64, Rank financed or assisted 126 British films at a cost of £24·88 million.[4] The Rank Organisation was losing heavily on its films and cut back severely on production, but in 1965 the organisation financed a co-production scheme with the NFFC, whereby each subscribed £500,000 towards films to be made at Pinewood.

Production costs had risen compared with the two previous years and while the NFFC report finds it impossible to say why, 'There is no doubt that the major factor has been the increase in fees and remuneration payable to personnel—producers, directors, artists, writers, technicians and craft labour. These account for 50 per cent of the total cost'.

How is the money spent?

258

We take an example from the NFFC's 1957 report based on the budgets of seven films costing more than £175,000:

	£s	Percentage of Total
Story and Script	7,660	3·3
Producer and Director	17,147	7·5
Production Unit salaries	32,072	14·0
Craft labour	21,452	9·3
Sets, materials and properties	10,525	4·6
Acting	39,117	17·0
Film and Laboratory charges	13,860	6·0
Studio facilities	26,065	11·3
*Type factor	27,811	12·1
Finance charges	12,203	5·3
INSURANCE		
Premiums	4,853	2·1
Claims (credit)	3,501	1·5
Producing company's overheads	10,670	4·6
SUNDRY		
Transport, Publicity, Entertainment	10,113	4·4

* This is explained as items which vary according to the type of film: location, music, costume etc.[5]

Four of the seven films in the £175,000 or more category exceeded their budget; a further eleven out of twenty-five, costing £175,000 or less, exceeded their budget.[6] It is not surprising that John Terry, the corporation's managing director, talks of films as 'a strange and difficult commodity. . . . Unlike most other products', he writes, 'it is impossible to know in advance how much it will cost to manufacture and quite impossible to assess in advance even the approximate figure for which it will sell'.[7]

On these quicksands British films, so far from sinking, have wonderfully survived. Indeed, it is remarkable what an upsurge of spirit informs the 1950s in the second half of the decade.

In 1957, the British Film Production Fund, until then a voluntary organisation was made statutory as the British

Film Fund Agency, and given another ten years of life. The Fund had been an important factor in saving production from bankruptcy, but in actual cash it had fallen short of expectation and in the seven years (since 1950) had raised only £18 million. This was well below the estimate of £3½ million annually predicted for it in 1953, and it fell lower still the following year.

These signs strengthened the case for a continuance of State subsidy and in 1957, the NFFC, like the Fund, was granted a further ten years of life, though it was compelled to work under heavy handicaps of debt for years to come. Permission to lend money to producers, which had been withdrawn in 1957, was now renewed.

Chapter 28

Transition in the 1950s

The 1950s do not show any marked departure from tradition until we reach the end of the decade with *Room at the Top*, *Look Back in Anger* and other controversial pieces. In the meantime the old experienced hands are still in command and the old experienced films are still being produced, some of them great successes. The men who are to remake British cinema have not yet arrived.

With their arrival, the old tradition of great starry productions in luxury settings is swept away, the mass movie sustained by a personality cult is in retreat. The film now becomes part of the great debate of the mid-century and is absorbed in the cultural revolution.

Other countries undergo a like transformation. In France the influential young writers of *Cahiers du Cinéma*, exponents of fashionable critical theory, are abandoning criticism to make films themselves and put their ideas into practice. They dispense with stars and sets, work on location, and film as cheaply as possible. They are the makers of the French New Wave and as the 1950s peter out the wave breaks on the stolid English shore and makes a stimulating impact. Chabrol's *Le Beau Serge*, Truffaut's *Les Quatre Cent Coups*, Resnais' *Hiroshima Mon Amour*, are celebrated at film festivals and in the film journals. Jean Luc-Godard triggers off an intense coterie worship.

In Italy Fellini and Antonioni are transforming the scene and we are to hear much of *La Dolce Vita* and *L'Avventura* and other films which are closely identified with their directors. The American film of the 1950s is still an all-out Hollywood product, fertile and confident as ever. We need

261

recall only a few of them: Stanley Donen's *On the Town*, Joe Manciewicz's *All About Eve*, Vincent Minnelli's *An American in Paris*, Elia Kazan's *On the Waterfront*, Alfred Hitchcock's *The Trouble with Harry*, Otto Preminger's *Anatomy of a Murder*, Orson Welles's *Touch of Evil*.

Out of the mainstream, not to be imitated, are the films of Ingmar Bergman, *Smiles of a Summer Night*, *The Seventh Seal*, *Wild Strawberries*, work steeped in the poetic spirit and of a quality rare enough to make a Bergman film an event.

Allowing for our known habit of over-praising whatever is foreign and under-praising whatever is British, the films made in our own studios compare well enough with those of other countries, and by 1960 equal and in some cases surpass them.

The French films seem more original and sparkling but are entirely dependent on good lively scripts. The Americans have a greater surface brilliance (even their 'profundity' seems somehow on the surface); the Italians are moving out of their neo-realist phase into comedy and spectacle.

Carol Reed, following up his success with *The Third Man*, made Joseph Conrad's *An Outcast of the Islands* (1951), a film which turned out to be a bad choice and failed to satisfy the critics on several counts. The crowded incident and scenic panoply of the novel were emphasised, it was said, at the expense of the characters which hardly had time to develop; Conrad's intricate plot construction had not been worked out. The *Spectator* and the *New Statesman* were both critical, though William Whitebait admits to the excitement of scene and story.

There were, too, differences of opinion about the acting, especially that of Trevor Howard as Willems, the outcast, of whom Winnington observed that Carol Reed had failed to get a performance out of him, while other critics found nothing but praise for it.

Outright approval came, not surprisingly, from Pauline Kael, who said *The Outcast* 'is not only better than any previous film drawn from Joseph Conrad's work, but also contains some of the most remarkable sequences ever filmed by the English director . . . even with its flaws, it's a brilliant work'.[1]

Reed's *The Key* (1957) with its starry cast—Sophia Loren, Trevor Howard, William Holden, Oscar Homolka—must be accounted a failure. It is difficult to accept Miss Loren, in this doom-charged film, as a sort of consolation prize for tug-boat skippers risking their lives in war. She is the centre of a story which lacks credibility, so that in this case rejection of the part is rejection of the whole.

Our Man in Havana (1959) is again a collaboration between Reed and Graham Greene and shows a return to form. A spy story set in pre-Castro Cuba, it is in the category of traditional entertainment we noted at the beginning of this chapter. Again it has a cast of unexceptionable box-office appeal—Alec Guinness, Ralph Richardson, Noel Coward, Burl Ives among them—and from the opening scenes of Guinness's arrival as the pale ineffectual spy, it perfectly renders the hot, seedy atmosphere of the novel. In fact, it retains all those qualities we have unthinkingly come to take for granted in a Carol Reed film.

Otherwise, there was no change; and no reason for change. Not since *The Stars Look Down* have his films shown any crusading spirit or commitment or interest in intellectual movements. Reed has always regarded himself as a story-teller and in this he is pre-eminently successful. When he made *Our Man in Havana* in 1959 he was one of the few British directors whose films were best-sellers all over the world and he was unlikely to show any startling change of style or viewpoint.

We left consideration of the work of Michael Powell and Emeric Pressburger with *The Small Back Room* which they produced in 1949. After this they made *The Elusive Pimpernel* (1950), 'a disaster', Powell said of it,[2] and *The Tales of Hoffman* (1951), both for Alexander Korda. The critical reception of the Offenbach film was damning, Philip Hope-Wallace, for opera, and A. V. Coton, for ballet, seeking to dispatch the two vulgarians from the cinema who had dared to invade their territory. Nor were they alone. It is seldom

263

that a major production by such a respected team receives such a mauling.

Some major talents were enlisted—Leonid Massine, Robert Helpmann, Moira Shearer, Frederick Ashton, Sir Thomas Beecham, and the Royal Philharmonic Orchestra, Hein Heckroth, who designed the sets, Dennis Arundell, who wrote the libretto. It was a constellation which, in the view of some critics, shed little light on the subject.

Paul Rotha asks whether 'this bizarre and eccentric picture is a new form of cinema—an amalgam of operatic singing, rich music, mimed ballet, cinematic animation and movie camera trickeries—or are Messrs Powell and Pressburger pulling our legs?' He advised Powell to return to the simplicities of his island film, *The Edge of the World*.

The *Spectator* praises the courage of the producer 'in attempting to employ *all* the arts and crafts together'. *The Tales of Hoffman*, viewed today, does indeed emerge as a fantastication of all the arts, but its lack of unity cannot obscure its distinct merits, a brio, an overflowing visual brilliance which sweeps it along; its musical achievement is acknowledged even by some of its severest critics.

Thorold Dickinson's *Secret People* (1951) is the story of a woman refugee, Maria Brent, who comes to London from a foreign country to stay with her daughter and father-in-law. She has been involved in revolutionary work with an old friend of hers, Louis Kelman, in her own country. Now she is caught up in an assassination plot in Soho which misfires and ends in the death of a waitress and later in her own.

Secret People has the clear-out characterisation and tight construction we find in other Dickinson films, the concern with humanity, the personal dilemma, the stricken conscience. Its theatrical treatment is manifest in the choice of Valentina Cortese as Maria and Serge Reggiani as the terrorist Louis. Audrey Hepburn as a night club dancer does not look like star material.

In 1953 Dickinson directed *Hill 24 Doesn't Answer*, produced in Israel, a rare example of the committed type of film long before the genre had made its appearance.

Dickinson had gone to Israel to advise the government on film production, but finding they were only geared to documentary, he stayed on and directed *Hill 24 Doesn't Answer*, the first film to be produced there in English. It was a highly charged political subject, half fact, half fiction, and dealt with the setting up of the Israel state and the British withdrawal. Its star was Haya Harareet, the film was shown at the Cannes Film Festival of 1955, and did well there. As a result of this outstanding success Dickinson was put in charge of the United Nations film services from 1956 to 1960.

In 1951 David Lean made *The Sound Barrier* from a script by Terence Rattigan, with Ralph Richardson, Ann Todd and Nigel Patrick in the leading parts, and in 1937 the more celebrated and contentious *The Bridge on the River Kwai*. In between came *Hobson's Choice* (1954) and *Summer Madness* (1955).

Time has somewhat blunted the lesson of *The Sound Barrier*, we are no longer so moved by the tale of lives cast away to prove a theory in aero-dynamics or to show that it is possible to get nowhere faster.

David Lean's Academy award film had a keener perception of the conventional values in such a story; it went beyond the death of pilots, the ordeals of wives, the inhumanities of science. Its real strength lay in the air, in the power of engines, in the picture it drew of dangerous machines creating lines of beauty at the speed of rockets. Lean's films, like Antonioni's, flourish on space.

The Bridge on the River Kwai (1957) had a wider relevance to human destiny, for the horrors of the Japanese war were still present in people's minds, the film had its moral basis in the conduct of war and of the individual in war. Pierre Boulle's novel, serious in intent, was a skilful mixture of popular elements. The characters are easily assimilated. Alec Guinness is the soldier with the one-track mind who thinks the bridge he is building under Japanese orders is more important than the war he is fighting. There are admirable parts for Jack Hawkins as leader of the Commandos, for William Holden as the cynical American who

265

escapes the prison camp, for Sessue Hayawaka as the camp commander.

'A good, tough film of action', said the *Spectator*, 'a credit to British film making. . . . Its conclusion—that war is madness—is not startling. What is interesting about it is that it shows up war from various points of view. . . . One ends up stimulated, wondering and confused. Heroism one cannot fail to admire, but where does it begin and where does it end?'.[3]

Arthur Knight in the American *Saturday Review* writes of 'an affecting dramatic, suspenseful motion picture', but something seems to inhibit his total acceptance of it. Pauline Kael shares the bewilderment of a number of English critics at the film's unsatisfactory ending (the blowing up of the bridge) which is never adequately explained, and this leads her to marvel at the indifference of audiences to what is really going on in a film, what Miss Kael describes as 'the destruction of the narrative sense'.[4]

Genevieve (1955), directed by Henry Cornelius, a farcical comedy of young people in a car race, is to be remembered because it caught a mood and was the unexpected hit of the year. A thing of charm and high spirits, it gave opportunities to Kenneth More and Kay Kendall in a series of cleverly contrived situations, but the writing and invention, a more difficult art, belong to the American, William Rose, who exposed the lunacies of the Englishman at play with a clear but affectionate eye.

With Michael Anderson's *The Dam Busters* (1955), commemorating Wing-Commander Guy Gibson, VC, and the destruction of the Mohne dam by the RAF, we return to the semi-documentary. The experiments with the bomb which is to destroy the dam and must be able to bounce along the water, the hazards of time and space, surpass the grimmest flights of fiction. Here there are no fine distinctions of duty or moral obligation, the parallel is rather with *Target for Tonight*, of airmen undertaking a dangerous mission in the almost certain knowledge of losing their lives.

During the next few years there is a sprinkling of war films—Asquith's fine *Orders to Kill* (1958) and Lewis

266

Gilbert's *Sink the Bismarck* (1960) are among them—but British producers mostly steer clear of war, they are feeling their way towards new themes and ideas.

Among writers discovering, or rather rediscovering, them is Wolf Mankowitz, some of whose work in fiction has been compared with that of Dickens. He began as a protégé of Korda and is represented in the fifties by *A Bespoke Overcoat* (1955), *A Kid For Two Farthings* (1956), and in 1959 by the musical film *Expresso Bongo*, which Val Guest directed.

A Kid for Two Farthings (1955) directed by Carol Reed and shown at the Cannes Film Festival, is the story of a small boy and his goat in the East End of London, of his father, a Jewish tailor, and of the richly human characters surrounding him. It had a quality of unsophisticated truth that critics approved, and when they compared it with the lush offerings of the big renters, preferred. The uniqueness of the film lay in its poetic evocation of the Jewish community in the East End.

Mankowitz has written innumerable scripts for Anglo-American production—plays, stories and documentaries, and his work shows a mastery of an astonishing variety of forms.

With Laurence Olivier's *Richard III* (1955) we are at the high point of the 1950s. It is without doubt the finest of his Shakespeare trilogy and was so adjudged by the majority of the critics. Olivier's production is a reminder how seldom we have to do with elevated themes, great characters or great issues, but are palmed off with petty domestic brawls or conventional villains treading the well-worn paths of gangsterdom and mayhem. One has to go far back in time to recall the archetypal villain such as Jew Suss or Citizen Kane, who shakes empires and passes into myth.

Though we have not concerned ourselves with the specialist film in this book, one outstanding example of it must be mentioned, namely, Halas and Batchelor's *Animal Farm* (1954). George Orwell's satire is compelling material for the cartoonist and this is the first occasion on which carica- ture is used in a British film for political ends. Considering the general indifference to social criticism in the cinema of the time, it is surprising that it was made at all, and even more surprising that it was shown. It foreshadowed the more critical attitudes which were to re-vitalise the screen in the late 1950s and 1960s. In that period great things were to be done.

Part VII

Into the 1970s

Chapter 29

New Men, New Cinema

Room at the Top (1959) is commonly spoken of as a turning point in British cinema and a forerunner of the new realism. In fact, a radical rethinking, a shift of mood and purpose are already making themselves felt in the mid-fifties.

New men were on the scene with new visions of cinema, the most influential of them being a group of actors, writers and directors from the Royal Court Theatre. They were all young men in their thirties, Tony Richardson, John Osborne, Karel Reisz, Lindsay Anderson and (working independently) John Schlesinger. They were the temporal successors to David Lean, Carol Reed, Michael Powell and others of an earlier generation.

The newcomers were on common ground in their opposition to the existing order and their resolve to challenge it, and they frequently though not invariably, chose working-class themes. When they arrived the literature of protest was in full spate, the Angry Young Men were baying from the stage of the Royal Court Theatre and John Osborne, Arnold Wesker, Alan Sillitoe, John Braine and Kingsley Amis were interpreting the mood of a prosperous and vocal working class. In 1957 Richard Hoggett's *The Uses of Literacy* was published and drew attention to the influence of the mass media, particularly newspapers and magazines, on the working class.

Of the writers who depicted working-class life Roger Manvell said: 'They were convinced that their background and speech idiom had as much right to literary and dramatic expression as those of the middle class who had been

271

dominant in both literature and theatre for long enough—or so it seemed to them.'[1]

With few exceptions directors of British films were rarely to be found championing causes or proclaiming allegiances. They did not speak publicly for they had nothing to say, and they were aware that any film of a political nature would at once be barred from the screen. Thus it had been for forty years.

This position was being radically transformed by the critical and questing spirit of the 1950s, by the militancy of the new writers and directors, and by the public itself, which recoiled in boredom or dismay from films it found increasingly devoid of meaning.

The first signs of change are already seen in the Free Cinema movement pioneered by Lindsay Anderson, Tony Richardson and Karel Reisz. The movement made statements about the human condition that were markedly personal, that laid emphasis on the individual and his environment and dealt with the pressures, corruptions and frustrations of everyday life. Free Cinema, as it happened, was anything but free, it was bound by the strongest commitment.

In 1955, on a grant from the British Film Institute, Tony Richardson and Karel Reisz made a short film, *Momma Don't Allow*, first offspring of the new movement. It is a study of a jazz club presided over by Chris Barber's band and recreates the mood and liturgy of jazz society at working-class level. It has no dialogue and yet it speaks clearly. Its touches of class-consciousness pre-figure the intense partisan-ship later to be found in films both by Richardson and Anderson.

Among the most impressive of the films made by this group is Lindsay Anderson's *Every Day Except Christmas* (1957), a documentary describing a working day at Covent Garden made for the Ford Company's *Look at Britain* series.

Here, in the words of the neo-realist, we witness 'life as it is and men as they are', the porters, the drivers, the salesmen, the buyers; the rhythm of laborious nights and rainy dawns when the produce comes in from the countryside and is sent to the shops and hotels. Walter Lassally's photography revels in the scene and produces a fragment of social history.

A year or two later, in 1958, Tony Richardson formed Woodfall Films with John Osborne, a partnership that was to have a decisive influence on English cinema. Harry Saltzman, the Canadian backer of the Beatles and James Bond films, was involved in this venture but did not stay long.

Woodfall arrives with large artistic resources based on the Royal Court Theatre and the English Stage Company. Such an array of directing, writing and acting talent had scarcely been seen under one roof since the days of Alexander Korda.

Woodfall's impact on the slumbering English movie scene was sharp, and produced a healthy intellectual turmoil, first with *Look Back In Anger*, then with such films as *The Entertainer, Saturday Night and Sunday Morning, The Knack, A Taste of Honey*. These films observe contemporary life critically or wittily but on the whole with deep misgiving; or they describe private worlds objectively and tolerantly as in *A Taste of Honey*. They created a taste and they met with a response.

Yet Woodfall's greatest success was not a contemporary subject but *Tom Jones* which reached the screen only through the intervention of United Artists after Bryanston and Columbia had turned it down. It was, they declared, too costly, an error of judgment which turned out to be costlier still, for *Tom Jones* was an unprecedented money-spinner.

Room at the Top, directed by Jack Clayton, still clung to some of the old box-office values. It was based on a bestseller, it relied on stars (Laurence Harvey and Simone Signoret) and it was made more or less regardless of cost. But at its core was a concern with human values and an honesty in expressing them which sharply differentiated it from its contemporaries. John Braine's hero, Joe Lampton, played by Laurence Harvey, is a brash Yorkshireman bent on forcing an opening for himself among the top people and becoming rich and successful. He does so, but brings about the death of one woman and tragedy to another.

273

The film made its impact by the frankness of its dialogue, the rough edges being smoothed over by the sensitive playing of Simone Signoret as the bored, wasted and seductive woman Joe falls in love with. The beating up which Joe suffers at the end was prelude to a whole crop of films in which violence is the symbol of a disintegrating society; at the same time *Room at the Top* released or helped to release a flood of sex films few of which had any serious motive.

The attention given to the film by the critics measured its importance. It was the big talking point. Penelope Houston in *Sight and Sound* analyses it at length and concludes that there is nothing great in it 'except occasionally in Simone Signoret's performance, but there is much that is vigorous, compelling and of the moment . . . it has the impact of genuine innovation; a new subject, a new setting, a new talent.'

Pauline Kael writes: 'Compared to the work of a great director like Renoir or De Sica, *Room at the Top* or *Sons and Lovers* or *Saturday Night and Sunday Morning* are a high-school girl's idea of cinema art', and she adds the characteristic death sentence: '*Room at the Top* got the worst possible reception from the American press'.[2] Her own view was on the whole favourable: 'The movie tells a story and it's absorbing and for the most part convincing in a way few American films have been.'

Roger Manvell finds in it 'a certain novelettishness belonging to an older style in British cinema (but) it had an authenticity in its sexual scenes which was new'.[3] This clamour of mixed opinion led, in England at any rate, to a great box-office success.

Clayton followed this up with an adaptation of Henry James's *Turn of the Screw* which he called *The Innocents* (1961). It stands outside the mass of contemporary cinema and shows him as a highly idiosyncratic director neither moved by fashion nor deflected by problems of adaptation, for there could hardly be material more intractable than a Henry James novel. These handicaps he mostly surmounted, but with, as it were, a divided success reflected in the divided opinions of critics.

274

Clayton, whose films are few, makes a further off-beat choice with his next film, *The Pumpkin Eater* (1964), from Penelope Mortimer's novel, a best-seller which had the advantage of a Harold Pinter script and dealt with the sexual and domestic woes of an unhappily married woman in London. It carried a sad conviction but being upper-middle-class and not working-class its reception was respectful rather than enthusiastic. The film produced a rarity for those days, a piece of emotional bravura from Ann Bancroft in the almost forgotten style of Bette Davis or Joan Crawford.

In 1967 Clayton made *Our Mother's House*, a psychological melodrama which starred Dirk Bogarde, but falls below Clayton's other work in interest.

Sons and Lovers (1960) which Jack Cardiff directed from a script by Gavin Lambert and T. E. B. Clarke, widens the field opened up by *Room at the Top* (1958). As an adaptation from the work of a writer of genius, *Sons and Lovers* should have made a greater noise in the world than *Room at the Top*, admirable though that novel is. But *Room at the Top*, with its biting modern idiom had the advantage of being a breakthrough, while *Sons and Lovers*, though smouldering with Lawrentian sex, is far less effective as narrative and in social point and relevance.

Today, the film looks innocuous enough. It is intelligently made, but it cannot, with all its intelligence, discover Lawrence's secret, which is literary and of the blood and has little to do with cinema. What it does, and quite successfully, is to capture in black-and-white the hard, unforgiving atmosphere of the coal-mines, the degrading conflicts in the Morel family which Lawrence describes, the poverty and meanness of spirit everywhere.

Trevor Howard and Wendy Hiller are strangely paired as Morel, husband and wife; Freddie Francis's photography drags beauty from the mean streets.

Stanley Kauffmann thought the film would satisfy neither the reader of the novel nor those 'who don't know or care' about it; the screen writers are 'hobbled by the book and cannot follow their best cinematic instincts'.[4] It thus becomes

275

'a series of illustrations of the novel'. Of the films which Jack Cardiff has made since, the most deserving of mention is *Young Cassidy* (1965), the story of Sean O'Casey's life; but it is tame beside Lawrence.

Tony Richardson's *Look Back in Anger* (1959), his first major film for Woodfall, did not reach the screen until three years after the stage production and by that time the passions in it had cooled and the style was becoming dated. To make it valid for the screen a number of changes were introduced. New scenes were added by John Osborne and a part written in for Edith Evans, Ma Tanner, who is only referred to in the play. Of the original cast only Mary Ure remained. The great speech, 'There aren't any good, brave causes left', was omitted. Nigel Kneale, an outstanding television dramatist, wrote the screen adaptation, Oswald Morris was the photographer, and Richard Burton and Claire Bloom added glamour to Royal Court prestige.

Interest in the film was immense but certain critics asked what all the fuss was about. The *Manchester Guardian* described it as a film with the anger diluted.[5]

'Jimmy (Porter) himself', wrote Isabel Quigly, 'no longer turns up as a surprise. At the tail of a fashion he once set, he now comes with a manner, a voice, opinions and grudges we all know too well. . . . Indeed, the angry young man, cosseted till his anger looks like petulance, has become a stock figure of our society, with its cult of the misfit, even of the gaolbird who publishes mis-spelt articles in the literary or glossy magazines'.[6]

'Customers unfamiliar with John Osborne's play may find it hard to figure out what made the original angry young man so angry', wrote Charles MacLaren,[7] a view reinforced by the *New Yorker* which found the character of Jimmy Porter insufferable, while the *Herald-Tribune* thought him 'the most unpleasant (hero) seen in a film for years'.

Yet there can be little doubt that *Look Back in Anger*, with *The Entertainer* which followed, stirred up the kind of controversy and stimulated the kind of enterprise urgently needed if our films were to hold their own against television, rock, pop, bingo and motoring.

Woodfall followed these successes with *Saturday Night and Sunday Morning*, *A Taste of Honey*, *The Knack*, *The Loneliness of the Long Distance Runner*, and *Tom Jones*. Woodfall plays a distinct and formative role in the cinema of the sixties.

The showing of *The Entertainer* was held up for three months because of disagreements with the film censor. It was given an X certificate instead of an A, thus limiting its area of release.

In the event the film provoked as much excitement as its predecessor and deep divisions of opinion on its merits. The play, it was said, lost a good deal in transition to the screen. 'For all the effectiveness of individual scenes', wrote Patrick Gibbs, 'I found the film as a whole rather remote, as if the director was attempting something after the style of Brecht's much discussed alienation'. Olivier's performance 'remains to be admired for its consistency and versatility'.[8]

'Bitter comment and romantic nostalgia, realistic dialogue in fantasy situations', Derek Prouse observed, 'with a sprinkling of topical references, fail to jell and the result is a film heading nowhere'.[9]

'A very depressing and a very good picture', Brendan Gill declared in the *New Yorker*, 'and I hope you will be brave enough to go and see it.'[10]

In *A Taste of Honey* (1961) Shelagh Delaney wrote a comedy about a Lancashire schoolgirl made pregnant by a coloured sailor who abandons her. She is befriended by a young homosexual and we are brought to a realisation of the life led by two human beings alienated from society and the frail attachments that make life possible for them. Tony Richardson, who produced the play, also produced and directed the film.

This was certainly a work of the time, bleak, realistic, built on solid kitchen-sink foundations. It had the kind of dingy truth George Orwell or Gissing dug out of their experiences but it is raised from that level by its humour and the wry wit of the writing. (Richardson also collaborated on the script.) The film brought into prominence a young actress of striking talents in Rita Tushingham and was well served by the naïvely tender performance of Melvin Murray (the homosexual), and by Dora Bryan as the tarty mother and Robert Stephens as her coarsely bright lover.

Alan Sillitoe's short story, *The Loneliness of the Long Distance Runner* (1962), which Richardson next made, pursues the theme of alienation in the story of a Borstal boy dragged into a public school and forced to train as a runner by a fanatical schoolmaster. He conceives the good life solely in terms of sport, as some people see it solely in terms of art, and bullies and harries his pupil to that end. The race is run and the runner, who could win, decides to lose. It is too slight a parable to make a really strong impact and its most effective scenes, those of bullying athleticism, are thinly spread.

Richardson then turned to *Tom Jones* (1963), the great novel which had, in a French critic's phrase, 'the march of an epic'. And, indeed, in terms of success it was epic enough and established its director as a world figure in movies. *Tom Jones*, compared with its predecessor, is as good red meat to soldier's skilly. Albert Finney's Tom is an explosion of high spirits which contrasts well with the high-stepping wit of Edith Evans, the charm of Susannah York and the vulgar humour of Hugh Griffiths.

Critical opinion was far from unanimous. Leonard Mosley saw it as a parody of parodies, a kind of *Carry On, Tom Jones*. The great novel was a sex romp.[11]

The Times has no objection to the sex element but puissantly adds: 'The only complaint that one has against this particular example is that, popular though it may be, it is just not a very good film. . . . What, then, has gone wrong?

'The basic fault is that *Tom Jones* seems from first to last . . . to be conjected, compiled almost, without the slightest signs of real gusto, real high spirits, real excitement even in the medium.'[12]

'The fact is', writes Philip Oakes, 'that in the most costly way—which squanders reputations as well as money—the film is a failure. A qualified failure, to be sure. John Osborne's screen play is properly bloody and bawdy . . . but

278

Richardson's handling of his cast is meddlesome, fitful and finicky. It could conceivably have been a breakthrough; a trail blazer for a new kind of intelligent escapism. But the chance has been bungled'.[13]

Felix Barker took a contrary view—'a glorious blend of artistry and entertainment . . . a most Hogarthian and rumbustious treat'.[14]

New York critics chose *Tom Jones* as the best film of 1963, Finney being declared the best actor and Richardson the best director.

Then after *Tom Jones* came a series of less fortunate films, the first being *The Loved One* (1965) from Evelyn Waugh's novel, which he made in Hollywood for MGM and for which nothing much can be said.

The Sailor from Gibraltar and *Mademoiselle* (both made in France in 1966) with *Red and Blue* (1967) failed to arouse any enthusiasm, yet they are far from being negligible or uninteresting. The last-named was a 35-minute film, starring Vanessa Redgrave in a story about an English cabaret singer in Paris, but it did not have much chance with the Rank theatres.

Mademoiselle, based on a scenario by Jean Genet, explored one of those perverse themes of the sixties in which evil gets the better of good and was the story of a sexually prim school teacher and her experience of love—'a half-hour anecdote', said one critic, 'blown up to feature-film proportions'.

Between 1968 and 1969 Richardson directed eleven films of which one, *The Charge of the Light Brigade*, when first shown in London, gave him the opportunity for a blistering attack on the film critics as incompetent and irresponsible. He sought to bar them from the press show. Mr Richardson's attack appeared in a letter to *The Times*. The critics replied. The publicity helped the film. In the tiny parish of the world premiere the affair made history but left film criticism exactly where it was.[15]

Chapter 30

The Changing Background— 1960s–1970s

New ideas had stirred the industry but the shape of things remained outwardly the same, the triangular structure stood firm, hermitically sealed in by the Government and the dollar. But with the decline of the old entertainment film and the rise of a more realistic cinema the prospect for the director became more attractive. Distributors, at a loss to know which way the film was going, were readier to listen to the ideas of writers and directors where before they had been guided by box-office charts and the parrot-cries of salesmen.

The large social and economic changes that had shaken the 1950s echoed into the 1960s, and these were receiving more than their usual share of attention from writers and dramatists. Pop art flourished. The Beatles sang and were compared with Beethoven. London became the centre of a swinging culture, above class; clothes were by Carnaby Street and conduct was permissive. Affluence was everywhere, but so, to a lesser extent, were poverty and crime. Crime soared into the headlines with the Great Train Robbery, the Moors Murders, and other spectacular cases. The Profumo scandal made the headlines and shook the Government. There were outbreaks of violence and anarchy and memory was still raw in the 1960s of the race riots at Notting Hill Gate in 1958.

For the cinema the permissive cult pushed back the frontiers to territory ever more violent and erotic and compelled a revision of film censorship. Until the 1939 war the function of the British Board of Film Censors had been mainly that of protecting children; the Board was the guardian of public morality, the voice of the establishment. It played safe with politics and upheld the stainless image of Britain abroad. Now the world had moved on, and the question was, for example: should Peter Watkins' film, *The War Game*, be shown, a subject commissioned by BBC Television and then banned? Should Joseph Strick's *Ulysses* be shown?

In 1953 the censor's office, concerned again for the welfare of young people, had introduced the X certificate as an alternative to the A, or adult certificate which could no longer contain the more violent and sexual cinema which had developed since the war. The 1960s carried screen permissiveness about as far as it could go and the BBFC realised that its censorship categories were badly in need of revision.

'The last decade (1960–70)', said John Trevelyan, secretary to the Board, 'has produced considerable liberalisation of censorship . . . reflecting what has appeared to be a liberalisation of public attitudes, but it has brought also a new explicitness and a vivid exploitation exceeding anything previously experienced; it has brought a sensationalism of sexual perversions of several varieties. This trend has been commercially successful so far, but it is doubtful, even so, whether it is widely acceptable'.[1]

In 1970 the Board revised its categories as follows:

Category U	Passed for general exhibition.
Category A	Passed for general exhibition but parents might prefer children under 14 years of age not to see the film.
Category AA	No persons under 14 can be admitted.
Category X	No persons under 18 years can be admitted.

The H certificate which had been devised for a time to classify Horror films was abandoned when the X certificate replaced it in 1953.

These changes reflected the more liberal policies pursued by John Trevelyan during his term of office. In a contribution to the *Society of Film and Television Arts Journal*,[2] which indicates how complex is the task of censorship, Trevelyan says: 'Violence and sex are, of course, the Board's main problem, in that order. . . . The Board was concerned with films which it felt could do actual harm and with films which it believes would give grave offence even to reasonable people.' For example, it paid particular attention to films which could affect drug-takers or stimulate sick minds. There was no proof, Trevelyan declared, that harm was caused either by screen violence or by sexual freedom, but conversely there was no proof that they did no harm 'to certain individuals'. Excessive violence could be stimulative and lead to the acceptance of violence in life as normal.

Trevelyan refers to André Glucksmann's study, *Violence on the Screen*, a painstaking survey of the evidence.[3] But Glucksmann's conclusions are hedged about with innumerable reservations and contradictions and declare finally that violence on the screen has no direct effect on behaviour.

The more liberal trend in censorship is apparent in 1966, when the BBFC issued nearly a hundred X certificates as a mark of increasing tolerance towards film producers. 'For some years', says *The Times*, reviewing the position in that year, 'production was confined to mildly pornographic rubbish and the X certificate acquired an unfortunate reputation.' After the success of *Room at the Top*, however, producers 'realised that the fresh wind already blowing through the theatre and through the literary world could be their salvation. People no longer went to "the pictures" once or twice a week as a matter of course, but an intelligent well-made film could still compete with the car and television'.[4]

That films such as *Cul de Sac*, *Night Games*, *The Family Way*, *The Marat-Sade* and *Blow Up* could be shown in the mid-sixties proves the success, or at least the breadth of the BBFC's policy. These films explored the new moralities and attitudes of the younger generation, and at the same time alienated numbers of older people whose minds were rusted up in the past. One aspect of this liberal tendency was the proliferation of film clubs in London and the provinces which were not subject to censorship. These widened the field and increased the popularity of the new productions,

282

and while some clubs dabbled in a good deal of pornography they also showed much that was original and stimulating.

In 1971 John Trevelyan retired after fourteen years as secretary to the BBFC and was succeeded by Stephen Murphy. Since 1965 Murphy had been senior programme officer with the Independent Television Authority. Some people who had been opposed to censorship of the arts in any form felt this to be the ideal moment to abandon censorship of the film altogether. But the industry thought otherwise, especially the exhibitors, and the Board was retained. Indeed there had been no serious move towards abolition. Murphy let it be known that he would pursue the same liberal policy as his predecessor, a policy which had been consistently encouraged by the leading film critics.

With changes in the cultural background went changes in audience reaction. The minority film was addressed to a livelier, younger and more discriminating audience, as faithful to cinema as the star worshippers of the Garbo-Crawford-Barrymore period.

The break-up of the mass audience proceeded quietly and was not at first seen as the revolution it undoubtedly was. The number of cinemas in 1971 was 1,553 and many were only half-filled. Showmen then realised that a small cinema full to capacity was better than a large one half empty. Hence began the radical reconstruction known as 'twinning', in which two small-sized cinemas were constructed out of a large one, or a complex of small cinemas formed a unit such as Cinecenta's multiple of four behind Leicester Square. The Empire Theatre had already, in 1962, reduced its 3,500 seats to half that number. A year or two later the Plaza gave birth to twins, so did the Saville and the Warner Theatres, and this happened all over the country. The Italian renaissance palaces of the 1930s were falling down and the mini-cinemas were springing up, and there was no shortage of films, largely continental, to supply them.

Block busters such as *The Sound of Music* and *South Pacific* which ground on for years at some obstinately super cinema were becoming a rarity. The mass audience was

283

confined to a few outposts such as the Dominion in London and such super cinemas as remained in the provinces.

In other respects the habits of the film trade still clung to it like barnacles. Nothing much had happened to change them since the Palache Report of 1944 which had rebuked 'undesirable practices in restraint of trade'. The recommendations that were to end these things were mostly swept under the carpet. Only two of importance were carried out—the ban on extensions to the Rank and ABC circuits, and the proposal of a film finance corporation, an idea that did not materialise until five years later (1949).

Twenty-two years after the Monopoly Report a more massive document came forth from the Monopolies Commission, *A Report on the Supply of Films for Exhibition in Cinemas* (1966).

This uninformative title was cover for an inquiry into every branch of the film industry and was really the same thing as the Monopoly Report. Again it called for greater competition. 'Competition is deficient', it warned, 'mainly because of the structure of the industry which results from the dominant position of ABC and Rank', to which were added the restrictive practices of the Kinematograph Renters' Society.[5]

It admitted that greater competition could be obtained by breaking up the circuits, 'but this would be a drastic step, the results of which would be uncertain'. ABC and Rank are recommended to give trial runs 'to films whose appeal to the public is in doubt'.

In 1967 the Federation of Films Unions produced yet another report. It was a review of film legislation, signed by George Elvin, the ACTT general secretary. It said of the Monopolies Commission's report that 'it merely throws a solution back to the monopolists', and it called for 'a greater British creative and financial participation in our films'. It repeated the charge that British production was dominated by the United States which produced films in Britain simply to benefit by the Eady levy. Finally, it emphasised that 70 per cent of screen time in 1967 was occupied by foreign films.

A third circuit, said the Federation, should be created to break the monopoly of ABC and Rank. This circuit, frequently proposed, was never to become a reality.

In 1968 the Cinematograph Films Council produced a report on all hitherto existing reports called a 'Review of Films Legislation', which led to a serious split in the Council's ranks. It recommended a continuation of the British Film Fund but was undecided about the quota and the future of the NFFC which had fallen on hard times and was in a state of suspended animation. A proposal for a National Film School was accepted on the understanding that it should be paid for partly by the British Film Fund and partly by the BBC and ITA.

Eight members of the Council, however, strongly opposed the report, Professor Sir Arnold Plant issuing a separate statement. The eight dissentient members went much further and described the Council's recommendations as 'not only vague or ambiguous or negative, but in many cases *a positive danger to the future of British film production*' (our italics). They demanded a reconstituted Films Council with experienced film-makers serving on it who had nothing to do with distribution or exhibition.

With so grave a split it is not surprising that the report was shelved and was soon collecting the dust which had settled on all the others.

A like sense of frustration was affecting the National Film-Finance Corporation. Through no fault of its own, it had always lost money and been saddled with debt. Now all things seemed to conspire against it. In 1969 the Corporation lost £149,239, not on production but simply in interest payments on the British Lion loan.[6] In 1970, because of trade uncertainty and the smaller number of films being made, it lost £304,786, the most promising film projects going 'automatically' to the major American companies instead of to the Corporation.

The Americans had simplified the financing of films by granting 100 per cent loans to producers for what they considered the right package. Independents found this simpler and more encouraging than the time-consuming methods of the NFFC. Now, however, with their own industry suffering a recession, the Americans were pulling out of British production and the fortunes of British film-makers were at their lowest.

It was at this moment, moreover, that the Government also decided to cut down on films. The Corporation's charter had been renewed for another ten years by the 1970 Films Act and it was empowered to borrow another £5 million for production. But a clause in the Act entitled the Department of Trade and Industry in certain circumstances to bring the corporation's activities to an end. When the Conservative Government of 1970 came to power, it did so.[7]

Discussions were held to save the NFFC from dissolution, and from these the idea was born of a consortium between the corporation and private interests. The Government were ready to advance £1 million 'on condition that the private sector will put up £3 for every £1 from public funds'—a proposal which Lord Goodman described as 'the greatest possible lunacy', since the money would have to come 'from people knowing nothing about films'.[8] So £3 million had to be found. A film made under the new arrangement would receive 50 per cent of its finance from the consortium and 50 per cent from the distributors. The new policy, of course, would be strictly commercial, though support would be given 'to films of artistic quality and technical merit'.

In the twenty years of its existence to 1969 the NFFC had financed more than 700 features and innumerable shorts, and in the five years to that date had earned £5 million in foreign currency. Among these productions were *Poor Cow*, *A Suitable Case for Treatment* and *Ulysses*, with many of like merit. The history of British film production from 1949 is to a large extent the history of the corporation.

The cost to the taxpayer (apart from the £3 million British Lion Loan) was just under £165,000 a year. That would seem cheap enough compared with the vast sums squandered or never even accounted for in ordinary commercial production. It is certain that no company riding the perilous seas of show business and expecting to keep afloat ever ventured into films with an initial debt of £3 million.

The situation of British films now was grave indeed. The twin pillars of government aid and American dollars that had sustained it for so long suddenly collapsed, leaving film producers stranded and with the prospect of having to fend for themselves.

During the time of economic vacuum when so much of promise in film-making had been brought to nothing, British Lion, which had made some 'mistaken decisions' and shown disappointing results, passed into other hands.

A series of take-over bids from within and without the film industry changed its fortunes in 1971–2. The first was from Star Associated, a prosperous entertainments complex owned by the Eckhart family of Leeds. While they were making up their minds a richer and more powerful investment company, Barclay Securities, stepped in and secured control, putting the future of Shepperton Studios in doubt. Hard upon this, however, came an offer from the City company, J. H. Vavasseur, to buy out the Barclay Securities group for £20 million, so that again a question mark hung over the studios.

These moves were of little interest to creative film men and some hundreds of technicians who saw in them merely another get-rich-quick deal made above their heads.

Launder and Gilliat and Roy Boulting withdrew from the scuffle in the summer of 1972 and the remaining directors— Lord Goodman, the chairman, Sir Max Rayne and John Boulting—resigned in January 1973, continuing to make films independently as Charter Films, the Boultings' original company. So a great chapter in British film production came to an end.

The same process that had changed the face of American film production, the take-over of creative and artistic interests by businessmen, overtook British Lion, and no one could say what the future was for film-makers or whether they had one. There were, however, some experienced film hands in the Vavasseur set up.

On the cultural front, as represented by the British Film Institute, a contrary mood of optimism prevailed. The Institute's energies in the 1960s were mainly directed to three areas: the development of the National Theatre in London, the setting up of regional theatres, and the field of experimental production.

The National Film Theatre had been established on the South Bank since 1952. Its success only made the more obvious the lack of similar facilities in other parts of the country. James Quinn, director of the Institute, had made a preliminary report to see what could be done, and his *Outside London* survey of 1966 made it clear that a regional theatre scheme would have strong support from academic and municipal bodies. The Institute could muster all the expertise for such an enterprise and went promptly to work. Nine regional theatres were set up in various cities from Brighton to Middlesborough. By 1967 they had become fifteen, the first major scheme being at Nottingham, with others at Manchester, Bradford, Sheffield and other cities.

In 1966 the John Player celebrity lectures were introduced and in 1970 a smaller theatre, NFT 2, is added to the main building. During these years the Institute owes much of its success to Miss Jennie Lee, the then Minister for the Arts, who responded to its appeals with grants of money. It is about this time, too, that we hear of further action towards a National Film School, and a committee is set up under Lord Lloyd to study the matter.

These plans did not all pass without criticism.

In 1970 some of the governors, among them Lindsay Anderson and Karel Reisz, attacked BFI policy and resigned from the board. They contended that the NFT programmes were too commercial and criticised *Sight and Sound* for taking too little interest in British films. The Institute was paying too much attention to production, and as a *Spectator* critic said, to 'trendy, over-arty ephemeral films'. *Sight and Sound* firmly rebuffed the charges.

An Action Committee did its best to unseat the whole board of governors but was overwhelmingly defeated on a postal vote. Thus the Institute overcame the most serious

288

crisis in its history. In 1971 Denis Forman succeeded Sir William Coldstream as chairman of the governors.

As if offering an example of what can be done in hard times, one department of the BFI had pursued the gentle art of filming on a shoe-string with some success, whatever attacks may have been made on it. This was the BFI Production Board. As an Experimental Film Fund under Sir Michael Balcon, it had functioned independently on a contribution from the Eady levy. By 1966 it was receiving an annual grant of £10,000 and became the British Film Institute Production Board, no longer independent but under the control of the governors.

Several of the Board's more promising films were shown publicly, among them Don Levy's full-length feature *Herostratus* (1967), Richard Saunders' *The Park* (1967) and Tony Scott's *Loving Memory* (1970) which opened the NFT 2 theatre and was also shown at the Cannes Film Festival. The finances of the Board were minimal and Saunders' other film, *Jack Pudding*, ran out of money and Production was held up for exceeding its budget.[9]

These and other events are recorded in Ivan Butler's book, *To Encourage the Art of the Film*, in which the Institute's origins, history and achievements are examined in detail, though not altogether impartially. Nevertheless it is the only full account of the BFI in a single volume and is written in the spirit of incorrigible optimism which, at this juncture, animates, and sometimes over-animates the Institute. It was a policy which put the BFI firmly on the map. In 1971 Stanley Reed, the director, resigned on account of ill health and was succeeded by Professor Keith Lucas, former head of the School of Film and Television at the Royal College of Art.

In the industry itself one of the projects which had been put forward in the late 1950s to stimulate the output of films was co-production in Europe, and this was now a very live issue in Wardour Street politics. Since the 1920s British films had been regularly produced abroad, for there were fewer restrictions and money was easier.

But now these films were more difficult to finance and more difficult to sell. Co-production was complicated by the language question and by the continuous clash of opinion between unions and employers. Yet there were great commercial advantages in it. Put in the simplest terms, a Franco-Italian production would be regarded in France as a French film and in Italy as an Italian film, each getting the commercial benefits of the partner-country. In the United Kingdom this dual nationality produced quota and levy benefits.

In 1963 the producers speak of a milestone being passed that year with the signing of the first co-production treaty with France. But this milestone turned out to be a millstone; and so it was with the Anglo-Italian treaty of 1967. Only two films, one French, one Italian, were produced in five or six years. Lack of agreement on stories and on working conditions, aggravated by old suspicions and resentments, made progress impossible and the vision of European co-operation was for the time being set aside.

Nevertheless, the producers soldiered on, convinced as ever of benefits to come, and in 1971 the British Film Producers' Association annual report refers to co-production treaties with Canada and Australia. It also notes the appointment of Mrs Gwyneth Dunwoody, former Parliamentary Secretary to the Board of Trade, as director of the producers' association.

In that year too the government-sponsored National Film School was opened under the direction of Professor Colin Young from the University of California, and a new phase began in the education of Britain's potential film-makers. Professor Young's reported intention was for 'an open-minded, undogmatic, socially responsible (school) closely connected with contemporary life'. A first batch of twenty-five students was enrolled to carry out this policy.

It is perhaps time to consider some of the industry's films which were already moving in this direction in the 1960s.

Chapter 31

The Director as Super-Star

After thirty or forty years the director is coming into his own and seemingly has full control of his medium. But has he? For the greater part of the cinema's history he has been a more or less gifted hack required only to put a story on the screen. Now his involvement is deeper, his knowledge wider, he is likely to be writer and director, or director and producer both, conceivably all three. As *auteur*, or sole begetter of the film, he lends himself to academic discussion in Europe and America. He enjoys a prestige comparable to that of his contemporary, the stage director, at this moment in theatrical history the super-star upon whom all, or most depends.

Yet the experience of film directors is still scarred with the old disillusionments. The art and the business are really as far apart as ever; they size each other up like prize fighters and are soon in head-on collision.

In France the film has undergone an extraordinary metamorphosis at the hands of Luc-Godard, Resnais, Truffaut and the critics of *Cahiers du Cinéma*. Conventions of plot and construction are cast aside, new techniques fabricated, the instant, the casual, the improvised; the youthful, the mad, the poetic; jump cuts, freezes, split screens—all are enlisted. In England there is a keen awareness of these innovations which are received with caution as a *nouveau vague* soon likely to exhaust itself.[1]

The American film, rethinking its terms of reference and clinging largely to well-tried formulas, adjusts to the new writing and the changed behaviour patterns. So we find a mixed programme of traditional and avant-garde films.

Unfamiliar names crop up—John Cassavetes, Shirley Clarke, Joseph Strick. From these and the old movie-makers a confident stream of films gushes forth in the early 1960s: *The Connection* (Shirley Clarke), *The Apartment* (Billy Wilder), *Psycho* (Alfred Hitchcock), *West Side Story* (Robert Wise), *The Man Who Shot Liberty Valance* (John Ford), *The Manchurian Candidate* (John Frankenheimer), *Dr Strangelove* (Stanley Kubrick), *The Balcony* (Joseph Strick) and *My Fair Lady* (George Cukor). Some of these such as *The Connection* and *The Balcony* break new ground. But these new waves, Roger Manvell warns us, 'are strictly for the cults'.[2] They are nevertheless a prelude to a cinema reflecting a steadily disintegrating society.

John Schlesinger

With John Schlesinger the whole permissive scene of the 1960s comes into focus. Schlesinger, born in 1926, began his career as a director of television documentaries, *Terminus*, which he made in 1961 for British Transport Films, being much praised and a prize-winner.

His first full-length feature, *A Kind of Loving* (1962), adapted from Stan Barstow's novel by Keith Waterhouse and Willis Hall, is a North country story about a young draughtsman and his misbegotten love for a girl at the office (parts played by Alan Bates and June Ritchie). She is trapped in digs with a possessive mother-in-law (Thora Hird) and lives a life of betrayed hopes and unprivate joy. Today the pace of this film, at least for the first half, seems intolerably slow but it has some fine moments and it is honest. Stanley Kauffmann notes that 'the British have taken a somewhat longer time than the rest of the Western world to admit the working man as a protagonist in art'. Having done so, he adds, they are in danger of 'getting drunk on drabness'.[3]

The film has one or two incidents (for that time) of shock humour (like the visit to the chemist for contraceptives) and is put together with great competence by Keith Waterhouse and Willis Hall. It reveals the sharp impressionistic style Schlesinger is to develop later. But its fault is that it is too like *Room at the Top* and *Saturday Night and Sunday Morning*. 'If it had had the candour to say so, its real theme is not social discontent . . . but the misogyny that has been simmering under the surface of half the interesting plays and films in England since 1956.'[4]

Billy Liar (1963), from a novel and play by the same writing team, observes the hostile world with the eye of fantasy, the young undertaker's clerk (Tom Courtenay) working out his frustrations by calculated lies or in hallucinatory visions of power and success.

Darling (1965) comes in for rougher treatment. It is about the sex life, including an abortion, of a young girl, Julie Christie, model, movie-actress and wife, who is too shallow to have any identity. It is a fun film with undertones faintly derisive of those involved. 'It seems to hark back', says Penelope Houston, 'to those distant days of the television satire industry . . . when it was impossible to open a newspaper without encountering a story about Christine Keeler.* The film's cynicism, its assumptions, the things it is interested in and the points it wants to make, give one the feeling of reading over files of old gossip columns. . . . It has all the snap and crackle of the cornflakes advertisement.'[5]

Clearly this was a genre without much future for Schlesinger, who decided to abandon the flip style for more substantial themes. He chose *Far from the Madding Crowd* (1967), an ambitious but as it happened unfortunate choice, for although it was a film of tremendous good looks it had very little else. Neither Julie Christie's Bathsheba nor Peter Finch's Boldwood were fully realised figures, nor did the brooding thickly-plotted melodrama emerge; it was Wessex without Hardy's thunder.

Schlesinger's next film *Midnight Cowboy* (1969) was as startling a contrast as his choice of Hardy. Though not a British film it is included here as an inseparable phase of his development, and, as it happened, his first big international success.

He selects New York as the setting for a story commenting on the gross materialism and the divided soul of America.

* Miss Keeler was involved in a scandal with a Cabinet Minister.

293

A handsome young kitchen-hand from Texas comes to the big city to try his luck with the rich sex-starved women there. He picks up a strange down-at-heels companion, Ratso (Dustin Hoffman), who strikes up an oddly touching friendship with him and leads Voight into some hilarious and sordid adventures.

Schlesinger has by now matured and refined his style which scores equally on the levels of wit and compassion. The call-girl Voight meets coming out of the hotel evokes a brilliantly witty scene, but his murderous encounter with the elderly pervert seems a gratuitous act of violence. It is nevertheless a film of many strengths and pleasures.

Its reception was overwhelmingly cordial. 'Far in advance of anything he (Schlesinger) has done over here', said John Russell Taylor in *The Times*. 'Compared with *Billy Liar* how much more assured is the handling. . .' If the sentimentality at the end is hard to take, 'the film never loses a certain saving acerbity, a sharp eye for the realities of life even within a fantasy situation'.[6] Derek Prouse, while not uncritical, finds it a very considerable . . . a new achievement, the more so as Schlesinger is working in a new locale.

As for its more vicious scenes, at this stage of movie history displays of sado-masochistic violence are common form and part of the message. But such scenes need the endistancing, the perspective, in other words the poetry which in this instance is lacking.

Sunday, Bloody Sunday (1971) has the advantage of a script by Penelope Gilliat, its excellences are clearly the result of a sympathetic collaboration between writer and director.

The young artist's (Murray Head's) two-sided love affair with a Jewish doctor (Peter Finch) and a disorientated career woman (Glenda Jackson) reflects the same anxious but fond disorder we find in Losey's *Accident*. The pangs of homosexual love and heterosexual love are bitterly but kindly observed. But here there is no violence, events move within a framework of restraint. It is a film of manners as well as of morals and this gives it an uncommon distinction.

John Coleman makes the point that the film is about 'the absence of certainty, about the way some of us live, perhaps, considering its homosexuality, an "us" as opposed to a "them" movie? . . . The film says, not that we must love one another and/or die, but that we ought to accommodate the difficulties of our own life . . . make the best of our own confusions'. The film 'keeps its cool under stress . . . its method is the mask of art'.[7]

Joseph Losey

Joseph Losey, an American, born in 1909, spent his early years in the theatre where he came under the influence of Brecht. He directed *Galileo* with Charles Laughton. He was among the first batch of Hollywood directors to be black-listed by McCarthy, an experience he has described as 'absolutely terrifying'.

It is chastening to read in Tom Milne's book, *Losey on Losey*, of the pressures brought to bear on directors at that time, 'an almost physical thing', Losey declares. 'What was so terrifying about the atmosphere was seeing people succumb, and seeing all protest disappear. Because if you did protest, you'd had it; if you were a university professor, or anybody, who dared to speak out, if you dared to say or do anything, it was the end.'[8]

Losey had attended Marxist study groups, had joined with Brecht in Washington in active protest, and in 1948 was directing for Adrian Scott, producer of Losey's first feature, *The Boy with Green Hair* (1948). Scott was soon axed for his un-American activities. Losey made a number of films under increasingly bleak circumstances and after directing *Big Night* in 1951 he came to England and sought a new identity and career.

'His films, both American and English, are almost entirely concerned either with violence in modern society or with difficult sexual relationships, sometimes with both', says Roger Manvell.[9]

The account given here is confined to his films in England since 1959.*

---

* Losey's last Hollywood film was *The Big Night* in 1951, followed, in England, by *Stranger on the Prowl* (1952), *The Sleeping Tiger* (1954), *Intimate Stranger* (1956), *Time Without Pity* (1957), *The Gypsy and the Gentleman*

Blind Date (1959), from a story by Leigh Howard, was evidently a rush job, though a Losey film, whatever its shortcomings, is never negligible. *The Criminal* (1960) an examination of prison life, shows Losey's continuing concern with man and his environment, in this instance a gambler sent to gaol (Stanley Baker), and his treatment at the hands of society, the members of that society being no less criminal, perhaps, than he is.

The Damned (1962), is a far more assured film and is a story of the Teddy boys of the 1950s viewed from a town in the West country. Losey fixes his Teds and their girl friends with an objective eye but his social pre-occupations frequently surrender to sheer love of action and the fascination the English scene has for him.

These films, made under difficulties, did little to advance Losey's reputation and they seem to have received at the time, too little critical attention. It is not until we come to *The Servant* (1963), from Robin Maugham's novel, that his outstanding merits as a director are appreciated.

The script, by Harold Pinter, taut and brooding, is well adapted to a tale of the corrupting relationship of master and servant (William Fox and Dirk Bogarde) and the ambivalent sex interplay in which two young women (Sarah Miles and Wendy Craig) are entangled with the men.

Harold Pinter must share the honours of the film with Losey, who could not have hoped for a more flattering press than it received—'flawless', 'masterpiece', 'brilliant', 'profound'—and Losey's slowly maturing fame took a leap forward.

His detestation of wars and of man betrayed or exploited by his fellow men led him by a process of natural selection to *King and Country* (1964), again with Dirk Bogarde whose reputation is rising fast. In this story, with its Kafka-like overtones, mindless forces seem to bear down on the luckless Private Hamp (Tom Courtenay) who walks away from the front in war-time because he can't take it any more. He is

(1957), *Blind Date* (1959), *The Criminal* (1960), *The Damned* (1962), *Eve* (1962), *The Servant* (1963), *King and Country* (1964), *Modesty Blaise* (1966), *Accident* (1967), *Boom* (1968), *Secret Ceremony* (1968), *The Go-Between* (1971).

court-martialled and shot in a scene of chilling horror. This time the critics were less impressed, though the film has enduring qualities, indeed some great moments.

Modesty Blaise (1966), a film not of Losey's choice, followed in 1966, and in 1967 *Accident*, again with a script by Harold Pinter. It shows the influence of Resnais and is a superb study of an in-grown order of academics at Oxford.

There is a car smash, a man is killed, but his girl companion, a student, survives unhurt. What led to the smash is then told in a long flashback of cross-relationships— devious, secret, sexual—but ever present in the minds of the protagonists.

The girl who survived the crash, an Austrian (Jacqueline Sassard), throws into confusion the lives of three Oxford men, two of them tutors, the third an upper-class undergraduate.

It is a subtle, powerful and visually exciting work, revealing Losey in possession of gifts he has laboured long to make perfect. Again praise of the film is general and especially of Stanley Baker's remarkable performance as one of the tutors.

Boom (1968), from a Tennessee Williams play, is a wildly fanciful legend of love and death staged in a dazzling white marble villa in the Mediterranean, which was built specially for the occasion. It was, they said, cheaper. The extravagance of its decor enclosing the nightmare figures of Elizabeth Taylor, Richard Burton and Noel Coward is visually entertaining but the tale told seems hardly worth so much talent.

Secret Ceremony (1968), described by Pauline Kael as 'a Gothic version of "folie a deux"—truly terrible', gives Elizabeth Taylor the part of a prostitute. She has lost a child of her own and is involved in a Freudian fantasy with Mia Farrow, who claims to be her daughter.

Losey then turned from this intellectual moonshine to *Figures in a Landscape* (1970), concerning a pair of ex-soldiers hunted to death by the pilot of an army helicopter. It is a parable of man at zero investigating the destructive world he has created for himself. Losey uses a film of action to explore an ambiguous contemporary theme.

These films provide an unexpected prelude to Losey's

most poetic and most English work, *The Go-Between* (1971) from L. P. Hartley's novel. The strength of the film, as most critics could not fail to point out, was in its lyrical evocation of the English countryside at the turn of the century.

Yet all the skill of Harold Pinter's script cannot conceal the basic unreality of this story about a boy used as a messenger between the high-born daughter of the house ((Julie Christie) and the muscular farmer (Alan Bates) who is her secret lover.

The *New Statesman* critic considered *The Go-Between* (and *Death in Venice*) two of the most over-rated films of the year,[10] but this was one of the few discords in the choirs of praise.

'To me', said Patrick Gibbs, 'the period picture is so persuasive and so beautifully composed that I never tired of the round of croquet games, picnics, swimming parties and country visits in which a splendidly stately . . . old house, dating, it looks to me, from the late eighteenth century, is seldom out of sight'.[11]

This summoning up of Edwardian England, like pages from a book of Golden Hours, gave *The Go-Between* its quality of truth. The sense of place, so compelling in a Losey film, made up for some of the deficiencies of character in the novel. A film made with such art is rare enough in British cinema, its faults throw into relief its qualities.

*Peter Brook**

Peter Brook's position in the cinema is not easy to define. The films he has made do not readily identify him as a film director in the sense we understand it when speaking, say, of Carol Reed or John Schlesinger or Bryan Forbes. For one thing, most of his films have appeared at infrequent intervals varying with other commitments, plays, operas, festivals and cultural journeys to the ends of the earth. This waywardness hinders reputation in the world of repeated sensation which is cinema. Continuity is lacking. For another thing, Brook's fabled achievements in the theatre tower above

* I am indebted to J. C. Trewin's biography, *Peter Brook*, for information relating to him in this chapter.

his films and tend to diminish them. The question is asked: Is he film or is he theatre? Absurd question, for he is both. Yet audiences and the great men in Wardour Street like to stick labels on their favourites, they must be one thing or the other. Judged by these criteria Brook's case is parlous indeed.

Moreover, he prefers always the difficult to the easy way and he passes on the difficulty to his always astounded audience. They respond with joy and excitement in the theatre, but less exultantly in the cinema. Because he falls into no category but his own it is difficult to find a parallel to his work in that of any other director. Perhaps the nearest in purpose if not in method is Lindsay Anderson, as deeply involved in theatre as in film and sharing with Peter Brook the mood of social and cultural protest.

By an irony scarcely noticed in the clamour of show business, the two feature films Lindsay Anderson made established him as a film director of world fame while the seven films Brook made have failed to do so.

How are we to account for this?

Setting aside such manifest propaganda pieces as *Tell Me Lies*, Brook seems deliberately to choose subjects of esoteric or intellectual interest, his cinema has a specific appeal to the egghead minority and not always to them. Anderson, on the other hand, selects themes of humanity or protest presented in striking physical forms but always broad enough in appeal to reach a mass audience. Brook has still to widen his appeal to that audience (assuming he seeks it) to create for film the taste he has created for his own kind of revivifying drama.

Brook's conception of cinema springs directly from the theatre he has pioneered and is an extension of the ideas and beliefs set forth in his book, *The Empty Space*.

That revolutionary handbook asserts the need for a new life-enhancing drama to replace 'the deadly theatre' sanctified by an effete middle class for generations. Brook wanted a miracle and by his genius he achieved one, indeed a number of miracles. Could he now do the same for the cinema?

'And vex the heels of all the yesterdays?'

Peter Brook was born in London in 1925 of Russian parents, and in 1944, while still at Oxford, directed his first amateur film, Sterne's *Sentimental Journey.* It was noticed by C. A. Lejeune in the *Observer,* not unfavourably. A year later at the age of 20 he is directing Cocteau's *The Infernal Machine* and in the immediately succeeding years Shakespeare and Shaw and plays and operas innumerable. These occupy him until the 1950s.

He then turned to films and directed *The Beggar's Opera* (1953), *Moderato Cantabile* (1960), *Lord of the Flies* (1963), *The Marat-Sade* (1967), *Tell Me Lies* (1968) and *King Lear* (1971).

The Beggar's Opera, in which he is associated with Laurence Olivier, got off to a bad start. Brook wanted to shoot it in black and white, the producers wanted it in colour. There were serious back-stage disagreements and when the film was screened, Olivier as Macheath was said not to have a voice.

Raymond Durgnat observes of the opera: 'All the ingredients abound for a glorious gallimaufry of Gainsborough melodrama (highwaymen, hangings, tarts and sluts. . .).'[12] Brook was of all people the least likely to produce a Gainsborough melodrama. But his own style of camera work, in this case rapid and pointed, the designs of Georges Wakhevitch, the songs of Christopher Fry, the script by Denis Cannan, failed to yield up a satisfying film. J. C. Trewin tells us that it 'did leave an impression curiously faint', and that it cost £250,000.

Brook did not make another film for seven years when he directed Jeanne Moreau in a story by Margaret Duras and Gerard Jarlot, *Moderato Cantabile.* The love affair of a married woman and a man employed by her husband is mysteriously set in motion by the murder of a third person. Brook attempts to pierce the surface of this unique experience and expose the reality; he strives to pin down the thought, the passion of the lovers with Proustian exactitude. It did not enthral the critics who sat on their high horses and looked down sorrowfully and the film got no further on release than a cult piece in a suburban film club. Peter

300

Brook himself 'liked it more than anything he had done', and he explains his treatment of it with his usual lucidity.

'We take out everything that dramatises the story', he writes. 'We take away the element of narrative. We avoid big scenes in the dramatic sense, and avoid underlining and pointing anything, avoid anything in the camera work, in the movement of the camera, the lighting, the music and the cutting that might dramatise it; eventually one has done a process of total elimination.'

In this technique of avoidance what is left?

'Character, mood, idea, conflict and emotion.'

This is Brook's cinema, as radical, unorthodox and unpredictable as Luc-Godard's but without Godard's flowing and masterful movement, his enchantment and surprise. Brook pursues the unattainable; if the prospect before him contains no challenge or is within reach, it is of no interest to him. But this is often a poor prospect for the filmgoer, and for Brook himself *Moderato Cantabile* did little to add to his reputation.

Again, in 1963, he chose as intractable a subject as could be found in William Golding's allegorical novel, *Lord of the Flies*, from a script by Peter Shaffer. The film was shown at the Cannes Film Festival, after which it took a year to reach London.

Richard Roud, reviewing it in the *Guardian*, recognises that men like Brook are badly needed in British films, is at pains to encourage him, but is inhibited by the work itself 'On the simplest of levels', he declares, '*Lord of the Flies* is a failure; one just does not believe it. Golding's novel about a group of boys marooned on an island and their gradual reversion to savagery is—or seemed at the time—an extremely powerful allegory. But allegory is the hardest of forms for the cinema to achieve.'[13]

It was made harder still in this case because Brook had finally to drop Peter Shaffer's script, which he regretted having to do, but it would have needed a film six hours long. There were other scripts, nine in number, but in the end Brook improvised from the novel, a characteristic act of defiance in circumstances of superhuman difficulty.

The broad critical view is that William Golding's novel is more or less unfilmable and by boys of 12 and 14 unactable. The miracle wrought in the theatre when directed to the screen does not work, the subtleties of the novel are not translatable in visual terms. Brook's visual terms are his own and in most of his film we are all too conscious of them for comfort. He rejects the notion urged by some critics that he is theatrical and that he fails to give his camera mobility. And indeed what is wrong with the theatrical in cinema? The cinema feeds on what it needs.

However, even that extraordinarily powerful and disturbing work, *Marat Sade*,* 'a film of the play as Weiss wrote it',[14] exhibiting Brook's virtuosity at full stretch, does not do much better and receives the kind of criticism which withholds outright praise and loads itself with ifs and buts. It received 'an almost universally hostile reception', said *Sight and Sound*, 'mainly on the grounds of theatricality'.[15] Yet it leaves a disturbing and ineffaceable impression.

Tell Me Lies is based on the stage production of Brook's *U.S.* It is the most personal and deeply felt of his films, a cry of rage against Vietnam. But it is a hurried piece of work (this appears to have been inevitable), it is weakened by excess and by too many blows from the sledge-hammer. In short, it lacks art.

King Lear, made in Denmark and raised to a sombre nobility by Paul Scofield's king, receives respectful but not excited appraisal by the critics. As with all Brook's work, they acknowledge a master but as clearly they realise something is missing.

David Robinson, writing of Lear, says: 'Yet it seems always characteristic of his (Brook's) films, in contrast with his stage work, that at the last moment he loses his nerve, loses confidence in his material, and feels the compunction aggressively to assert a "cinematographic" personality and style. . . . In Lear he has correctly identified a disjointed and staccato quality; but he has incautiously emphasised it

* Its full title is *Marat Sade: the persecution and murder of Marat as performed by the inmates of the asylum of Charenton under the direction of the Marquis de Sade.*

not only with passages of epileptic camerawork and a violent mannerist cutting with which he disjoins the phrases of soliloquies. He has also chosen to cut out lines and, most peculiarly, individual words . . . the play and Schofield's performance too seem obscured behind all the cinemato-graphic devices and effects.'[16]

All this, he adds, is the more frustrating since there are marvellous moments, fine insights.

Our cinema is not over-gifted with either genius or idealism but could do with an infusion of both, and these qualities are embodied in the work of Peter Brook. Whether con-ditions call for as marked a change in film as *The Empty Space* calls for in the theatre is doubtful, for the film has staged its own revolution and is not stultified by bourgeois tradition.

Lindsay Anderson

Lindsay Anderson is that rare phenomenon in films, the wholly political animal. He addresses himself exclusively to the social scene. As critic and propagandist, as director of films and plays, he is of one piece, of single vision, breathing revolutionary fire. That he is no dreamer of abstractions may be inferred from a reading of his book, *Making a Film* (1952), a masterly factual report from the studio floor that describes the day-to-day making of Thorold Dickinson's *Secret People*.

Anderson was born in India in 1923, went to Cheltenham College and then to Oxford, and directed his first short film, *Meet the Pioneers*, as an amateur in 1948. It was a docu-mentary about conveyor belts. He was already writing about films while still an undergraduate, helping to edit the critical film magazine, *Sequence*, with Gavin Lambert and Peter Ericcson. In the succeeding years on small means or none he made a number of short films for various sponsors, such as *Wakefield Express* and *Thursday's Children* about the Royal School for the Deaf at Margate, examples of the Free Cinema movement he pioneered with Tony Richardson and others.

It is not until 1963 that we hear of his first feature film, *This Sporting Life*, which followed a series of plays he had

303

directed for the Royal Court Theatre; it is another five years before he makes his second feature, *If.* . . . This time-consuming interval in Anderson's career, however usefully employed, is due as much to his uncompromising nature as to the failure of the industry to recognise an extraordinary talent.

This Sporting Life (1963) is based on the novel by David Storey and describes the career of a young Yorkshire miner (Albert Finney) and his love affair with a widow older than himself (Rachel Roberts), and his own vulgarly posh life as a football star. The miner's love, forced without understanding on the widow, shatters her personality and she dies of a brain haemorrhage. It is one of those studies of failure to communicate, of irresponsibility, of false and wounding relationships which become almost a commonplace in the sociological cinema of the sixties.

Anderson was able to find precisely the style of direction needed for this theme, dynamic and intimate, much of it in close-up, especially the fine rugger sequences. It was in every way an astonishing performance for a director making his first feature film, though critics were apt to overlook his long labours in documentary and television.

The *Guardian* critic, unimpressed, speaks of the film's 'new wave pretentiousness and cliché-ridden script and direction'.[17]

Penelope Gilliat takes a directly opposite view and considers the film a stupendous achievement. 'It has a blow like a fist. I've never seen an English picture that gave such expression to the violence and the capacity for pain that there is in the English character.'[18]

Stanley Kauffmann comes nearer to defining Anderson's intentions when he says 'we get a sense of sport as microcosm, less a game than raw antagonism, and outlet for energy and hate and frustration that society no longer provides elsewhere'.[19]

That view prepares us for the much more concentrated outburst of hate and destructiveness to be found in *If.* . . (1968). *If.* . . describes a murderous rebellion organised by three boys at an English public school. It is not, says

304

Anderson, an attack on the public school system, it is a metaphor for a much wider evil which the public school system promotes and preserves. Or again it may be viewed as a fantasy; each must interpret the film in his own way.

The ambiguity is therefore deliberate and the school's sado-masochistic rituals of caning and torture, the fantasies of sex, the nude headmaster's wife, the slaughter on Speech Day—these are the elements of a dream, a nightmare, a vision. Alternatively, it is from end to end a piece of nonsense put together with unnecessary art.

'One-sided . . . very close to the borders of Fascism', said the BBC critics. Dilys Powell goes at once to the meaning: 'It is not just about an imaginary public school. It is about the rigid ideas and the authoritarian society which Mr Anderson and his collaborators see rooted in a public school.'[20] Penelope Mortimer describes *If . . .* as Anderson's master work. 'Everyone has taken a tremendous risk and a tremendous artistic success has been achieved.'[21]

Pauline Kael, making a comparison between *If . . .* and Vigo's *Zero for Conduct* observes: 'When *Zero for Conduct* was attacked in France as violent, perverse, and obscene, there was no doubt that, as André Bazin said, "for Vigo the school is nothing less than society itself". Anderson's model for *If . . .* is a key film both aesthetically and politically, and Anderson's school, following the same plan, seems meant as a mirror of society, and his conscious aim in all that stuff about rigidity and sadism and the rot of the upper classes seems to be to demonstrate that our society drives us to violence as the only solution—that it is only the pure act that can come out of all this. Anderson's adults are grotesques, but, unlike Vigo's, they are presented literally and may even be intended to be taken realistically as proof of the effects of stultifying traditions.

'They will probably be taken by most adults in the audience as evidence of conditions that must be improved, and by at least some students as evidence that the only thing to do is to blow everyone up—after all, killing them isn't like killing real people, because they don't seem to have any honest emotions."[22]

What then, if we choose to interpret the film as reality? The school is destroyed, parents and staff murdered, violence is celebrated; waste and vacuum remain.

Anderson's own clearly expressed intention is that of metaphor. But it is metaphor with an explosivs charge.

'The film is, I think, deeply anarchistic', he says. 'People persistently misunderstand the term anarchistic, and think it just means wildly chucking bombs about, but anarchy is a social and political philosophy which now puts the highest value on responsibility. The notion of someone who wants to change the world is not the notion of an irresponsible person.'[23]

Ken Russell

Ken Russell, born in 1927, is of the increasing number who learned their trade in television, and we first hear of him in connection with the BBC 2 programmes of the 1960s. He had been directing a number of ten-minute films about the arts since 1959, including some for Huw Weldon in the *Monitor* series. From here he moved on to longer documentaries—on the dance craze, on the guitar, on pop art, on the ballet, on a variety of things—as a result of which he was asked to produce some full-length studies of great artists of the last century.

It was these biographies, chiefly of composers, which drew attention to a director with a startlingly fresh approach and with the ability to give new life to a genre already becoming atrophied. He has little use for the formal biography or hushed tribute but looks for what lies behind it, and as in other investigations of the Victorian cupboard, the skeletons produced are often surprising. Indeed, his work for the BBC displayed a unique gift for sparking off controversy.

In films Russell seems equally determined to shock and scandalise, but this, though he gives it a greater emphasis, is in the prevailing mood. As a director he cultivates the big dramatic effect and, like Fellini, floods the screen with erotic imagery and incessant visual fireworks. His work always shows a definite point of view and his phenomenal technical mastery is obvious.

Between 1961 and 1970 he made television biographies of Prokofiev, Elgar, Bartok, Debussy, Delius and Richard Strauss. In between he made a full-length comedy film, *French Dressing* (1964), and the Len Deighton spy story, *Billion Dollar Brain* (1967). He is always commuting between the small and the big screen. When *Billion Dollar Brain* failed he went back to do the portrait of Delius and after that returned to films to make *Women in Love*.

It was his biography of Richard Strauss that raised a storm, chiefly because it denounced the composer as a man of influence in Germany who could have stood up to the Nazis, and perhaps even helped to change the course of events, but failed to do so. Public clamour over this programme rose to such heights that questions were asked about it in Parliament, an absurdity that only added to Russell's prestige. In an American interview he had described current television biography as being 'filled with terrible clichés', 'Deification of an artist', he declared, 'is wrong, he should be presented as a human being who, despite his faults, manages to create lasting works of art.'[24]

It is in the light of these events that we must consider Russell's first notable film production, *Women In Love* (1969).

D. H. Lawrence's novel, produced and adapted by Larry Kramer, is basically the story of two sisters, Gudrun and Ursula, in the Midlands, and their relationship with Gerald Crich, the aristocrat and Rupert Birkin, the teacher. The two men are also seen in a parallel intimacy which moves towards a never quite explicit homosexuality. Through the exploration of these loves Lawrence develops his metaphysic of sex but his final meaning is left obscure.

The proposal to film *Women in Love* was bitterly attacked by Dr Leavis, who declared that it was 'an obscene undertaking to "write it again" for the screen. . . . No one', he declared, 'who had any inkling of the kind of *thing* the novel is or how the "significance" of a great work of literature is conveyed, or what kind of thing "significance" is, could lend himself to such an outrage. Great writers, even when they're dead, ought to be protected.'

This could well have influenced subsequent criticism,

307

which ranged from the cautious or indifferent to the total rave, but on the whole was enthusiastic. Patrick Gibbs, after a closely reasoned analysis, finds the film merely pleasant. 'What is left is a pleasant enough period piece, often very well acted, tracing one not very remarkable pair of lovers who marry and another whose affair ends tragically with death in the Alpine snows. Pleasant?—the word gives everything away. There's something here of his people, plot and scene, but very little of D. H. Lawrence.'[25]

This view is echoed in *Sight and Sound* which considers Larry Kramer has made a film '*about* the novel, rather than of it', and that it will offend many Lawrentians.[26] David Robinson regards the film as 'an interpretation rather than a translation of the novel; and I think you have to be a committed Lawrentian properly to judge it as such'.[27]

John Russell Taylor, confessedly anti-Lawrence, comments: 'Lawrence was determined in *Women In Love* to have his say on the obsessive subject of man, woman, and the quest for "the ultimate sensual experience" and cared little if the result might seem merely absurd to those not on his wave-length. . . . Mr Russell rushes at his subject in exactly the same wholehearted way, sparing us nothing, and he goes on to describe the naked roamings through the dewy woods, etc. . . . The result is ludicrous, but really rather likeable.'[28]

The only approval unreservedly given is that for the players, Glenda Jackson's Gudrun, who received the Actress of the Year Award from the New York critics, and Jennie Linden's Ursula; and again for Alan Bates as Birkin and Oliver Reed as Crich (though physically they bear little resemblance to Lawrence's originals).

Russell's love of theatricality and excess was suited to the fevered dialogue and exalted sensuality of the novel (typified by the famous naked wrestling match between the two men). Much was made of this by the press and the public interest was prodigious.

After such a triumph one would suppose Russell free to film what he chose and he resolved on a return to his biographical manner. This was *The Music Lovers* (1971), based on the life of Tchaikovsky. The screenplay was by Melvyn Bragg.

Tchaikovsky (Richard Chamberlain) is presented as a tormented genius doomed to encompass his own destruction. A homosexual, his attachment to Count Chiluvsky, with its hint of scandal, becomes a menace to his career and he rushes into marriage with the immature and neurotic Nina Milukova in the hope of settling down. But his work has suffered, he has developed a hatred of all physical involvement and his failure to consummate the marriage drives Nina insane. She ends her life in a lunatic asylum and Tchaikovsky kills himself by drinking poisoned water.

Russell punctuates his narrative with intervals, turbulent or peaceful, in which we see the composer at work and the famous symphonies act as counterpoint to stormy or lyrical moments. We see also his relations with his patron, Madame von Meek, and his sister, Sasha and go-getting brother, Modeste.

Though severely handled by some critics, *The Music Lovers* pleased all but the most tone-deaf to its appeal. 'A grotesque "life" of Tschaikovsky, in almost every particular, the film is an insult.'[29] 'Tschaikovsky has been made the excuse for a crude melodrama about sex', said the BFI's *Monthly Bulletin*.[30] 'The sad thing is that behind it all lurks an exuberance, an enjoyment in the sheer act of film-making which many of our more sober directors lack.' Sad indeed, for this provided most of the entertainment. 'A mixture of semi-truths and fanciful conjecture on the lines of Russell's now infamous Strauss biography', said *Sight and Sound*.[31]

Christopher Hudson, recalling Russell's fondness for rococo excess, says: 'As it happens, Tschaikovsky's life was sufficiently extravagant and melodramatic to be enhanced, not distorted, by this approach.' He condemns the 'slow-motion romps through woodland' and the stripping scene in the railway carriage when Nina tries to force her husband's interest. 'This scene is as repellent as it was meant to be, and seems unfair to Nine, not to mention Glenda Jackson, the actress.'[32] But on the whole the writer approves.

If anyone supposed that the objections raised to *The*

Music Lovers would in any way influence Russell's style they were quickly undeceived, for *The Devils* (1971) seemed simply to write larger all the excesses of its predecessor.

The film had an impeccable provenance, being derived from a play by John Whiting based on Aldous Huxley's *The Devils of Loudon*, set in seventeenth-century provincial France. The central character is Urbain Grandier (Oliver Reed), a lecherous priest adored by the hunch-backed Prioress of the convent (Vanessa Redgrave) whom he never sees.

The Prioress's frustrations and sexual fantasies are shared by the nuns and attributed to possession by the Devil, and in a series of obscene rituals they are ordered to be exorcised. The priest is denounced, tortured, and burned alive, and the walls of Loudon destroyed.

Russell makes the most of the burnings, executions, flagellations, blasphemies, and the nude gambollings of the nuns which are sometimes carried to absurdity. The critical reaction was predictably one of abhorrence.

'A hymn to sado-masochism. It is vulgar, camp and hysterical. His (Russell's) camera gloats and dwells and if the effect is pornographic, it's because, as with all pornography, we don't care what happens to anyone.'[33] 'This grotesque charade of queer courtiers, nude nuns and rhubarbing spectators begins to look uncannily like a companion piece to *Hellzappopin'*.'[34]

But the director has his supporters. 'Ken Russell is a baroque travesty artist, a homicidal farceur and *The Devils* is, despite, or maybe because of, the censorious growls that have greeted it, the best film he has made. . . . It's as bright and confidently tasteless as a postcard from Lourdes, as awful as a What-a-way-to-spend-Easter joke, as touching and painful as a communion service.'[35]

We share the view of the awfulness and tastelessness but it is possible to take these things too seriously and to dwell obsessively on the idea of films as works of art. Russell's unrestrained showmanship, after all, is an effect the cinema has prided itself on since its birth. A view which cuts off the filmgoer from these common pleasures is surely suspect, and

310

without reality. In the context of show business, there is something absurd in damning a film outright while tens of thousands of citizens are queueing up to see it. This is what happened to *The Devils*, as to many another film branded as vulgar, tasteless, and so on.

'To condemn because the multitude admire', said Hazlitt, 'is as essentially vulgar as to admire because they admire. There is no exercise of taste or judgement in either case'.

Russell has made seven feature films (up to the time of *Savage Messiah*) and any number of shorts and television features. He has sometimes been charged with putting his technical brilliance at the service of undeserving themes, but the truth is that all his work is intelligent above the average. He appears to pay little heed to critics but heads straight for his audience.

He has shown an equal facility in the handling of many different ideas, he has the boundless invention of the artist who is also a prodigy, like Balzac, and he has made one film at least, *Women in Love*, which has been called a masterpiece. However provocative or tasteless his films may be, they are never insignificant. Whatever he is making commands attention. Whatever he says is said with force and imagination. Russell is now in mid-career and a director with so interesting a past is pretty certain to have as interesting a future. He is in as good a position as any man to astonish us.

Bryan Forbes

With Bryan Forbes we are conscious of a talent, of a series of talents, skilled, original, arresting even in one or two cases, but of a different order from that we have been discussing.

Like most people struggling to get ahead in the film business, Forbes has been making films for a good many years before he takes on the full directorial responsibility.

Born in 1926, he was only 22 when he adapted *The Small Back Room* from Nigel Balchin's novel, for Powell and Pressburger. This was followed by *The Wooden Horse*, *Cockleshell Heroes* and other films. From writing and acting

311

he advanced to directing and producing, and after nearly twenty years, being then in great demand, he was appointed to the top production job at Associated British studios at Elstree, the company at that time undergoing a process of reorganisation. This was in 1968 though the assignment did not continue for long. Such dizzy elevation was all very well, but studio topmanship merely took Forbes away from what he was best at doing, though he did as a matter of fact make a film of his own, *The Raging Moon*, during that period.

The Angry Silence, which he wrote and produced with Richard Attenborough, does not strictly belong to the sixties as it was made in 1959, but it is sixties in temper and it signals the approach of a new talent which has been quietly simmering away for years before coming to the boil.

Directed by Guy Green, *The Angry Silence* approached realistically the subject of trade unionism which the Boultings had viewed satirically (*I'm All Right, Jack*). Richard Attenborough plays the part of a dissident factory hand who refuses to join a wildcat strike and is sent to Coventry by his mates and deserted by the bosses.

Any stirring up of thought about trade unionism could be expected to cause trouble and in fact did so. The film sufficiently made its point to bring protests from trade unionists, and Attenborough felt compelled to go out and answer them personally.

Critics (not all) respected the film for its serious tone and its sharply written dialogue, Forbes excelling in those scenes of domestic strife between Attenborough and his wife (Pier Angeli). But the rough idiom of the pubs and the factory is also there and the film had the merit of being about something.

Such a subject underlines the difficulty of using politically motivated themes, however skilfully disguised as entertainment. The employers must be villains, the workers oppressed and worthy citizens, issues must be blurred. 'No bad mark anywhere against the unions', said C. A. Lejeune of the film.[36] Nevertheless, in the movie climate of the time, only then beginning to shrug off its complacency, it was an effort worth making and brought its money back. All the big distributors had turned it down.[37]

In 1959 Bryan Forbes, Richard Attenborough and Jack Hawkins had formed their own company, Allied Film Makers, and produced *The League of Gentlemen*, a comedy of crooks, then *Whistle Down the Wind*, the first film Forbes directed. This was an attempt to examine, through the eyes of a child, the Christian ethic in a context of doubt and unbelief, with a teenager (Hayley Mills), and her young friends confronting a man whom they believe to be Christ on earth but who is in fact an escaped murderer. Here again Forbes plunges into a thorny subject of primary interest to himself but of the most dubious popular appeal. (He incidentally introduces an actor of great promise in Alan Bates.)

With *The L-Shaped Room* (1962) we are in the back streets of Notting Hill Gate where the lodgers share the emptiness of their flea-bitten rooms, and make what they can of their love affairs. Tom Bell, as the writer and factory worker in love with the French girl, Leslie Caron, learns from a friendly Negro in the house, Brock Peters, that she is already pregnant by another man. What will he do? Who will look after her? Not Tom Bell. The girl goes back to France. It is a little irony of the time, amusing, bitter, in the contemporary mood. Cicely Courtneidge as a veteran music hall star, and Avis Bunnage as a landlady, are brought in to lighten our darkness and raise our spirits.

The fascination that the strange and the abnormal in human character seem to have for Forbes leads him to the experiment of *Seance on a Wet Afternoon* (1964) which he wrote, directed and produced. It concerns a half-demented medium who feels that her talents are unrecognised and is ready to go to any lengths, even murder, to reach the top in her career. She kidnaps the child of rich parents for a ransom and when the story has become a nation-wide sensation, restores it by 'psychic' means to its home.

The mingling of action—the kidnapping and the chase— with the supernatural, is expertly managed and works on both levels, and the acting of Kim Stanley and Richard

313

Attenborough as the central characters creates a cumulative horror that is chilling. Here again an unlikely story repaid the courage needed to make it.

King Rat (1965), made in Hollywood, returns us to the familiar terrain of graft, corruption and humour in a Japanese prison camp. *The Wrong Box* (1966) from the R. L. Stevenson story followed; and then a characteristically off-beat subject for Edith Evans, *The Whisperers* (1966). It is a study in decay reflected in the musings of the splendid, ruined old lady, Dame of the British Empire, dreaming of her past in her shabby old tenement, impervious to the meanness and ingratitude of those around her.

If this was not great movie-making—it needed a few quite ordinary thrills to keep it going—there was a magnificent theatricality in Dame Edith's performance, acting of an order hardly ever found in films, and not always wanted. Otherwise, with its heavy grey texture, its appeal was very much a matter of taste.

Deadfall (1968), a chic thriller for Michael Caine about jewel thieves, is well below form and in the general opinion so is *The Mad Woman of Chaillot* (1969), made in France. Yet this is a film of many charms and deserved better than it got. Forbes took over the direction from John Huston in the early stages, not a good omen.

Based on a modest play by Girardoux, it is blown up to a full-scale spectacle for Katharine Hepburn, Charles Boyer and Yul Brynner. An international gang in Paris conspire for the possession of oil beneath the home of the Countess Aurelia (Miss Hepburn) in Chaillot, and in an elaborate charade she turns the tables on them. Though the film evoked little sympathy, it was far from lacking in interest. It had some well-managed scenes, particularly the meeting of the conspirators in Paris; as spectacle (including Miss Hepburn) it was fantastic and beautiful. In short, it was one of those bad films more worth looking at than some good ones.

That Forbes is a romantic might be deduced from a number of instances, and he next produced an example in *The Raging Moon* (1971). Lacking a realistic foundation, it is a good deal less successful than *The L-Shaped Room*. He takes the case of two young cripples in wheel-chairs and the problems facing them in ordinary life and in love. Delicately and intelligently played by Nanette Newman and Malcolm McDowell, it looked promising but somehow refused to come to life.

We take this as an indication of a certain narrowness of vision which distinguishes Forbes' work from that examined in the previous pages. The private world, however well observed, needs the touch that is to take it beyond the general to a universal significance.

Forbes sponsored a number of productions while at Associated British, of which *The Railway Children* (1971) and *Tales from Beatrix Potter* (1971) did phenomenally well. Shortly after this the industry entered on one of its periods of acute depression and the barometer of production fell to zero.

315

Conclusion

Once again film production is at a standstill and at the end of 1971 a good 50 per cent of the technicians in the industry are out of work, and at a time, too, when both commercially and artistically British films are at their highest level. It is a more serious position than anything that has happened since 1948, for the causes do not lie entirely within the business itself but are governed by events in America and by what is happening in the world outside.

We have been opposed, in this study, to government intervention and to dependence on America in the belief that films, whether works of art or not, are not made by governments, and that American interests, having swallowed the British industry whole, have undermined its efforts and destroyed its independence.

All this is held to pernicious nonsense by the best authorities. Yet what do we find?

That both the Government and America, having supported British films largely for reasons of material gain, abandon them the instant that interest is threatened, leaving British production completely in the lurch. Can we be certain the same thing will not happen again?

Viewing the British industry in retrospect, no one of sense can make sense of it, only loss. Loss in 1937, loss in 1948, loss in 1971. Loss to producers, loss to technicians and to the creative talents on which the whole structure depends. And most of the time the spectacle of the two major circuits dictating to producers what kind of films they should make, and where and how they should be released, perhaps (if the film is a really good one) in some remote cinema where failure is certain.

No wonder the great men in the City did not respond to the invitation of the great men in the Government to keep British films afloat.

In the meantime new methods had been devised to reduce costs by using mobile studios on location. Smaller studios were being used for interiors, the preposterous salaries were being cut down. Good films have been made and are still being made on sane budgets. Are we to say, with the examples before us of Losey, Schlesinger, Anderson, Richardson, Forbes and a dozen others, that there is no future for British cinema?

These names are the best assurance that a future exists and is sufficiently bright. What our directors have always lacked is continuity of output, so that they can neither develop their ideas with certainty nor plan ahead. All is sweat, gamble and frustration. Nothing settles down, no roots are struck, the future of the industry is next Monday.

'Yes—oh dear yes, nothing stands still, I wish it would,' said E. M. Forster in another context, but it would do for our own.

The old hands running the business whom only fire, hemlock or assassination could be expected to remove, have done enough damage. The new generation of film-makers has a different concept of film-making and may take less money on order to make more of it. It has brought us an intellectually richer cinema which spreads a wider influence than ever in its history and has gained honours at numberless festivals. But it seems not to have brought the money into the market which would fill our studios and increase employment.

It is the perpetuating muddle of the film's economy that finally forces us to the view (which we have all along opposed) that British subsidies and American dollars are necessary to keep our cinema alive and well. (See Bernstein, Appendix II).

It was not always so. The film was launched in the beginning by a few devoted and quick-sighted men who saw it as an end in itself and their deepest satisfaction. Then it was enough to love the cinema in order to make it. It grew into a great business. Today it is still a business, and that's the trouble. For everyone engaged in it waits too long and too often for his opportunity.

Appendix I

Documentary: The Last Word

by John Grierson

In the following article, which he recorded on tape, Grierson discusses many aspects of the movement he founded and the course it has taken since post-war days.

Here is one way of looking at it when we were developing documentary in the twenties, and the reality of it in the thirties. We thought of ourselves as involved in a movement. That is why there is a special significance in the fact that one is constantly being asked: Are you disappointed or otherwise in what happened?

The only other film men who could be asked that kind of question have been, of course, the leaders of schools, that is to say, the Russian school of Eisenstein, Pudovkin, and so on, or the very great school of slapstick—of Sennett and Hal Roach. There are not many of them who can be isolated in aesthetic or other fundamental worth from the general flow of box-office film from Hollywood and other entertainment centres.

The documentary film school is more easily detachable than any. It had some ambitions in the field of entertainment, but only in so far as it had duties to audiences and a need for circulation.

It had very considerable aesthetic ambitions at one time and in fact from time to time it achieved important aesthetic results—I think particularly in the mid-thirties and during the war. But it has always been liable to sacrifice its aesthetic ambition for a continuing hold on the reporting of events and the demonstration of public problems and the persuasion of audiences generally.

Now there are two phases in the development of the documentary film movement. In the beginning we set out

318

to use the film to report on what we saw, and to report on the world in which we lived. It was in a period of growing social consciousness—it was during the early period, the great wave of social democracy, and we almost inevitably associated development of the documentary film with the progress of the working class, the developments in science and technology, the growth of international relationships of one kind and another, and the social problems thrown up in our modern surroundings.

This was Phase One. Obviously, this interest didn't come naturally to the showmen of show business represented by the film theatres. But there were, in fact, occasions when our interests coincided. For example, there were many in show business interested in the new realism and its dramatic potential, and some documentary films did very well at the box-office. It was not on the cards that the show business would take to its bosom our conception of documentary film as the positive public enlightener.

My own greatest contribution to the documentary film was almost certainly that I conceived it as involving quite new relationships which could not, or could only occasionally, be equated with what was then described as the entertainment catering business. In so doing I looked immediately to—looked immediately for, an audience outside the theatres, and I looked immediately to the need for financial support outside the film business. That was, I think, the revolutionary equation involved in the setting up of the documentary development.

So the documentary film movement as a movement was founded on the conception of a non-theatrical audience that is today a vast array of specialised audiences, and we used to say at the time that there was more seating capacity outside the theatres than there was inside the theatres, and that was true enough, and it was founded on the expectation of financial support from governmental and other authorities concerned with the use of the film, or logically likely to be concerned with the use of the film for public enlightenment of one kind or another.

I shall return to this Phase One, for I had a lot to do with

319

its control on all levels including the aesthetic, but if you are to get the early development of the documentary film into proper perspective, you have to realise the completely *new* public situation that created Phase Two. It was, of course, the coming of television.

It immediately provided the documentary film with all it had dreamt of from its earliest days—at least with most of the essentials it had dreamt of. It provided a national audience which was not exclusively interested in entertainment. It provided a continuing source of finance in most of the fields of public interest in which the documentary film had interested itself from the earlier days. The exposition of social problems, the development on all the horizons of science and technical progress, the dramatic problems of international relationships—all became the normal consideration for TV producers in their contact with community service.

So you must see the BBC in Britain as taking over the documentary film movement which I directed in the thiries. They didn't take it over altogether, but certainly they took over to a very large extent. For the leadership of documentary today in the United Kingdom you must look to people like Huw Weldon. Similar takeovers have occurred particularly in most of the—I think, all of the—technically developed countries. There has not been the same takeover by television in the under-developed countries.

In some ways TV has done far better in the—what we used to call, rather pompously—creative treatment of the actual, than we ever did in the thirties. For one thing TV undertook a national responsibility in the matter of news coverage, and in so doing has associated itself with the great journalistic tradition of Fleet Street, In fact. it took over many of its important people from Fleet Street.

In some of the fields that were, shall we say, excellently covered by film in the thirties, very high standards have been maintained. In TV or, shall we say, in the TV era of the documentary film, I am thinking especially of the nature films, the films describing technological, scientific and other explorations—and I am thinking of the world of discovery generally.

TV has kept up the standard. In the field of news in depth there were again excellent things done in the film phase—or the first TV phase. I'm thinking of *The March of Time.* I'm thinking of *World in Action* which came from Canada and was in some respects an advance in the coverage of news in depth—an advance on *The March of Time.* But the supply of news in depth that we see today on TV is much larger than it ever was, more widely ranging and more complete. And I'm sure, too, that it draws on a wider range of expertise than we could do with our resources during the pre-television period of the documentary film.

The documentary film of the late thirties and the war films dealt importantly with social problems and some of the most precious cinematic moments were arrived at in these particular films. Well, television has on the whole maintained that same documentary interest in social problems. TV, moreover, while inheriting the Fleet Street tradition, has also inherited some of the traditions of show business. I'm thinking of its having rather especially the tradition of Western European theatre. This is reflected in a treatment of actuality which, while it makes its own impact, is inclined to be more sympathetically dramatic than the British documentary film tradition of the thirties permitted.

Then again, in spite of TV's self-conscious association with the literary world, and my! how they're boring with it—there are inner factors in TV that seem to prevent the pursuit of the aesthetic qualities which the documentary films, Phase One, most certainly achieved. Taking only British documentary films of the thirties, for example, British TV has produced nothing of such pure cinematic quality as some of the sequences in, say, *The Song of Ceylon, Coal Face* or *Night Mail*, or war films like *Listen to Britain*.

Phase Two of the documentary film movement, that is to say, the TV phase of the documentary film, in which it may be said to have been nationally stabilised and very truly nationalised, has its roots in the old newsreels of the cinema and in the documentary film movement financed in Britain by the Government, and it has the great blessing of roots in both Fleet Street and the West End Theatre, as I've noted.

L

But it is very significantly not deeply rooted in the traditions of film-making, much less in those finer excursions of the cinema that once associated the documentary film not only with the pursuit of film poetry, but strangely enough with the pursuit of new horizons of sound effects. One of the oddest things to me in the whole history of the cinema and TV is that this pursuit of new effects from the soundtrack, which was finding all sorts of good things about the middle thirties, has not been continued in the later period.

I think that much has been lost and I would have thought that what we indicated in the documentary film in, say, 1935 was certain to be taken up, not only by film and TV in the TV phase, but by radio itself. On these particular and specific grounds I would fault this, certainly fault the later, development of the documentary film in Britain in its TV phase.

It could be that the organisation of TV is too monstrous to permit the poetics to emerge, but it's as well to remember that Whitehall, which did not permit them, is a pretty monstrous place in itself. It could be that TV, even at the BBC, breeds a pre-occupation with time-serving—time-serving in the sense of undue pursuit of the immediate, and that this doesn't permit the more patient pursuit of excellence.

But however we excuse it, my own view is that the TV people will never be truly in possession of the medium, never feel truly in possession of the medium, no matter how much they feel blood brothers with Fleet Street, or blood brothers with the West End theatre or the University Common Room—they won't feel truly in possession until they get round to having a conscience in the matter of cinematic quality in its true sense—that film thing which Mack Sennett once described mystically as the Bubble.

But whatever the shortcomings—if there is a shortcoming—and it's important in the development of the art of the cinema—it should not obscure the fact that by and large TV in Britain—there I include the BBC, ITN and Granada's *World in Action*—probably represents a more considered national use of the documentary film in general than we see in any other TV system in the English-speaking world.

Now this short division of documentary development between the pre-TV phase and the post-TV phase should, I think, answer some of the questions about what we praised in the past and what we praise in the present and where, if any, the disappointments lie. The great thing about Phase One was, of course, the development in the late twenties and thirties of the idea that the film industry was not sufficiently developing the cinema's capacity for observing real life, not sufficiently developing the cinema as the servant of public purposes.

The important thing was—some of us saw the road wide open for the invasion of the film country by other interests of entertainment pure and simple, and our tying of cinema to a new world of associations based on the public purpose. One of the by-products was the extraordinary loyalty of the documentary people among themselves during the thirties, and this applied not only to the great British co-operative, which is the largest and best of all, but to the relationships in the British group and some of the groups in other countries.

It seems that the sense of public purpose did bind them together and give them not only a co-operative approach to the task of cinema as a whole in the public service, but also a co-operative approach to film-making itself.

The word 'unit' derived, I think, from the documentary approach—the idea of film units—I mean the very phrase 'film units' was first used by the documentary people, and it did mean that all sorts of people worked together and in almost any combination, and today it's difficult indeed to say who in particular was responsible for a particular film. I don't say that that sort of co-operation—or spirit of co-operative—can arise on every occasion, or be built into any particular set of circumstances, but it is worth noting as one of the special manifestations of the documentary film in its first phase—the fact that public purpose can create very powerful co-operative efforts in the cinema.

This applies, of course, not only to the documentary film group in the thirties in England but also specially to the documentary film group at the Crown Film Unit during the war, and it would apply equally to the National Film Board in Canada over a very long period indeed.

One of the things that might be worth noting is the fact that scarcely any individual succeeded notably in the documentary film outside the co-operative and outside the documentary's fundamental relationship with public purposes and finance deriving from it. Flaherty represented the greatest example of the independent outlook of a man still looking for a place in the normal world of entertainment for his documentary kind of film.

Now, it is an historical fact that he did not finish one single film he ever started under the auspices or in association with the film industry. In the last resort, after *Elephant Boy*, he had to seek the sanctuary of the documentary co-operative. In fact, all question of personal documentary talent apart, the documentary co-operative, representing the alliance of documentary-makers with public purpose and public finance, represents the basic reality of the documentary film in Phase One. Nor, as I have noted, did public purpose preclude some exciting aesthetic results which belong to the story of cinematic achievement in general.

Several factors contributed to the aesthetic efforts and discoveries of the documentary film. We were, in the early days, much pre-occupied with the fact that we were dealing with a new medium. We were, day in, day out, involved in a process of discovery, the new horizons opened up by the cinema; we were involved in discovering a new language of expression and the grammar that went with it. Even when sound came we continued to explore the possibilities of the silent cinema as well as starting out on the new implications of the sound track.

To say the least we were not much tempted by the new relationships with the theatre which were very obvious with the coming of sound. We were almost, very especially first and last, the true film people. This was the case in the middle thirties.

But events overtook us. More and more there was an attempt to describe and to discuss social problems and

324

contribute to both social and educational services. The simple powerful commentary on the sound track encouraged journalistic talents which, in the relatively dramatic form represented by the *March of Time* and *World in Action*, actually brought the documentary film more closely into touch with normal theatre audiences than ever before.

Certainly, the poetics of *The Song of Ceylon* and *Night Mail* days largely disappeared in England giving place to the journalistic use of the documentary film in terms of newsreel, in terms of news in depth, in terms of the discussion of social and other public problems. It disappeared in England, very expensively disappeared, with the Crown Film Unit.

Elsewhere, whenever there is a true tradition, the documentary film prospers, good films of the poetic order continue to be made all over the world and they allow that it is in the tradition that they continue. The aesthetic excellence in the documentary film in recent years has come from countries like Canada, Holland and Poland, India and Yugoslavia, Sweden and France, Italy and Hungary, and, yes, from as far afield as Bolivia. In almost every case, the old formula obtains.

There has been public sponsorship to public ends which has been wise enought to permit aesthetic effort. In all cases, too, production has been in and for the film world of theatrical and non-theatrical distribution, and outside the domain of television. In many respects, therefore, the old Phase One of documentary film development still rules many parts of the world. Where TV has not been developed, and in countries too far-flung or scattered to permit wholesale TV coverage, the old laws which gave special life to the cinema still obtain.

In many countries the film contributes even more vitally to the public service than it ever needed to do in the Western world and this is especially so in the under-developed countries where there is progressive use of the film and progressive use of travelling film theatres for basic education in matters like health and hygiene and technique of production. In this connection we ought to remember for the record that no country saw this need as much as the UK or did more to lay the foundation of these services now being carried on in the under-developed countries.

It was from the early thirties of basic interest to the British documentary group, and I suppose from the very early days of the Empire Marketing Board which first articulated the idea of film services to under-developed countries. We were perhaps unique in first realising that one principal task was to train native units to do their own national film work and in their own way. Nor is this the least of the achievements of the British documentary film co-operative in its Phase One, the creation or encouragement of documentary film units all over the world.

There is no parallel to this activity, so far as I know, and no parallel to this influence today, not even at the United Nations. So in a fashion the old Phase One of documentary is as alive today as it ever was, but in other countries than Britain, it represents the documentary film in the very direct service of public purposes and in the very specific use of documentary film in educational and social fields. It frequently represents fidelity to the tradition of film-making as such, which is missed in the TV era in TV's pursuit of the mass audience and TV's show business pursuit of immediate impacts.

However, we may not sell short the very real progress which the documentary film has made in the TV period along certain lines. We never had in the documentary film days a newsreel service anything like the newsreel service given out today by TV, nationally and internationally. We never had the same coverage of public affairs even in the old film days, or anything like the support of expertise of every kind.

Appendix II

Post-war Trends in Cinema-going

In reply to the questions (*a*) What effect has television had on your cinemas since the war? (*b*) What has been the success of British films at Granada Theatres compared with European and American films?, Lord Bernstein, chairman of Granada, made these comments:

(*a*) 'During the immediate post-war years when the BBC only were operating, the effect on audience attendances was minimal, but with the advent of commercial television and the resultant choice of programmes, admissions declined sharply.

'The older age group who had been accustomed to attending cinemas regularly once or twice a week stayed at home, with the result that audiences which at one time prior to the advent of TV were composed of people from, say, 10 to 65, were after the introduction of commercial TV composed of the age group 10 to 25.'

After referring to other factors in the decline, such as motoring and various leisure activities, the report continues:

'Whilst TV is often blamed for the decline in cinema-going, we must not overlook the benefit it has brought to the cinema. It is true to say that it has stimulated the appreciation of films, and that cinema-goers today (1971) take a far more intelligent interest in films that did their predecessors. TV programmes dealing with films have without doubt played a large part in making the public more aware of what the cinema has to offer.

'Television continues to play its part in deterring people from visiting the cinema because during any one week there are shown a number of films on television, some of which

327

are comparatively recent, i.e., five years old, and in many cases they are films which are superior to those which are currently being shown in their local cinema.

'Because the advent of television changed the market to a much younger age group, the majority of films being made are geared for that market and do little to attract back the older age groups.'

(*b*) 'Over the past six years British films accounted for over 52 per cent of the top ten grossing films of each year. The overall percentage over this period was 51.66 British to 48.33 foreign and it maybe of interest to note that of the foreign films in the top ten each year a Disney picture was included.

'The quality has never been better . . . from *A Man for All Seasons* to the *Carry Ons*. Directors such as Ken Russell, Charles Jarrott, Jack Gold (all of whom started on TV) and stalwarts such as David Lean, Tony Richardson and the Boulting brothers continue to make successful films.'

On the question of the withdrawal of the Americans from British film production, the report adds: 'While one would like to think it were possible to "go it alone" in British film production, one has to be realistic and recognise that this is *not economically feasible,* and therefore American participation *is* necessary if there is to be a flow of product into British cinemas.'

Notes

CHAPTER 1

Publication details are given more fully in the Bibliography.

1. Letter from Will Day to the author, 8 October 1934.
2. *Origins of the Motion Picture* by D. B. Thomas, pp. 17, 26.
3. *Birt Acres*, reprinted by Tantivy Press, 1963.
4. *Edwardian England* edited by S. Nowell Smith, p. 193.
5. *'Film and the Cultural Tradition'* by Raymond Williams, BBC broadcast, 18 February 1971.
6. *Marcel Proust* by George D. Painter, Vol. 2, p. 160.
7. *Specimens of English Dramatic Criticism*, (World's Classics), p. 233.
8. *French Film*, by Roy Armes, p. 14.
9. *A Million and One Nights* by Terry Ramsaye, Vol. 2, pp. 566 and 571.
10. *Kino* by Jay Leyda, p. 410.
11. *The Liveliest Art* by Arthur Knight, p. 207.
12. *The Film Till Now* by Paul Rotha, p. 314 (revised edition, 1949).
13. *The British Film Industry*, A Report by Political and Economic Planning, 1952, p. 32.

CHAPTER 2

1. *History of the British Film* by Rachael Low, Vol. 3, p. 79.
2. Ibid., Vol. 2, p. 97.
3. Ibid., Vol. 2, p. 21.
4. Ibid., Vol. 2, p. 111.
5. *Came the Dawn* by Cecil Hepworth, p. 28.
6. Ibid., p. 42.
7. Ibid., pp. 122–3.
8. *Let's Go to the Pictures* by Iris Barry, p. 242

CHAPTER 3

1. *The British Film Industry* (PEP), 1952, p. 32.
2. *Film Censors and the Law* by Neville Hunnings, p. 50.
3. *The Factual Film*, p. 210.
4. *Film Censors and the Law*, p. 88.
5. *History of the British Film* by Rachael Low, Vol. 2, p. 64.
6. Ibid., Vol. 3, p. 105.

CHAPTER 4

1. *Flashback* by George Pearson, p. 27.
2. *Reminiscences of a Pioneer Film Producer* by G. B. Samuelson (1938).
3. *Flashback* p. 41.
4. Ibid., p. 95.
5. Ibid., p. 134.
6. *The Silent Picture*, Spring 1969, (George Pearson issue).
7. *Flashback*, p. 188.
8. *The Times*, 19 November 1930.

CHAPTER 5

1. *History of the British Film* by Rachael Low, Vol. 4, pp. 191, 203; *The Liveliest Art* by Arthur Knight, p. 148.
2. *The Times*, 13 May 1929.
3. *Michael Balcon Presents*, pp. 20 and 58.
4. *History of the British Film*, Vol. 4, p. 135.

CHAPTER 6

1. *The Silent Picture*, Summer/Autumn 1971.
2. *The Factual Film*, p. 31.
3. *The British Film Institute: Twenty-five Years*, 1958.
4. *Outlook*, BFI Report, 1966, p. 30.

CHAPTER 7

1. Letter to author from F. E. Hutchinson.
2. 1965 figures. See *A Competitive Cinema*, p. 142.
3. Ibid., p. 44.
4. *The British Film Industry* (PEP), 1952, p. 124.
5. *History of the British Film*, by Rachael Low, Vol. 2, p. 54.
6. *The British Film Industry* (PEP), 1952, p. 43.

CHAPTER 8

1. *History of the British Film* by Rachael Low, Vol. 2, p. 23.
2. *The Times*, article by the author, 20 September 1967.
3. *The Kine Year Book, 1915*, p. 17.
4. *The British Film Industry* (PEP), 1952, pp. 45–47.
5. Ibid., p. 59.
6. *Money Behind the Screen* by F. D. Klingender and S. Legg, p. 15.
7. *The British Film Industry* (PEP), 1952, p. 59.

CHAPTER 9

1. See *A Competitive Cinema* (Institute of Economic Affairs), p. 108.
2. Monopolies Commission Report, 1966, para. 81.
3. Rank, interview with the author, 18 June 1963.
4. Sir John Davis, interview with the author, 28 June 1971.

CHAPTER 10

1. *Behind The Screen* by Klingender and Legg, p. 54.
2. *The British Film Industry* (PEP), 1952, p. 114.
3. *The Factual Film*, p. 190.
4. Ibid., p. 191.
5. *The British Film Industry* (PEP), 1952, p. 75.

CHAPTER 11

1. See Baynham Honri's technical survey in *The History of the British Film* by Rachael Low, Vol. 3, p. 241.
2. *The History of the British Film*, Vol. 2, p. 139.

CHAPTER 12

1. *Hitchcock* by Eric Rohmer and Claude Chabrol, p. 13.
2. *The Films of Alfred Hitchcock* by George Perry, pp. 10, 12.
3. *Hitchcock* by François Truffaut (Secker & Warburg), p. 49.
4. *The Times*, 23 September 1930.
5. Author's interview with Hitchcock, 1960.
6. *The Times*, 27 February 1968.
7. *The Film Till Now* by Paul Rotha, p. 320.
8. *Celluloid: The Film Today* by Paul Rotha, p. 171.
9. Graham Greene, the *Spectator*, 15 November 1935.

CHAPTER 13

1. *The Elstree Story*, Associated British Picture Corporation, 1967.
2. *The Observer*, 26 February 1933.
3. Ibid., 2 December 1934.
4. *The Sunday Times*, 2 December 1934.
5. *Punch*, 12 December 1934.
6. Basil Wright, the *Spectator*, 1 January 1939.
7. Graham Greene, the *Spectator*, 16 June 1939.
8. *Twenty-five Thousand Sunsets* by Herbert Wilcox, p. 2.
9. *My First 100 Years in Hollywood* by Jack Warner, pp. 100, 104 and 180.

10. Robert Clark, interview with the author, 3 August 1969.
11. *Histoire du Cinéma* by René Jeanne and Charles Ford, pp. 291, 292f.

CHAPTER 14

1. *Film Censors and the Law* by Neville March Hunnings (Allen & Unwin, 1967), p. 73.
2. Ibid., p. 97.
3. Ibid., p. 98.
4. Ibid., p. 108.
5. Ibid., p. 118.
6. Ibid., pp. 117–19.
7. Ibid., p. 102.

CHAPTER 15

1. BBC Television Interview, 27 December 1968.
2. *Alexander Korda* by Paul Tabori, p. 110.
3. Alexander Korda, interview with the author, 24 October 1933.
4. *The Daily Telegraph*, 2 February 1934.
5. *The Times*, 2 February 1934.
6. *The Listener*, 8 March 1936.
7. The *New Statesman*, 2 August 1941.
8. *The Film Year Book, 1947–1948*, pp. 44–45.

CHAPTER 16

1. BFI Edinburgh Festival programme, 1968.
2. Ibid., 1968.
3. *The Filmgoer's Companion* by Leslie Halliwell, p. 303.
4. *The Film Till Now* by Paul Rotha and Richard Griffith, p. 520.
5. Ibid., p. 522.
6. *Documentary Film* by Paul Rotha, p. 119.
7. *The Observer*, 29 April 1934.
8. *Footnotes to the Film* edited by Charles Davy, pp. 61–2.

CHAPTER 17

1. *Agee on Film* by James Agee, p. 365.
2. *Thirty Years with G. B. S.* by Blanche Patch, pp. 118–19, 123.
3. *Meeting at the Sphinx* by Marjorie Deans, p. vii.
4. *Thirty Years with G. B. S.*, p. 127.
5. *Meeting at the Sphinx*, p. 96.

CHAPTER 18

1. Lindsay Anderson in *The Sunday Times Magazine*, October 1970.
2. John Grierson, preface to *Documentary Film* by Paul Rotha, p. 7.
3. *Documentary Film* by Paul Rotha, p. 7.
4. *The Factual Film*, p. 45.
5. Ibid., p. 63.
6. *Kino* by Jay Leyda, p. 178.
7. *The Factual Film*, pp. 53, 55.
8. Ibid., p. 77.
9. *The Cinema Quarterly*, Summer 1933.

CHAPTER 19

1. *History of England* by A. J. P. Taylor, p. 315.
2. *Michael Balcon Presents*, pp. 134–5.
3. *Sight and Sound*, Spring 1969, p. 101.
4. *Art of the Cinema in Ten European Countries*, p. 210.
5. *Agee on Film* by James Agee, p. 17.
6. Eric Maschwitz, Arthur MacRae, Flt./Officer Jenny Nicholson, Gerald Kersh and Sgt. Guy Trosper.
7. The *Manchester Guardian*, 2 August 1945.

CHAPTER 20

1. BFI *Monthly Film Bulletin*, October 1941.
2. *The Film Till Now* by Paul Rotha and Richard Griffith, p. 560.
3. William Whitebait, the *New Statesman*, 2 May 1942.
4. Ibid., 26 September 1942.
5. *The Film Till Now* by Paul Rotha and Richard Griffith, p. 53.
6. C. A. Lejeune, *The Observer*, 7 May 1944.

CHAPTER 21

1. *Film* by Roger Manvell (Penguin revised edition), p. 66.
2. *Agee on Film* by James Agee, pp. 207–208.
3. Richard Winnington, the *News Chronicle*, 9 June 1949.
4. Ibid., 7 May 1944.
5. *The Art of the Cinema in Ten European Countries*, Lindsay Anderson, p. 214.
6. Dilys Powell, *The Sunday Times*, 4 April 1944.

333

CHAPTER 22
1. Palache Report, p. 6, para. 7.
2. Ibid., p. 35, para. 1.

CHAPTER 23
1. *Tendencies to Monopoly in the Cinematograph Film Industry* (Report of a Committee appointed by the Cinematograph Films Council), 1944.
2. Ibid., p. 36, para. 2.
3. *The British Film Industry* (PEP), 1952, p. 98.
4. Ibid., p. 114.
5. Report of Film Studio Committee (Gater Report), p. 14.
6. Ibid. Appendix iv.
7. Report of the Working Party on Film Production Costs, p. 6, para. 6.
8. *A Competitive Cinema*, Institute of Economic Affairs, 1966, p. 171.
9. *The British Film Industry* (PEP) 1952, p. 235.
10. Ibid., p. 237.

CHAPTER 24
1. *The Decline of the Cinema* by John Spraos, p. 19.
2. *A Grammar of the Film* by Raymond Spottiswoode, p. 142.
3. *The British Film Industry* (PEP) 1958, p. 150.

CHAPTER 25
1. *The British Film Industry* (PEP), 1952, p. 100.
2. *Art of the Cinema in Ten European Countries*, pp. 212–13.
3. *Films, 1945–1950* by Denis Forman.
4. *British Film Academy Journal*, Autumn 1955, reprinted in SFTA Journal, July-August 1969, p. 3.
5. William Whitebait, the *New Statesman*, 9 November 1946.
6. *Films, 1945–1950* by Denis Forman.

CHAPTER 26
1. *Michael Balcon Presents* by Sir Michael Balcon, p. 112.
2. *Michael Balcon's Twenty-five Years in Films* edited by Monja Danischevsky, p. 7.
3. Paul Dehn, *Sunday Chronicle*, 23 February 1947.

4. Dilys Powell, *The Sunday Times*, 1 May 1949.
5. C. A. Lejeune, *The Observer*, 1 July 1951.
6. *Michael Balcon Presents*, p. 187.
7. Ibid., pp. 194.

CHAPTER 27

1. *A Competitive Cinema* (Institute of Economic Affairs), 1966, p. 33.
2. Ibid., p. 34.
3. NFFC Annual Report, 1957, p. 2, para. 5.
4. Monopolies Commission Report, 1966, para, 137.
5. NFFC Report, 1957, p. 12, Appendix C.
6. Ibid., p. 10, Appendix B. (under item 8).
7. From an article in *The Cinema* celebrating the Hundredth anniversary of the Piccadilly branch of the National Provincial Bank.

CHAPTER 28

1. *Kiss Kiss, Bang Bang*, by Pauline Kael, p. 327.
2. Interview with Michael Powell by Kevin Gough-Yates, NFT booklet, 1971, p. 8.
3. Isabel Quigly, the *Spectator*, 11 October 1957.
4. *I Lost it at the Movies* by Pauline Kael, pp. 8–9.

CHAPTER 29

1. *New Cinema in Britain* by Roger Manvell, p. 40.
2. *I Lost it at the Movies* by Pauline Kael, p. 68.
3. *New Cinema in Britain*, p. 44.
4. *A World on Film* by Stanley Kauffmann, pp. 97–8.
5. The *Manchester Guardian*, 27 May 1959.
6. The *Spectator*, 5 June 1959.
7. *Time and Tide*, 6 June 1959.
8. Partick Gibbs, *The Daily Telegraph*, 26 July 1960.
9. Derek Prouse, *The Sunday Times*, 31 July 1960.
10. Brendan Gill, *The New Yorker*, 15 October 1960.
11. The *Daily Express*, 27 June 1963.
12. *The Times*, 27 June 1963.
13. *The Sunday Times*, 30 June 1963.
14. The *Evening News*, 27 June 1963.
15. *The Times*, 9 April 1968.

CHAPTER 30

1. *Society of Film and Television Arts Journal*, July 1970.
2. Ibid., July 1970.
3. *Violence on the Screen* by Andre Glucksmann, BFI, 1971.
4. *The Times*, 'Britain's Changing Society' series, 6 April 1966, p. 1.
5. Report on Supply of Films for Exhibition in Cinemas, 1966, p. 64.
6. Annual report of NFFC, p. 1, para. 4.
7. Ibid., 1971, p. 1, para. 4.
8. *Cinema Today*, p. 1, 11 December 1971.
9. *To Encourage the Art of the Film* by Ivan Butler, pp. 153–4.

CHAPTER 31

1. *The Contemporary Cinema* by Penelope Houston, pp. 109, 110.
2. *New Cinema in the U.S.A.* by Roger Manvell, p. 8.
3. *A World of Film* by Stanley Kauffmann, p. 200.
4. Penelope Gilliat, *The Observer*, 15 April 1962.
5. *Sight and Sound*,
6. *The Times*, 10 October 1969.
7. The *New Statesman*, 2 July 1971.
8. *Losey on Losey* edited by Tom Milne, p. 91.
9. *New Cinema in Britain* by Roger Manvell, p. 103.
10. The *New Statesman*, 31 December 1971.
11. Patrick Gibbs, *The Daily Telegraph*, 11 October 1971.
12. *A Mirror for England* by Raymond Durgnat, p. 112.
13. Richard Roud, the *Guardian*, 31 August, 1964.
14. *Peter Brook* by J. C. Trewin, p. 160.
15. *Sight and Sound*, Spring/Summer 1967.
16. David Robinson, *The Financial Times*, 23 July 1971.
17. The *Guardian*, 6 February 1963.
18. Penelope Gilliat, *The Observer*, 10 February 1963.
19. *A World on Film* by Stanley Kauffmann, p. 210.
20. Dilys Powell, *The Sunday Times*, 22 December 1968.
21. Penelope Mortimer, *The Observer*, 22 December 1968.
22. *Going Steady* by Pauline Kael, p. 283.
23. Elizabeth Sussex, *The Times*, 29 November 1968.
24. Gene D. Phillips in *Film Comment*, Mass., U.S.A., 21 October 1970.
25. Patrick Gibbs, the *Daily Telegraph*, 11 November 1969.
26. Ian Leslie Christie, *Sight and Sound*, Winter 1969/70, p. 50.
27. David Robinson, *The Financial Times*, 14 November 1969.
28. John Russell Taylor, *The Times*, 11 November 1969.

29. Margaret Hinxman, *The Sunday Times*, 2 February 1971.
30. *BFI Monthly Film Bulletin*, March 1971, p. 108.
31. *Sight and Sound*, Spring 1971, p. 108.
32. Christopher Hudson, the *Spectator*, 6 February 1971.
33. George Melly, *The Observer*, 25 July 1971.
34. Tom Milne, *BFI Monthly Film Bulletin*, August 1971.
35. Jonathan Raban, the *New Statesman*, 30 August 1971.
36 C. A. Lejeune, *The Observer*, 13 March 1960.
37. *Sight and Sound*, Summer 1961, p. 111.

Bibliography

Agee on Film by James Agee (Peter Owen, 1941).
The American Cinema by Andrew Sarris (E. P. Dutton, 1968).
Lindsay Anderson by Elizabeth Sussex (Studio Vista, 1969).
Anger and After by John Russell Taylor (Methuen, 1962).
Art of the Cinema in Ten European Countries edited by Alan Lovell, Council for Cultural Co-operation in Europe, 1967.
The Art of the Film by Ernest Lindgren (Allen & Unwin, 1948, 2nd ed. 1963).
The Battle of Britain: The Making of a Film by Leonard Mosley (Weidenfeld & Nicolson, 1969).
British Cinema by Denis Gifford (Zwemmer, 1968).
The British Film Catalogue, 1895–1970 (David & Charles, 1973).
Peter Brook, a Biography by J. C. Trewin (Macdonald, 1971).
The British Film Industry (A report by Political and Economic Planning, 1952 and 1958).
Buster Keaton by David Robinson (Secker & Warburg 1969 and Thames & Hudson, 1970).
Came the Dawn by Cecil Hepworth (Phoenix House, 1951).
Celluloid: The Film Today by Paul Rotha (Longmans, 1931).
The Celluloid Sacrifice by Alexander Walker (Michael Joseph, 1966).
Charlie Chaplin by Isabel Quigly (Studio Vista, 1968).
Cinema by C. A. Lejeune (Alexander Maclehose, 1931).
The Cinema, 1952 edited by Roger Manvell and R. K. Neilson Baxter (Pelican, 1952).
The Cinema and the Public by Walter Ashley (Ivor Nicholson & Watson, 1934).
Cinema Eye, Cinema Ear by John Russell Taylor (Methuen, 1964).
Comedy Films by John Montgomery (Allen & Unwin, 1954).
A Competitive Cinema by Terence Kelly (Institute of Economic Affairs, 1966).
A Concise History of the Cinema, two volumes, edited by Peter Cowie (Zwemmer, 1971).
The Contemporary Cinema by Penelope Houston (Penguin, 1963).
The Decline of the Cinema by John Spraos (Allen & Unwin, 1962).
The Disciple and his Devil by Valerie Pascal (McGraw Hill, 1970).
A Discovery of Cinema by Thorold Dickinson (Oxford University Press, 1970).
Documentary Film by Paul Rotha (Faber & Faber, 1936).
Early American Cinema by Anthony Slide (Zwemmer, 1970).

338

Edwardian England edited by Simon Nowell-Smith (Oxford University Press, 1964).

The Empty Space by Peter Brook (MacGibbon & Kee, 1964; Penguin, 1972).

English History by A. J. P. Taylor (Oxford University Press, 1965).

The Elstree Story (Printed by Associated British Picture Corporation, 1967).

The Factual Film: A Survey by the Arts Enquiry (published by PEP and Oxford University Press, 1947).

Film by Roger Manvell (Pelican Books, 1944).

Film as Film by V. F. Perkins (Pelican Books, 1972).

Film Censors and the Law by Neville March Hunnings (Allen & Unwin, 1967).

Film Makers on Film Making edited by Harry Geduld (Pelican, 1967).

The Film in National Life by A. C. Cameron (Allen & Unwin, 1932).

The Film and the Public by Roger Manvell (Pelican, 1955).

The Film Till Now by Paul Rotha and Richard Griffith (Vision Press & Mayfair Publishing Co., 1949).

The Filmgoers' Companion by Leslie Halliwell (MacGibbon & Kee, 1968).

The Film Year Book, 1947–48 (published by Kinomatograph Weekly).

Films 1945–50 by Denis Forman (Longmans for the British Council, 1952).

The Films of Alfred Hitchcock by George Perry (Studio Vista, 1965).

The First Twenty-five Years (British Film Institute, 1958).

Flashback: The Autobiography of a British Film Maker by George Pearson (Allen & Unwin, 1957).

Footnotes to the Film edited by Charles Davy (Lovat Dickson, 1938).

French Cinema since 1946 by Roy Armes (2 vols) (Zwemmer, 1966).

French Films by Roy Armes (Studio Vista, 1970).

Friese-Greene by Ray Allister (Marsland Publications, 1951).

Garbo and the Night Watchman edited by Alistair Cooke (Secker & Warburg, 1971).

Going Steady by Pauline Kael (Temple Smith, 1968).

A Grammar of the Film by Raymond Spottiswoode, 1st ed. (Jonathan Cape, 1937).

Grierson on Documentary edited by Forsyth Hardy (Collins, 1946).

Hamlet, The Film and the Play edited by Alan Dent (World Film Publications, 1948).

Histoire encyclopaedique du cinéma by René Jeanne and Charles Ford. Volume I, 1895–1929 (Paris, Robert Lafont).

Histoire du cinéma mondiale by Georges Sadoul (Paris, Flammarion, 1959).

The History of the British Film by Rachael Low. Vols. I–IV (Allen & Unwin).

History of the Film by Maurice Bardeche and Robert Brasillac, translated and edited by Iris Barry (Allen & Unwin, 1938).

A History of the Movies by Benjamin Hampton (Noel Douglas, 1932).
Hitchcock by Francis Truffaut (Secker & Warburg, 1968).
Hitchcock by Eric Rohmer and Claude Chabrol (Editions Universitaires, Paris, 1957).
Horror Movies by Carlos Clarens (Secker & Warburg, 1968).
The House that Stoll Built by Felix Barker (Frederick Muller, 1957).
How it Happened Here by Kevin Brownlow, Cinema One Series (Secker & Warburg in association with BFI, 1968).
I Blow My Own Horn by Jesse Lasky (Gollancz, 1957).
I Lost it at the Movies by Pauline Kael (Jonathan Cape, 1966).
The Innocent Eye, the Life of Robert J. Flaherty, based on research material by Paul Rotha and Basil Wright, 1963.
Inside Pictures by Ernest Betts (Cresset Press, 1960).
Journey to the End of the Night by Louis Ferdinand Celine (Penguin, 1934).
The Kine Year Book, 1915.
Kino by Jay Leyda (Allen & Unwin, 1960).
Kiss, Kiss, Bang, Bang by Pauline Kael (Calders & Boyars, 1970).
Alexander Korda by Paul Tabori (Oldbourne, 1949).
Let's Go to the Pictures by Iris Barry (Chatto & Windus, 1926).
Life and Adventures of Carl Laemmle by John Drinkwater (Heinemann 1931).
Lindsay Anderson by Elizabeth Sussex (Studio Vista, 1969).
The Lion's Share by Bosley Crowther (E. P. Dutton, 1957).
The Liveliest Art by Arthur Knight (Mentor Books, by arrangement with the Macmillan Company, 1959).
Losey on Losey by Tom Milne, Cinema One Series (Secker & Warburg in association with Sight and Sound, 1967).
Cinema of Joseph Losey by James Leahy (Zwemmer, 1967).
Making a Film by Lindsay Anderson (Allen & Unwin, 1952).
Marcel Proust by G. D. Painter (2 vols) (Chatto & Windus, 1959 and 1965).
Meeting at the Sphinx by Marjorie Deans (Macdonald, n.d.).
Michael Balcon Presents: A Lifetime in Films (Hutchinson, 1969).
Michael Balcon's Twenty-five years in Films edited by M. Danischewsky (World Film Publications, 1947).
A Million and One Nights by Terry Ramsaye (Simon & Schuster, 1926).
A Mirror for England by Raymond Durgnat (Faber, 1970).
Money Behind the Screen by F. D. Klingender and Stuart Legg (Lawrence & Wishart, 1937).
Monthly Film Bulletins published by the British Film Institute.
The Movies by Richard Griffith and Arthur Mayer (Spring Books, 1963).
Mr Rank, The Story of J. Arthur Rank and British Films by Alan Wood (Hodder & Stoughton, 1952).
My First Hundred Years in Hollywood by Jack Warner (Random House, 1964).

New Cinema in Britain by Roger Manvell (Studio Vista, 1969).

New Cinema in Europe by Roger Manvell (Studio Vista, 1966).

New Cinema in the U.S.A. by Roger Manvell (Studio Vista, 1968).

A Pictorial History of the Talkies by Daniel Blum (Hamlyn, 1968).

Prater Violet by Christopher Isherwood (Penguin Modern Classics, 1961).

The Pleasure-Dome by Graham Greene (Secker & Warburg, 1972).

The Rise of the American Film by Lewis Jacobs (Teachers' College Press, New York, 1968).

The Romance of Soho by E. Beresford Chancellor (Country Life, 1931).

Secrets of Nature by Mary Field and Percy Smith (Faber, 1934).

Shots in the Dark (Allan Wingate, 1951).

The Silent Cinema by Liam O'Leary (Studio Vista, 1965).

Specimens of English Dramatic Criticism, World's Classics series (Oxford University Press, 1945), p. 233.

Spotlight on Films by Egon Larson (Max Parrish, 1950).

Sunday, Bloody Sunday, The Script of the John Schlesinger Film (Corgi Books, 1971).

The Theatre of the Absurd by Martin Esslin (Eyre & Spottiswoode, and Pelican Books, 1968).

Thirty Years with G. B. S. by Blanche Patch (Gollancz, 1951).

This Film Business by Rudolph Messel (Ernest Benn, 1928).

To Encourage the Art of the Film: The Story of the British Film Institute by Ivan Butler (Robert Hale, 1971).

Twenty Years of British Film, 1925–1945 (Falcon Press, 1947).

Twenty-five thousand Sunsets by Herbert Wilcox (Bodley Head, 1967).

The Uses of Literacy by Richard Hoggett (Pelican Books, 1958).

Upton Sinclair Presents William Fox. Published by the author (Los Angeles, U.S.A., 1933).

Violence on the Screen by André Glucksmann (British Film Institute, Education Dept., 1971).

Where We Came In by Charles Oakley (Allen & Unwin, 1964).

World Cinema: A Short History by David Robinson (Eyre Methuen, 1973).

A World on Film by Stanley Kauffmann (Dell Publishing Co., 1958).

The Year's Work in Films, 1949 (British Council, 1949).

ARTICLES AND DOCUMENTS

Birt Acres, pamphlet by H. Tummel (Tantivy Press, 1963).

British Film Institute Monthly Bulletins (March 1971, August 1971).

British Board of Film Censors leaflet (1970).

'Censorship: The BBFC View' by John Trevelyan, *Journal of the Society of Film and Television Arts* (Spring and Summer 1971).

Cinematograph Films Acts, 1927–66 (H.M. Stationery Office, Summer, 1933).

The Cinema Quarterly (Summer 1933).

341

The Film Business

The Development of the Cinema by Roger Manvell (London School of Film Technique, 1968).

Federation of Film Unions—Review of Film Legislation Policy (1967).

Film and the Cultural Tradition, BBC Broadcast by Raymond Williams, 1971.

'Films: A Report on the Supply for Exhibition in Cinemas', Monopolies Commission Report (H.M. Stationery Office, 1966).

The First Colour Motion Pictures by D. B. Thomas, Science Museum Monograph, (H.M. Stationery Office, 1969).

'Gainsborough Portraits' by James Mason, The Sunday Times Magazine (1 November 1970).

Guide to British Film Production (British Film Producers' Association, 1966).

Journal of the Society of Film and Television Arts (July/August 1969).

Michael Powell by Kevil Gough-Yates (National Film Theatre in conjunction with John Player & Sons, 1971).

National Film Finance Corporation's Annual Reports, 1957–68 (H.M. Stationery Office).

Origins of the Motion Picture by David B. Thomas, Science Museum Monograph (H.M. Stationery Office, 1964).

Outlook, British Film Institute (1966, 1967, 1968).

Reminiscences of a Pioneer Film Producer by G. B. Samuelson, based on research by Harold Dunham. Privately printed, 1938.

Review of Films Legislation, Cinematograph Films Council (H.M. Stationery Office, 1968).

Review of Films Legislation and Policy. Issued by ACTT for the Federation of Film Unions, 1967.

Report of the Film Studio Committee (The Gater Report) (H.M. Stationery Office, 1948).

Report of the Working Party on Production Costs (H.M. Stationery Office, 1949).

The Silent Picture, No. 2 (Tantivy Press, 1969), p. 6.

Tendencies to Monopoly in the Cinematograph Film Industry (H.M. Stationery Office, 1944).

Victor Saville by Cyril B. Rollins & Robert J. Waring (British Film Institute, 1972).

Index

343

345